The New History and the Old

The New History and the Old

Gertrude Himmelfarb

The Belknap Press of
Harvard University Press

Cambridge, Massachusetts
and London, England

This book is printed on acid-free paper, and its binding materials
have been chosen for strength and durability.

Library of Congress Cataloging-in-Publication Data
Himmelfarb, Gertrude.
   The new history and the old.

   Bibliography: p.
   Includes index.
   1. Historiography.   I. Title
D13.H445   1987   907'.2   87-327
ISBN 0-674-61580-8 (cloth)
ISBN 0-674-61581-6 (paper)

For Celia and Harold Kaplan

Contents

The New History and the Old

The past is full of life, eager to irritate us, provoke and insult us, tempt us to destroy or repaint it. The only reason people want to be masters of the future is to change the past. They are fighting for access to the laboratories where photographs are retouched and biographies and histories rewritten.

—Milan Kundera, *The Book of Laughter and Forgetting*

Introduction

The "Old New Social History" and the "New Old Social History": thus one eminent social historian (Charles Tilly) distinguishes his mode of history from that of another eminent social historian (Lawrence Stone).[1] Recalling the history of this genre, one might be tempted to add some additional "old's" and "new's" to accommodate the several varieties that have emerged since James Harvey Robinson proclaimed the advent of the "New History."

Even in 1912, when Robinson issued that manifesto, the "new history" was not all that new. In 1898 the *American Historical Review*, bastion of the old history, published an essay, "Features of the New History," commending the "new" *Kulturgeschichte* as practiced by Karl Lamprecht—which itself was not so new, Jakob Burckhardt's classic work on the Renaissance having appeared almost half a century earlier. Lamprecht's new history was not quite Burckhardt's; nor was Robinson's Lamprecht's. But they had much in common with one another and with later versions of the new history, for they all rejected the basic premises of the old history: that the proper subject of history is essentially political and that the natural mode of historical writing is essentially narrative. Lamprecht's "genetic" method, emphasizing causation rather than narration, presaged the "analytic" method favored today. And Robinson's plea for a history of the "common man," which would dispense with the "trifling details" of dynasties and wars and utilize the findings of "anthropologists, economists, psychologists, and sociologists," is still the agenda of the new history.[2]

England had its own founding father in J. R. Green, whose *History of the English People* (1877–80) professed to take as its subject the "English People" rather than "English Kings or English Conquests," and to be concerned more with the Elizabethan Poor Laws than with the Armada and more with Methodism than with Jacobitism.[3] Less than half a century later H. G. Wells published an un-Victorian and irreverent version of the new history in the form of an *Outline of History,* in which a "world-historical" figure like Napoleon was seen strutting upon the crest of history like a "cockerel on a dunghill."[4] Determined to democratize history as well as debunk it ("demystify," the Marxist would say), Wells described his history as the "common adventure of all mankind," of all classes and all nations.[5] And he was pleased to report that his book was not only about the common man, it was for the common man, the common reader—in evidence of which he cited the sale of over two million copies in little more than a decade. Although most professional historians were as disdainful of Wells as he was of them, they could not ignore his work or its thesis. Reviewing the *Outline* in the *American Historical Review,* Carl Becker (himself often identified as a new historian) confessed that Wells's "new history" was too new for his tastes, too insistent upon judging the past by the standards of the present—or rather by Wells's vision of the future, when the "Great Society," the "Federal World State," would have ushered in a truly democratic and universal era.[6] If that prophecy now seems quaint, some of Wells's other fancies have come to pass. In 1900 he offered a "prospectus" for a history of mankind that would take into account all the forces of social change: biologic, demographic, geographic, economic. Later, in his autobiography, Wells remarked that if he were a multimillionaire, he would establish "Professorships of Analytic History" to endow a new breed of historians—"human ecologists."[7]

As it happened, the French had already started to produce that new breed. The *Annales d'histoire économique et sociale* was founded in 1929 in opposition to the political and diplomatic historians who dominated the academic establishment—the Sorbonnistes, as they were contemptuously called. That epithet lost some of its sting when the *Annales* moved from Strasbourg to Paris, where one of its editors (Marc Bloch) joined the faculty of the Sorbonne and the other (Lucien Febvre) the Collège de France. With the establishment after the war of the Sixième

Section of the Ecole Pratique des Hautes Etudes, the Annalistes acquired a powerful institutional base, and under the editorship of Fernand Braudel their journal became the most influential historical organ in France, possibly in the world.[8] It has also proved to be remarkably innovative. Going well beyond the more traditional forms of economic and social history, it now derives both its subjects and its methods from anthropology, sociology, demography, geography, psychology, even semiotics and linguistics.

While Americans have been developing their own modes of new history—econometric and cliometric, black and ethnic, feminist and sexual, psychoanalytic and populist—they have also been much influenced by their colleagues abroad. A large contingent of historians may be found making annual or sabbatical pilgrimages to Paris to take instruction from the masters. Others look to Britain for inspiration, especially to the Marxists, whose work has been used to fortify the indigenous tradition of radical history (typified by Robinson's student and collaborator, Charles A. Beard). Thus E. P. Thompson's *Making of the English Working Class* has become the model for the making of the American working class; Eric Hobsbawm's concept of "primitive rebels" is taken as the prototype of inner-city gangs; and Perry Anderson's version of "Althusserian" Marxism is the point of departure for discussions of the theory and methodology of Marxism.

If the new history, as we know it today, is not as novel as some of its younger enthusiasts might think, neither is the old history as archaic as its critics assume. The old history, traditional history, has had a long time to assimilate and accommodate itself to the new. Indeed, even before the advent of the new, it was never as homogeneous or simplistic as the stereotype has it. German history managed to make room for a Burckhardt as well as a Ranke, for cultural history as well as political and "scientific" history. The English Whig historians, descending from Burke and Macauley, came in many sizes and shapes, including some notably un-Whiggish types. And their contemporaries in France had a breadth and liberality of spirit that even the Annalistes admire; one of the complaints of the new historians is that the Sorbonnistes abandoned the grand tradition of Guizot, Thierry, and Michelet. Nor are the great American classics merely political chronicles. Bancroft's history was not only a paean to Jacksonian democracy; it also reflected his predilection for German idealism and romanticism. And Parkman's "history of the American forest," as he called his work on the Great West,[9] was as rooted in anthropology, geography, and ecology as the work of any new historian; the wilderness was as surely his hero as the Mediterranean was Braudel's.

The new history, then, is older than one might think, and the old not quite so antiquated. But what is undeniably new is the triumph of the new. In the historical profession as a whole the new history is now the new orthodoxy. This is not to say that the old history is no longer being written. Political, constitutional, diplomatic, military, and intellectual histories continue to be written by some eminent senior historians and even some enterprising young ones. (Although more often the old history is rewritten in the light of the new. Thus political history is quantified and sociologized, and intellectual history—the study of ideas—is converted into *mentalité* history—the study of popular beliefs and attitudes.) Yet the old history, if not entirely superseded, has been largely displaced. What was once at the center of the profession is now at the periphery. What once defined history is now a footnote to history.

In the spirit of collegiality, some historians (old and new alike) have argued that all this is of little consequence so long as a mood of tolerance prevails, so long as each historian can "do his own thing"— or, as has been said, "go to heaven his own way."[10] Others, taking a more cynical view of the matter, belittle the new history as yet another academic fashion that will disappear as soon as the novelty wears off, or as soon as some more venturesome novices assert themselves by rebelling against their elders. (In the profession this is known as revisionism.) In fact, this particular fashion has survived several generations and has become more entrenched with the passing of time. By now there are historians—serious, reputable, senior historians—who know no other kind of history and can do no other kind. For them the new history has lost its distinctive character. They recognize no legitimate criticism of the genre as such, any more than of history as such. To the argument that quantitative history, for example, has a tendency to elevate method over substance, permitting statistics to define the subject, they reply that this is no different from constitutional history, which takes its themes from whatever documents are available. To the charge that social history tends to be unduly concerned with the minutiae of everyday life, they respond by pointing to the no less tedious machinations that make up a good deal of political history. The issue, we are told, is not the new history or the old, but good history or bad.

This is a tempting resolution of the matter. Who can refuse the appeal to good history? Who can deny that there is much bad in the old and much good in the new? Who can be so churlish as to revive old disputes and resist the call to rapprochement? Who indeed, except perhaps an intellectual historian who finds that ideas are not so easily reconciled, that important questions are at stake which have not yet been resolved, that the two modes of history reflect differences in subject and method which are tantamount to different conceptions of history, and that the new history has significant implications not only for the history of historiography but for the history of ideas as well.

The chapters of this volume deal with one or another mode, method, or aspect of the new history and the old. They testify to a variety that appears to contradict the singularity of "new history" and "old history," that may even seem to defy the labels "new" and "old." Yet for all the variations and qualifications contained within them, the categories have a reality that cannot be denied. That reality is reflected in common usage. "New history" has become the accepted shorthand term for modes of history that may not be consistent with one another but that do represent, singly and collectively, a challenge to traditional history.

The challenge is serious only because of the dominance ("hegemony," the new historian would say) of the new history in the profession today.[11] Indeed, it is the fact of dominance that is crucial to the argument of this book. Again and again I make the point that the issue is not the new history as such but rather the decisive role it has assumed and the superior claims made on its behalf. No one—certainly not I—can reasonably object to a study of popular unrest in Paris from 1557 to 1572; or of vagrants, beggars, and bandits in Cuba from 1878 to 1895; or of women's work in manufacturing in Central Europe from 1648 to 1870; or of stature and nutrition in the Hapsburg monarchy in the eighteenth century. But when, as recently happened, these constitute the entire contents (apart from book reviews), not of the *Journal of Social History* but of the *American Historical Review*,[12] and when the editors and editorial board of the *Review* see nothing noteworthy in this grouping of articles—indeed do not recognize them as belonging to a distinctive genre—one may find cause for reflection and concern.

It is this species of the new history, social history, that is the subject of the opening chapter of this volume. "History with the politics left out" is the way G. M. Trevelyan described social history almost half a century ago. The phrase is now used facetiously, but it does characterize a mode of history that either ignores politics, or relegates it to the realm of "epiphenomena," or recognizes it as a subject deserving of study only when it has been transmuted into social or political science. When such a history professes to be "total" history, or even the dominant and superior form of history, the implications are momentous—not only for the writing of history but for the historian's conception of the polity and of the human beings who are the subject both of the polity and of history.

The chapter on the "New History" focuses on quantohistory and psychohistory, each of which exhibits its own kind of determinism and its own methodological problems. "Two Nations or Five Classes" describes an exercise in sociological history and contrasts the abstractions and models of this type of history with the "moral imagination" of the Victorians. "The 'Group'" deals with the influential school of British Marxist history: its origins in the Communist Party, its ideological commitments and revisionist strategies, its relation to non-Marxist history and to the new history.

The paired essays in the following chapters analyze specific works and themes of the new history. The first, on social history, considers the views of two founding fathers of that genre and reflects on its present status. The second presents psychohistorical interpretations of two major English thinkers, which serve as case studies of the method itself. The third, comparing recent historical works on France and England, concludes that one of the supposed casualties of the new history, national history, may not yet be as defunct as is sometimes claimed.

The counterpoint to the new history is generally taken to be "Whig history," which is preeminently political in subject and narrative in form. "Who Now Reads Macaulay?" points out that Victorian historians of all political persuasions, Tories and Radicals as well as Whigs, shared the view that the history of a people is primarily the story of its political heritage and that English history is peculiarly the story of a "liberal descent." "History and the Idea of Progress" traces an idea that is often associated with Whig history but is in fact characteristic of a long line of thinkers who differed about what constituted progress but agreed that some concept of progress was necessary to give meaning to history by bringing the past into a continuum with the present and the future. "Does History Talk Sense?" suggests that the challenge to traditional history does not come only from the new history: the conservative philosopher Michael Oakeshott is in this respect more radical than Nietzsche, and Nietzsche more Whiggish than Oakeshott; for Nietzsche's historical muse makes sense of the past by speaking to our present concerns, whereas Oakeshott's is a beloved mistress who cannot "talk sense" because the past itself is dead.

Most of the chapters of this book were published in the 1980s, the earliest, "Clio and the New History," in 1975. The "Frenchness of France" has not previously been published, and a somewhat different version of the essay on Macaulay appeared in my volume of essays, *Marriage and Morals among the Victorians*. All the essays but one have been edited, expanded, and in some cases extensively rewritten. The one exception is "History With the Politics Left Out," which is included here in essentially its original form. When it was first published in 1984, it provoked a good deal of controversy, and rather than blunt the issues by revision, I chose to keep the original intact and add a Postscript by way of commentary.

The passionate response to that essay, favorable as well as critical, caused me to reconsider an opinion I had come to a few years earlier. In 1980, in a review of *The Past before Us* (a volume of historiographic essays commissioned by the American Historical Association), I wrote of "intimations" in this book and elsewhere that some new historians were becoming sensitive to the concerns of traditional historians. I predicted that "the 'humanization' of social history will eventually lead, not to a restoration of the old history, but to an accommodation in which old and new can live together."[13] I came to this conclusion despite other intimations in the same work that so far from seeking an accommodation with the old history, some new historians were embarking on a still more radical mission. In his contribution to that volume Carl Degler observed that while a great deal of attention was being directed to the history of women and the family, these subjects had still not been properly integrated into the "mainstream" of history, and that this could be achieved only by altering our conception of history and our sense of the past: "In sum, what is meant by history or the past will have to be changed before these two subdisciplines become an integral part of it."[14]

Since the publication of *The Past before Us* the demand for "mainstreaming" has been echoed by other subdisciplines dealing with workers, blacks, ethnic groups, and social and sexual "deviants." One might well wonder whether anything would remain of the discipline of history if these subdisciplines were brought into the mainstream, and whether such an effort of integration would not result in the disintegration of the whole. The "total" history that some new historians pride themselves on might turn out to be a total dissolution of history—history in any form recognizable to either the new or the old historian. This is, in effect, the prescription offered by Theodore Zeldin (discussed in Chapter 7); pursuing the historical revolution to its end, Zeldin seeks the liberation of history from all the categories and concepts (cause, time, class, nation) that still enslave it.

Even some of the Annalistes are beginning to suspect that they have unleashed a force they cannot control. The very disciplines they have used to subvert the conventions of the old history threaten to subvert history itself. It is curious to find the editors of a collection of essays by prominent Annalistes complaining of the "aggression of social sciences," and still more curious to hear of the effect of that aggression on history: "The field which it [history] used to occupy alone as the systematic explanation of society in its time dimension has been invaded by other sciences with ill-defined boundaries which threaten to absorb and dissolve it."[15] The same volume contains an essay by one of the editors with the provocative title "The Return of the Event." But the "return" heralded there is not of the kind of "event" familiar in traditional history. On the contrary, Pierre Nora confirms "the effacement of the event, the negation of its importance and its dissolution," as the great triumph of the new history. It is quite another event that he sees as returning: one that has been produced by the mass media of modern industrial society and that is often indistinguishable from a "nonevent" or "illusion," a "sign" or a "function."[16]

A similar retreat, more semantic than substantive, may be noted in the United States, where one of the founders of the new history has called for a "new old history" to correct the excesses of the new and restore some of the virtues of the old. But the *"mentalité* history" that Lawrence Stone invokes as the distinctive mode of this "new old history" is nothing like traditional intellectual or even cultural history. And the "revival of narrative" he points to—the "narration of a single event" exemplified by Emmanuel Le Roy Ladurie's *Montaillou,* Carlo Cipolla's *Faith, Reason and the Plague in Seventeenth Century Tuscany,* Eric Hobsbawm's *Primitive Rebels,* E. P. Thompson's *Whigs and Hunters*—is far from the old narrative history, where the narration was not of a single event but precisely of a series of events chronologically connected so as to tell a story over a significant span of time.

One is not surprised to find other signs of misgiving and dissidence. Orthodoxies breed heresies; dominance generates discontent. As the new history loses the glamour of novelty, the old acquires a new allure. More and more often one hears confessions of nostalgia for an old-fashioned history that has dramatic movement and literary grace; for a political history that regards constitutions and laws as something more than ploys in the manipulation of power; for an intellectual history that takes serious ideas seriously, as ideas, rather than as instruments of production and consumption; even for a social history that does not presume to be dominant or superior, let alone "total." It may be that we are witnessing the beginning of yet another wave of historical revisionism—not the restoration of an old regime (historians are skeptical of such restorations) but the inauguration of a new regime.

It is tempting to say (as I once did) that we can now look forward to a real accommodation of new and old, a merging of the best of both. It is a pleasing prospect but not a very hopeful one. At a time when the "old new" historian adamantly rejects the small, tentative overtures of the "new old" historian, one can hardly be sanguine about the prospects of reconciliation with the "old old" historian. There is a good deal at stake, not only in terms of professional interests (careers dependent upon particular subjects, methods, and institutional affiliations), but of philosophical convictions—ideas about history, politics, society, even human nature. The new historian cannot concede the preeminence of politics in the Aristotelian sense, which supposes man to be a "political animal"; and the old historian cannot admit the superiority, let alone totality, of a mode of history that takes man to be a "social animal." Nor can the new historian conceal his contempt for a history that persists in studying "important people, significant events, and successful historical movements";[17] nor the old historian find it anything but bizarre that such subjects should be derided and that *l'histoire historisante* should be used as an invidious term.[18] So long as new historians announce that "Mickey Mouse may in fact be more important to an understanding of the 1930s than Franklin Roosevelt,"[19] or that "the history of menarche" should be recognized as "equal in importance to the history of monarchy,"[20] traditional historians will feel confirmed in their sense of the enormous gap separating the two modes of history.

One would like to think that reality will inevitably assert itself to produce a more sensitive and realistic history. But here too one cannot be sanguine. It was, after all, during the most catastrophic event in modern times that two of the greatest Annalistes affirmed their faith in a doctrine that belittled events and located reality in the "impersonal forces" of history. In his moving account of the fall of France in 1940, Marc Bloch alluded to the theory of history that contributed to the prevailing mood of "intellectual lethargy."

> We were all of us either specialists in the social sciences or workers in scientific laboratories, and maybe the very disciplines of those employments kept us, by a sort of fatalism, from embarking on individual action. We had grown used to seeing great impersonal forces at work in society as in nature. In the vast drag of these submarine swells, so cosmic as to seem irresistible, of what avail were the petty struggles of a few shipwrecked sailors? To think otherwise would have been to falsify history.[21]

Even then Bloch did not consider the possibility that this "cosmic" theory may have falsified history itself, that it was not only politically enervating but historically stultifying. One wonders whether that possibility occurred to him when he later joined the Resistance movement—and gave his life to it.

It was the same tragic event, the fall of France, that ironically provided another historian with the opportunity to launch an attack on *l'histoire événementielle*.[22] Historians have paid homage to Fernand Braudel, who managed to write the first draft of his monumental work, *The Mediterranean and the Mediterranean World in the Age of Philip II*, while confined in a prisoner-of-war camp in Germany during World War II. That work extolled *la longue durée:* the "inanimate" forces of geography, demography, and economy that were the "deeper realities" of history, compared with which the passions of Philip II and the ideas of the Renaissance were "cockleshells" tossed on the waters of history.[23] The book was indeed an impressive achievement, but also a profoundly ironic, even perverse one. For it was written at a time when Europe was being convulsed by the passions of a single man and by ideas that very nearly destroyed a people and a religion of considerable *durée*. Braudel himself has said that he wrote it in prison, partly as a "direct existential response to the tragic times I was passing through."

> All those occurrences which poured in upon us from the radio and the newspapers of our enemies, or even the news from London which our clandestine receivers gave us—I had to outdistance, reject, deny them. Down with occurrences, especially vexing ones! I had to believe that history, destiny, was written at a much more profound level.[24]

It is curious that historians, admiring the intrepid spirit that could bring forth so bold a theory in the midst of such tragic "occurrences," have failed to note the gross disparity between that theory and those occurrences—the extent to which the theory did indeed "outdistance, reject, deny them." It is still more curious that in the years following the war, as historians tried to assimilate the enormity of the individuals and ideas responsible for those "short-term events" (known as World War II and the Holocaust), the theory of history that belittled individuals, ideas, and above all events became increasingly influential. The irony is compounded by the fact that what Braudel took to be an "existential response" to reality—distancing himself from it and seeking a "much more profound level" of meaning—was exactly the opposite from the response of the Existentialists, who found meaning precisely in the actuality of events, however contingent and ephemeral. Because the Existentialists respected the meaning of events, they also respected the integrity of the individuals involved in them—the conscious, responsible, autonomous individuals whose actions were freely willed, even "gratuitous." Braudel, by denying the "underlying reality" of events, denied both the efficacy of individuals and the possibility of freedom. *The Mediterranean* concludes by asserting the triumph of the long term over the individuals doomed to live in the short term.

So when I think of the individual, I am always inclined to see him imprisoned within a destiny in which he himself has little hand, fixed in a landscape in which the infinite perspectives of the long term stretch into the distance both behind him and before. In historical analysis, as I see it, rightly or wrongly, the long term always wins in the end. Annihilating innumerable events—all those which cannot be accommodated in the main ongoing current and which are therefore ruthlessly swept to one side—it indubitably limits both the freedom of the individual and even the role of chance.[25]

If historians have shown themselves, on occasion, to be strangely resistant to historical reality, they have also proved to be peculiarly vulnerable to boredom. In his *Philosophical Dictionary* Robert Nisbet has an entry on "boredom"—nothing so pretentious as "ennui," "anomie," or "apathy," but the simple "insistent and universal" human trait of boredom. Toward the close of the article he quotes Bertrand Russell: "If life is to be saved from boredom, relieved only by disaster, means must be found of restoring individual initiative not only in things that are trivial but in the things that really matter."[26] Some new historians have confessed that their initial disaffection with traditional history came from boredom with the old subjects: dynasties and governments, wars and laws, treaties and documents. So it may be that a new generation of historians, bored with the "everyday life of common people" and the "long-term structures" of geography and demography, may find a renewed excitement in the drama of events, the power of ideas, and the dignity of individuals—"not only in things that are trivial but in the things that really matter."

"History with the Politics Left Out"

.1.

You, the philologist, boast of knowing everything about the furniture and clothing of the Romans and of being more intimate with the quarters, tribes and streets of Rome than with those of your own city. Why this pride? You know no more than did the potter, the cook, the cobbler, the summoner, the auctioneer of Rome.

—*Giambattista Vico, 1702*

When the history of menarche is widely recognized as equal in importance to the history of monarchy, we will have arrived.

—*Peter Stearns, 1976*

A few years ago, in a discussion of recent trends in the writing of history, one young historian proudly described his work as being on the "cutting edge of the discipline." He was writing a study of a New England town toward the end of the eighteenth century, an "in-depth" analysis of the life of its inhabitants: their occupations and earnings, living and working conditions, familial and sexual relations, habits, attitudes, and social institutions. He regretted that he had to confine himself to that one town, but some of his colleagues were doing comparable studies of other towns and their collective efforts would constitute a "total history" of that time and place. I asked him whether his study, or their collective studies, had any bearing on what I, admittedly not a specialist in American history, took to be the most momentous event of that time and place, indeed one of the most momentous events in all of modern history: the founding of the United States of America, the first major republic of modern times. He conceded that from his themes and sources—parish registers, tax rolls, census reports, legal records, polling lists, land titles—he could not "get to," as he said, the founding of the United States. But he denied that this was the crucial event I took it to be. What was crucial were the lives and experiences of the mass of the people. That was the subject of his history; it was the "new history," social history. My rebuttal—that even ordinary people (perhaps most of all ordinary people) had been profoundly affected in the most ordinary aspects of their lives by the

13

founding of the republic, by political events, institutions, and ideas that had created a new polity and with it a new society—seemed to him naive and old-fashioned.

There was, in fact, something anachronistic about this exchange. The "new history"—or rather the new "new history," as distinct from the old "new history" sired by James Harvey Robinson and Charles Beard early in the century—is itself no longer new. If it is dated from the founding of the *Annales* more than half a century ago, it is by now well into middle age. Indeed, it is so firmly entrenched in the profession that while young novitiates flaunt their boldness and originality, they are comfortably enjoying the perquisites of a well-endowed establishment. And some of its leading proponents and practitioners (François Furet and Lawrence Stone) find reason to complain of the excesses and defects of what has become the new orthodoxy.[1]

Nor is the new history as monolithic as the label suggests. It encompasses a variety of subjects and methods, some of which are mutually exclusive. Yet there are characteristics that unite it, and even more that differentiate it from the old history. Thus the new history tends to be analytic rather than narrative, thematic rather than chronological. It relies more upon statistical tables, oral interviews, sociological models, and psychoanalytic theories than upon constitutions, treaties, parliamentary debates, political writings, or party manifestos. Where the old history typically concerns itself with regimes and administrations, legislation and politics, diplomacy and foreign policy, wars and revolutions, the new history focuses on classes and ethnic groups, social problems and institutions, cities and communities, work and play, family and sex, birth and death, childhood and old age, crime and insanity. Where the old features kings, presidents, politicians, leaders, political theorists, the new takes as its subject the "anonymous masses." The old is "history from above," "elitist history," as is now said; the new is "history from below," "populist history."

The new history is by now old enough to have provoked a fair amount of criticism. The analytic approach, it has been said, fails to capture the dynamic movement of history; the quantitative method narrows and trivializes history by confining inquiry to subjects and sources capable of being quantified; psychoanalytic interpretations derive more from a priori theories than from empirical evidence; sociological models are too abstract to elucidate specific historical situations; the prevalent ideological bias disposes the historian to identify with his subjects and endow them with his own attitudes and values; the populist mode cannot accommodate those notable individuals whose actions and ideas did, after all, help shape history; and the genre as a whole, in its variety of techniques and approaches, suggests a methodological permissiveness that seems to bear out Carl Becker's famous dictum, "Everyman his own historian."[2] All these criticisms and more have been discussed and debated. But there is another issue that has received less attention and that may be more significant. For the new history is preeminently social history, and as such it makes problematic the kind of history that has been the traditional concern of the historian—political history.

What does it mean to write history that cannot "get to" the founding of the American republic (or the development of the English constitution, or the course of the French Revolution)? What does it mean when this mode of history becomes the dominant mode, when it is practiced not on the periphery of the profession but at the very center, not as an ancillary field but as the main field—indeed, as some social historians insist, as "total" history?[3] What does it imply about one's sense of the past and of the present, about an American past and present devoid of the principles of liberty and right, checks and balances, self-government and good government, which were first enunciated by the founding fathers and incorporated in our Constitution?

It was almost fifty years ago, in his *English Social History*—one of the first English works to deal exclusively with social history, and under that label—that G. M. Trevelyan offered the famous definition of social history as "the history of a people with the politics left out." He hastened to add that it was difficult to leave out the politics from history, especially in the case of the English people. All he hoped to do was to "redress the balance," to recover that part of history, the history of daily life, which had been sorely neglected.[4] And he proposed to do so knowing that others were engaged (as he himself had been for most of his professional life) in the writing of conventional, political history. He would have thought it a travesty to redress the balance so far as to reverse it entirely, to make social history the dominant form of history, to have it supplant rather than supplement conventional history.

Trevelyan, after all, like his great-uncle Macaulay, was preeminently a Whig historian, cherishing the political institutions and traditions that had made England the liberal, progressive, enlightened country that he, like Macaulay, thought it to be. His Whig interpretation of English history, like the Whig mode of writing history—the "Whig fallacy," as it has been called—has fallen into disrepute.[5] When Herbert Butterfield exposed that fallacy more than half a century ago, he meant to caution the historian against the insidious habit of reading history backward, of seeking in the past the sources of those ideas and institutions we value in the present, thus ignoring the complexities, contingencies, and particularities that make the past peculiarly, irrevocably past. But he did not mean to counter a too intrusive present-mindedness with a too austere past-mindedness, to deny the continuity of past and present. If it is unhistorical to permit the present to determine the past, it is surely as unhistorical to prevent the past from informing the present. And it is surely unhistorical to belittle or ignore political ideas and institutions that were agitated and agonized over sometimes to the point of bloodshed—and have since become our heritage.

Unlike a Trevelyan or his modern counterpart for whom social history complements and supplements conventional history, the new social historian regards social history as the only meaningful kind of history, even as "total" history. In this sense, it is the new historian who is truly guilty of the Whig fallacy. For it is he, even more than the Whig, who permits the present to shape the past, who projects into the past his own idea of what is real and important. It was once only the Marxist who regarded politics as the "epiphenomenon" of history, the "superstructure" or "reflection" of the underlying economic and social "infrastructure." Today that view of politics has so penetrated our culture that in this respect it might well be said, "We are all Marxists now." Having failed in so much else—in providing an example of a communist society that is not tyrannical or authoritarian, in fulfilling Marx's predictions of the pauperization of the proletariat and proletarianization of the petty bourgeoisie, of the collapse of capitalism and triumph of worldwide revolution—Marxism has succeeded in this: in demeaning and denigrating political events, institutions, activities, and ideas.

In a sense the new social historian goes even further than the Marxist. Where the Marxist feels it necessary to prove, or at least assert, a causal relationship between economics and politics, the new historian may simply ignore the political dimension, making the social reality so comprehensive and ubiquitous that any form of government, any law or political institution, is automatically perceived as a form of "social control." Instead of the classic Marxist infrastructure—the mode of production and the social relations deriving from that mode—the new infrastructure is the daily life of ordinary people: the relations of the sexes as well as of classes, the condition of criminals and the insane as well as of workers and peasants.

For the social historian, however, as for the Marxist, the infrastructure is what the historian thinks it is, not what contemporaries may have judged to be the most significant aspects of their lives and times. Like the Marxist, the social historian finds it all too easy to convict his subjects of "false consciousness," of not understanding their own reality. If he thinks at all about the discrepancy between his account of the past and that of contemporaries, he assumes that he is wiser than they, that the advantages of hindsight and the latest analytic techniques—econometrics, prosopography, psychology, or whatever—give him a more objective, more accurate view of the social reality. His is the "true" consciousness, theirs the "false."

The social historian does this in good conscience because the reality he attributes to the past is the reality he recognizes in the present. If he makes so much of work and play, sex and childhood, it is because these are the things that preoccupy him in his own culture, that he believes to be a more important part of the existential reality than the "merely formal" processes of government and politics. If he interprets the religion of the Victorians as a form of psychic compensation, a sublimation of social distress, an expression of alienation, it is because he cannot credit, for himself or his peers, convictions and experiences that are essentially religious rather than social or psychological. If he puts more credence in local history than in national history, in folk traditions than in political traditions, in oral and informal evidence than in written documents, in popular myths about witchcraft than in theories of statecraft, he is unwittingly telling us more about the political and intellectual culture he himself inhabits than about the culture he is ostensibly describing.

In imposing his own sense of reality on the past, the social historian exhibits all the faults of the Whig interpretation without its redeeming features. However fallacious the Whig assumptions about the origins of civil liberty, constitutional government, and representative institutions, there is nothing fallacious, nothing anachronistic, about attributing to the past a deep concern with political, parliamentary, and constitutional affairs. Social history, in devaluing the political realm, devalues history itself. It makes meaningless those aspects of the past which serious and influential contemporaries thought most meaningful. It makes meaningless not only the struggle over political authority but the very idea of legitimate political authority, of political rule that is not merely a euphemism for "social control," of rights and liberties that are not (as Jeremy Bentham thought them) "fictitious entities," of principles and practices that do not merely reflect (as Antonio Gramsci would have it) the "hegemony" of the ruling class. The social historian who professes to write a comprehensive, "total" history of England or America while leaving the politics out (again, I am not speaking of the historian for whom social history is a supplement to political history) is engaged in a far more radical reinterpretation of history than even he may suspect.

The truly radical effect of the new enterprise is to devalue not only political history but reason itself, reason in history and politics—the idea that political institutions are, at least in part, the product of a rational, conscious, deliberate attempt to organize public life so as to promote the public weal and the good life. In this respect the social historian is only following the example of his colleague the political scientist, who sees politics as essentially a game, with politicians jockeying for position, power, and the perquisites of office, playing upon the interests, passions, and prejudices of their constituents. This political process is presumed to be rational on the part of politicians only with respect to the means of attaining and retaining power, not the ends of power; and rational on the part of electors only with respect to the satisfaction of their particular interests, not the public interest. (The language of political science is itself suggestive: "politicians" rather than "statesmen," "constituencies" or "voters" rather than "citizens.")

On those occasions when the social historian applies himself to politics, it is this conception of politics that shapes his research.[6] Thus he quantifies the economic interests and class status of members of Parliament and their constituents; or psychoanalyzes the motives and behavior of those who seek power and those who install them in power; or describes the relationship of rulers and ruled in terms of "hegemony" and "deference"; or sees in the bureaucracy and "administrative momentum" the explanation of laws and policies; or looks in smoke-filled rooms and the corridors of power for the secrets of political decisions. He does everything, in short, except utilize the kind of sources—constitutions, laws, judicial decisions, debates, commentaries, treatises—which might suggest a rationality and deliberation that were not self-serving, that were directed to the ends rather than the means of power, that embodied some conception of the national interest and public welfare. The social historian finds precisely these sources suspect, as if formal documents are less trustworthy than private communications, as if forethought and deliberation imply Machiavellian attempts to conceal the truth, as if the ephemera of the moment (a casual remark or a hasty note) are more revealing than considered reflection and judgment, as if interests are more real than ideas and passion more compelling than reason.

In his inaugural lecture at Cambridge University in 1968, the eminent historian Geoffrey Elton commented on the title of his new chair.

> The chair is the chair of English Constitutional History. Now I chose that title myself, and I don't think I could have chosen worse, could I? I damned myself twice over. English Constitutional History, in the present climate of opinion. *One* adjective might have been forgiven. Perhaps Chinese Constitutional History would have been all right. Perhaps English Social History would have been wonderful. But no, I will pick them both: English Constitutional History.[7]

Elton, whose *Tudor Revolution in Government,* published in 1953, was itself something of a revolution in Tudor history and whom no one can accuse of being a stodgy old historian, went on to explain why he chose that outlandish title.

> The purpose of constitutional history is to study government, the manner in which men, having formed themselves into societies, then arrange for the orderly existence, through time, and in space, of those societies. It is therefore, like every other form of history, a form of social history, a form of the history of society. But it takes particular note of the question of

government. It is concerned with what is done to make that society into a properly structured, continuously living body, so that what goes wrong can be put right, so that the political action of which that society is capable can be efficiently and effectively conducted. Machinery, yes. But also thought, the doctrine, the teaching, the conventional notions. What does the society think its government is, how does it treat it, what does it do to amend it? What forms of change are possible, what reforms, and so on and so forth.[8]

Constitutional history, Elton argued, is central to the understanding of the past because it represents the efforts of a people to organize and govern itself as rationally and effectively as it can. But it is also central to the historical enterprise, because it represents the efforts of the historian to discover as best he can the objective truth about the past—to discover it, moreover, in those written documents that are the objective evidence of the past and thus the principal resource of the historian trying to reconstruct the past as objectively as he can. Those documents have to be interpreted and reinterpreted, amplified and supplemented by other kinds of evidence; but they cannot be denied, falsified, or ignored. And as those documents are the bequest of the past to the historian, so they are also the bequest of the past to the present.

Therefore, from the point of view both of the continuous work of historical research and from the point of view of teaching history, and from the point of view of conveying to the world and to the future a sense of the past and an understanding of the past, the study of government maintains, to my mind, its primacy. It can be most fully explicated, it can be most thoroughly described, it can be most clearly understood, it leaves fewer absolutely open questions, it can instruct in the use of reason better than anything else.[9]

"It can instruct in the use of reason"—that is the heart of the matter. No one knows better than Elton the degree to which politics, in the past as in the present, consists in the struggle for money, power, privilege, position. But he also understands that part of the political process consists in the attempt to restrain these self-serving motives, to create out of them, or to impose upon them, a structure of government that will serve society as a whole. The historian has many tasks, but his main task is "the creation of a right mind, and a right reason." "To discover the truth as best he can, to convey that truth as truthfully as he can, in order both to make the truth known and to enable man, by learning and knowing the truth, to distinguish the right from the wrong reason"—this, Elton assures us, is the "simple" task of the historian.[10]

A great deal is at stake in this simple task, nothing less than the restoration of reason to history. This is not Hegel's Reason, a transcendental spirit or idea infusing history, but a more mundane, pragmatic reason. It is the reason reflected in the rational ordering and organization of society by means of laws, constitutions, and political institutions; and the reason implied in the rational activity of the historian seeking to discover and transmit the truth about that society, so that later generations may be instructed about the past that is part of their own present and that they, in turn, will bequeath to future generations. The title of Elton's address, "The Future of the Past," is deliberately ambiguous: it is the future of history, as well as of the past, that is at issue.

When Elton delivered that lecture in the late sixties, he could not have foreseen the present state of the discipline. Or perhaps he did foresee it and was being as canny about the future as he was about the past. In any event, his remarks are today more pertinent than ever. For it is not only political history that the social historian denies or belittles. It is reason itself: the reason embodied in the polity, in the constitutions and laws that permit men to order their affairs in a rational manner—or, on occasion, in an irrational manner, which other men perceive as such and rationally, often heroically, struggle against. It is the reason transmitted to the present by way of constitutions and laws, which themselves specify the means for their amendment and reform. And it is the reason inherent in the historical enterprise itself, in the search for an objective truth that always eludes the individual historian but that always (or so it was once thought) informs and inspires his work.

This rationality is now consciously denied or unconsciously undermined by every form of the new history: by social history positing an infrastructure that supposedly goes deeper than mere political arrangements and is not amenable to reason or will; by anthropological history exploring such nonrational aspects of society as mating customs and eating habits; by psychoanalytic history dwelling upon the irrational, unconscious aspects of individual and collective behavior; by structuralist history emphasizing the long-term ecological "structures" and medium-term economic and social "conjunctures" at the expense of short-term politics and individuals; by *mentalité* history giving greater credence to popular beliefs than to the "elitist" ideas of philosophers; by oral history relying on verbal reminiscences rather than written documents; by *engagé* history priding itself on advocacy rather than mere analysis; by populist history seeking to recover not only the lives of ordinary people but intimate feelings that tend to be inaccessible and unknowable; by the new history of every description asking questions of the past which the past did not ask of itself, for which the evidence is sparse and unreliable and to which the answers are necessarily speculative, subjective, and dubious.

Again I must say—I cannot repeat it too often—that it is neither the subjects nor the methods of social history that are at issue but their dominance, which itself reflects the assumption, increasingly common in the profession, that these subjects and methods represent a higher form of history, more real and significant, more elemental and essential, than the old history. About this tendency there is no question: one need only look at the programs of the annual meetings of the American Historical Association, or at the newer historical journals, or at applications for grants, or at the titles of recent and prospective dissertations. If the process is not even more advanced, it is because the old generation of historians has not yet died out (although many have become converts to the new history) and because some among the younger generation have resisted the allure of the new even at risk to their careers.

It is tempting to think of this as a passing fad, one of those paroxysms of enthusiasm to which universities are so prone. Unfortunately universities have a way of institutionalizing such fads: it is called the tenure system. By now a generation of new historians—or several generations as these are calculated in academia—are tenured professors busily producing students in their image. For many young (and no longer so young) professors, and even more graduate students, social history is the only kind of history they know, certainly the only kind they respect. Rather than being a fad, it more nearly resembles a revo-

lution in the discipline. One recalls the revolution in education ushered
in by the progressive school three quarters of a century ago, and in
philosophy by the analytic school half a century ago, both of which still
dominate their disciplines (although they are now beginning to come
under attack). This is not to say that social history is or will become the
only mode of history. Political, constitutional, diplomatic, and intellectual history will survive, but not in the mainstream of historical studies; they will be on the periphery, as social history once was.

In America this revolution has already filtered down from graduate
programs to undergraduate schools and even high schools. A recent
documentary-essay question on the College Board Advanced Placement examination in American history was "How and why did the
lives and status of Northern middle-class women change between 1776
and 1876?"—a question described in the bulletin of the American
Historical Association as a "mainline topic."[11] A similar question on
the European history examination dealt with methods of child rearing
in England from the sixteenth through the eighteenth centuries.[12]
Again, the point is not the propriety of such questions but their prominence. These examinations send out signals to high schools throughout the country telling them what kind of history should be taught if
their students are to compete successfully for admission to college; in
effect, they establish something very like a national curriculum. And
given the limited time available for the study of history in our high
schools, the new subjects do not merely supplement the old; they
inevitably supplant them.

The practitioners of social history will say, And about time too. Why
should not women and children supplant kings and politicians? Why
should not the way ordinary people lived, loved, worked, and died take
precedence over the way they were governed? Such a reordering of
priorities would be eminently reasonable and humane—were it not for
the cost of that enterprise, a cost borne precisely by those ordinary
people about whom these historians are most solicitous. If ordinary
people are being "rescued from oblivion," as has been said, by the new
"history from below," they are also being demeaned, deprived of that
aspect of their lives which elevated them above the ordinary, which
brought them into relationship with something larger than their daily
lives, which made them feel part of the polity even when they were not

represented in it, and which made them fight so hard for representation precisely because they themselves attached so much importance to their political status.

When Macaulay prepared his readers for the famous third chapter of his *History of England*—the chapter describing "the history of the people as well as the history of the government," the conditions of life and work, the state of manners, morals, and culture—he said that he would "cheerfully bear the reproach of having descended below the dignity of history."[13] But it never occurred to him to go so far below the dignity of history as to dwell on the history of the people to the exclusion of, or even at the expense of, the history of the government. Still less did it occur to him to impugn the dignity of the people by dwelling on the least dignified aspects of their history. A recent book entitled *A Mad People's History of Madness,* consisting in extracts from writings by the mad, was hailed by one reviewer as "a welcome contribution to history from below."[14] It is only a matter of time before other critics will fault it for being insufficiently "from below," for including such eminences as the medieval mystic Margery Kempe instead of the truly lowly, anonymous madmen (and mad women, one must now hasten to add) in Bedlam and Bellevue.

For Macaulay the "dignity of history"—what an archaic ring that now has—was tantamount to the meaning of history. If political events, institutions, and ideas loom so large in his history, it is because he saw them as shaping and defining the past, giving form and meaning to the past as contemporaries experienced it, and to the story of the past as the historian tries to reconstruct it. From a different perspective some Marxists have taken exception to a mode of history that deprives the past of the meaning they find in it. Thus Elizabeth Fox-Genovese and Eugene Genovese have charged that social history, by romanticizing the ordinary life of ordinary people, denies the theory of immiseration that is the Marxist impulse for revolution and, by focusing upon daily life at the expense of politics, obfuscates the class struggle that is, finally, a political struggle, a struggle for power. Against this privatization and depoliticization of history, they cite Engels' *Origins of the Family, Private Property, and the State,* whose very title calls attention to the "decisive political terrain of historical process." Like Lenin attacking the "Left deviationists" for objectively playing into the hands of the counterrevolutionaries, the Genoveses rebuke those "ex-Marxists, ex-new Leftists, and ex-Communists" who perpetrate a "bourgeois swindle" by dwelling upon the daily lives of people instead of the class struggle.[15]

One can sympathize with the Marxist who finds that social history, once his ally, has turned against him, not deliberately but unwittingly, by distracting attention from the revolutionary struggle. One can also sympathize with the social historian who, for all his radical sympathies, finds Marxism inadequate or irrelevant in explaining the ordinary lives of ordinary people, to say nothing of the abnormal lives of deviants, criminals, and the insane. And one may forgive the conventional historian if he takes *Schadenfreude* in finding each of them exposing the weaknesses of the other, thus confirming what he has long said: that it is as much a distortion of history to ignore politics as to make the class struggle the determining fact of history.

After several decades of the new history, we can better appreciate what we are in danger of losing if we abandon the old. We will lose not only the unifying theme that has given coherence to history, not only the notable events, individuals, and institutions that have constituted our historical memory and our heritage, not only the narrative that has made history readable and memorable—not only, in short, a meaningful past—but also a conception of man as a rational, political animal. And that loss is even more difficult to sustain, for it involves a radical redefinition of human nature.

An eminent social historian has appealed to Aristotle for the ultimate vindication of his enterprise: "There is no better definition of human nature than Aristotle's, translated as he understood it: 'Man is a social animal'."[16] What Aristotle said, of course, is "Man is by nature a political animal."[17] It is not in the "household" or in the "village," Aristotle said, but only in the "polis" that man is truly human, decisively different from "bees or any other gregarious animals." The latter, after all, also inhabit households and villages (societies, as we would now say); they also eat, play, copulate, rear their young, provide sustenance for themselves (and, often, for their families), have social relations, and develop social structures. What they do not have is a polity, a government of laws and institutions by means of which—and only by means of which, Aristotle believed—man consciously, rationally tries to establish a just regime and pursue the good life. The social historian, rejecting any such "elitist" idea as the good life, seeking only to understand *any* life, indeed regarding it as a triumph of the historical imagination to explore the lowest depths of life, to probe the unconscious, unreflective, irrational aspects of life, denies that man is the distinctive, indeed unique, animal Aristotle thought him to be—a rational animal, which is to say, a political animal.

Postscript

When this essay was first published in *Harper's* in April 1984, it provoked even more controversy than I had expected. The editors solicited comments from some historians, and others volunteered their opinions, which ranged from effusive praise to unprintable vituperation. But it was not until I received the first batch of letters addressed to me privately, some commending my courage in saying publicly what they thought but had not dared say, others denouncing my ignorance, arrogance, and bigotry, that I realized just how sensitive a nerve I had struck.

In reprinting the essay, I planned to revise and expand it (as I have the other chapters of this volume). But since this might give me an unfair advantage over my critics, I have let the original version stand (except for small stylistic changes, elimination of duplication, and restoration of the footnotes and the original title). Instead, I shall take this opportunity to comment on the more important points raised in response to the essay. (Only those correspondents whose letters were published in *Harper's* will be mentioned by name.)

Because most of my critics seem to think that I am pronouncing an interdiction on all of social history, I have borrowed one of their techniques and performed a simple arithmetic calculation. I find that in the course of the paper I said, no fewer than *seven* times, that my objections are not to social history as such but to its claims of dominance, superiority, even "totality"—not to social history as it may complement or supplement traditional history but to that which would supplant it. Anticipating this misinterpretation, I opened one paragraph: "Again I must say—I cannot repeat it too often—that it is neither the subjects nor the methods of social history that are at issue but their dominance." But no amount of repetition seems to avail.

Indeed—as one of my correspondents pointed out—some of those who charged me with seeking to abolish social history expressed just that claim of superiority, that contempt for all other forms of history, which confirms exactly the point I was making.

The most moving letters I received were from graduate students relating their experiences with professors (including some eminent historians) who refused to approve or supervise dissertations on such "archaic" and "elitist" subjects as political and intellectual history. One of the students in my own seminar, when urged to expand his paper into a dissertation, told me that the professor within whose province that subject would fall warned him that a political and intellectual biography of the kind he was interested in was "old hat," that it would never be published and would hinder his career.

I am not persuaded, therefore, by Lawrence Stone, who took me to task for "flogging a dead or dying horse," citing his own prediction in 1979 that "social historians were beginning to turn back to more traditional modes of historical writing." While it is true, as I said in my article, that some historians have become uneasy with the "new orthodoxy," their misgivings are not reflected in the profession as a whole. Stone himself has had occasion more recently to repeat his criticisms, including the charge that the new history has erred in ignoring the political dimension of history.[18] And his own conception of a "new old history," as I have argued elsewhere in this volume, departs so little from the conventional new history that it does not address the issues I have raised.

Other historians who have warned against the new history have done so precisely because they are troubled by its dominance in the profession. In his presidential address to the American Historical Association in 1982, Gordon Craig described the prevailing attitude toward political history in general, and diplomatic history in particular, as varying "between condescension and antipathy." He pointed out that in the preceding half-dozen annual meetings of the association, the subject of international affairs averaged 5 sessions out of 128.[19] An analysis of more recent programs would show an even greater disproportion; and the few sessions ostensibly on political and diplomatic history are more often exercises in social history in the guise of political and diplomatic history. One of Stone's own colleagues, also a social historian, provides evidence to the same effect (although not in a critical spirit). Analyzing the history courses offered at eight American universities between 1948 and 1978, Robert Darnton finds that the number of courses in political history fell in proportion to the total number of courses offered, while the number in social history rose precipitously.[20]

Responding to my point about the filtering down of social history to the high schools, as demonstrated in the documentary-essay questions on Advanced Placement examinations, one historian who helped make up the examinations assured me that the questions reflected no such bias, that they were merely intended to test the ability of students to use source materials and to think logically and critically about historical facts, assumptions, and deductions. Yet a recent account of the "intellectual origins and impact" of the documentary-essay question, published in the American Historical Association newsletter, more than confirms my charge. This evidence is all the more telling because it comes from someone who fully approves both of social history and of the examinations.

> Overall, many AP American History teachers were involved with the "new" history, and some of the most committed members of this group served on the Committee of Examiners in AP American History where they shared their enthusiasm for these reforms with the college members of the committee. The individual most responsible for the development and introduction of the DBQ [documentary-based question] was Reverend Giles Hayes of the Delbarton School in Morristown, New Jersey. Reverend Hayes had a strong awareness and commitment to the "new" history of the 1960s, while being deeply influenced by the same era's inquiry movement.

This article also supports my claim that the examinations "send out signals" to high schools about the kind of history that should be taught and thus "establish something very like a national curriculum."

> The committee was aware that the DBQ advocated a change from past procedures and norms, and they pondered the implications of such an approach. Some members wondered if the test should be an agent of curriculum change or continue as a measurement of the content and skills of existing college-level American history courses. As noted, DBQ supporters such as Reverend Hayes believed the AP program should be on

the "cutting edge" of curricular reform, and this view eventually prevailed as the committee endorsed the DBQ.[21]

It is not surprising to find the same filtering-down process occurring in France, the home of the new history, but it is curious to observe the dismay of the Socialist government when confronted with the practical effects of a social history that is otherwise so congenial to them. In August 1983 a cabinet meeting discussed a recent survey showing that only a third of the children entering secondary schools could give the date of the French Revolution. "The deficiency of teaching history," François Mitterand declared, "has become a national danger."[22] Since then there has been much talk, among the parties of the Left as well as of the Right, about the need to restore some sense of political and narrative history, with an emphasis on notable individuals and within a framework of nationality. Even a few Annalistes are beginning to have second thoughts. Marc Ferro, codirector of the *Annales* and director of studies in the social sciences at the Ecole Pratique des Hautes Etudes, described the widespread practice in France of teaching history by having schoolchildren compile "single-street histories" of their own neighborhoods, thus showing them how to use documents and to question supposed facts rather than merely memorize dates and events. The result, he concluded, is that sometimes "children no longer know any history."[23]

That it is not only children who "no longer know any history" because they do not know any political history is occasionally conceded by other social historians. The American historian I quoted, who confessed that he could not "get to" the founding of the United States, has his confreres abroad. The eminent Annaliste François Furet has commented on the neglect of "one of the most classic areas of historiography," the French Revolution—classic because it inevitably calls for narrative treatment and also because it establishes "politics as the fountainhead and instrument of freedom." Yet this subject was "virtually absent," he found, from both the prewar and postwar sets of the *Annales,* "as if this locus classicus of national history were precisely the special preserve of the 'other' history."[24] Eric Hobsbawm too has pointed to "a possible weakness of the *Annales* approach, namely its difficulty in coping with what you call the great formative political events in a country's history: the Risorgimento in Italy, or indeed the French Revolution in France."[25]

Some critics took me to task for criticizing the practice of "asking questions of the past which the past did not ask of itself." Historians, they argue, habitually ask such questions. So they do and so they should. But my stricture, I made it clear, has to do with asking those questions "for which the evidence is sparse and unreliable and to which the answers are necessarily speculative, subjective, and dubious." I would obviously not object to questions for which the evidence is available and reliable—and, perhaps more important, which do not presuppose or predetermine the answers, which do not impose upon contemporaries the assumptions, values, and concerns of the historian. A typical example has just come to hand. A high-school history teacher, who chairs the Test Development Committee of the College Board's Advanced Placement European History section, describes an exercise to develop students' comprehension of material that might otherwise seem "opaque."

> One possible exercise assembles students representing nineteenth-century German Liberals, Conservatives, Catholics, Socialists, and Feminists with Chancellor Bismarck. Representatives from each discussion group "confront" Bismarck, expressing their approval or disapproval of his policies and confessing whether they have "sold out" to him.[26]

One does not know which is the greater historical distortion: the idea that Feminists represent a nineteenth-century German group on the order of Liberals, Conservatives, Catholics, and Socialists, or the image of these groups "confronting" Bismarck and confessing whether they have "sold out" to him.

Since Carl Degler is one of the critics who made this point, it may be fitting to cite an article he wrote many years ago, which impressed me then and continues to persuade me. The historian, he wrote, is guided less by "covering laws" that are presumed to be true in all times and places than by "participant-sources"—that is, contemporary evidence. Thus the historian might think it plausible that the American Revolution was caused by high taxes or the navigation laws, but if he finds no evidence for that in the contemporary literature he has to abandon the thesis; conversely, if he finds other reasons given at the time he has to take them seriously, however strange they may seem to him. "The careful historian," Degler concluded, "tries to think as his subjects did, and within their system of values."[27]

Another critic asks, "Have not the vast majority of people in the past thought that where they lived and how they made a living, who they married, and what happened to their children rather more 'basic and significant' than who won the last election?" He rebukes me for thinking that "yet another study of the intricacies of John C. Calhoun's political thought is far more valuable than an analysis of the family life of the four million slaves of the antebellum South." I would agree that an analysis of the family life of the four million slaves would be valuable (if it were more reliable and less speculative and tendentious than are many such studies), but not if it means being so contemptuous of "yet another study" of Calhoun—whose ideas and influence were, as it happens, of considerable significance for the lives of those four million slaves. Nor do I think it a sign of respect for "the vast majority of people" to suppose that they are less interested in "who won the last election" (or who won the last war?) than, perhaps, a Harvard professor who manages to be interested in national politics without neglecting his home, career, and family. This critic, it seems to me, is exhibiting a truly elitist bias—and a truly unhistorical one, considering the fact that so many "ordinary" people have been passionately concerned with political, ideological, and religious causes, often to the extent of sacrificing livelihood and even life.

I am also criticized for failing to appreciate the irrationality in history. "Nietzsche, Freud, and Kafka, and, more recently, Richard Hofstadter," I am reminded, "had made clear to everyone that human beings and the politics they practice are hardly guided only by reason." But I never suggested they are guided "only" by reason. Nor did Aristotle (without benefit of Nietzsche, Freud, Kafka, or Hofstadter). Aristotle's "political animal" had all the passions, impulses, interests, feelings, desires—and, yes, irrationality—known to modern man; but he was also presumed to be endowed with a "reason" that made him a human being rather than merely an animal. Nor did Aristotle (and nor did I) claim that politics is entirely a rational activity—only that it is that in part, and that that part is a vital and essential ingredient of political life.

There is even more involved in the idea of rationality than I ventured to suggest in my essay. For rationality is the precondition of freedom, of the free exercise of individual will. To the extent to which the political realm is more conducive to rational choice, compared with the social realm which is governed by material and economic concerns, it is in politics that the potentiality for freedom lies. This explains why social history tends to be more deterministic than political history, and why political history finds a natural ally in intellectual history. Herbert Butterfield, for all his criticism of Whig history, understood this well. "Over and above the structure of politics," he wrote in his critique of Lewis Namier, "we must have a political history that is set out in narrative form—an account of adult human beings, taking a hand in their fates and fortunes, pulling at the story in the direction they want to carry it, and making decisions of their own."[28] But perhaps my critics will be better disposed to the argument when it is made by one of their own. In urging his colleagues to reconsider the Annaliste aversion to political history, François Furet points to the intimate connection between political history and the idea of freedom:

> Thus, too, political history is primarily a narrative of human freedom as seen through change and progress. Although political history does describe the framework, that is, the constraints within which men act, its major function is to describe the thoughts, choices, and actions of men—primarily of great men. Politics is the quintessential realm of chance, and so of freedom. It gives history the structure of a novel, except that its plot must be composed of authentic facts verified according to the rules of evidence; and this history is indeed the true novel of nations.[29]

Clio and the New History $\cdot 2 \cdot$

A sociologist friend once complained to me of the amorphous state of his discipline. Sociology, he said, is totally undefined, in terms of both subject matter and methodology; no one knows what it is supposed to comprise or how it is supposed to do what it purports to do. He envied history its good fortune in having fixed boundaries and focal points—periods, countries, regimes, dramatic events, great leaders. And he admired its clear and firm notions of scholarly procedure: how one inquires into a historical problem, how one presents and documents one's findings, what constitutes admissible evidence and adequate proof. I gently disabused him. Whatever advantages history may once have enjoyed, it is rapidly unburdening itself of them all. In fact, it seems bent upon transforming itself into something like sociology—or anthropology, or psychology, or demography, or geography, or ethnology, or any other discipline that promises new vitality and new revelations. The situation is all the more curious because these other disciplines are themselves in a state of disarray. G. R. Elton once observed that historians were being enjoined to "call in Freud" at the very time when psychologists were "poised for a mass-flight from Freud."[1] More recently Clifford Geertz remarked that the anthropological perspective is very much "in" in the intellectual and academic community, while anthropologists themselves are suffering from acute self-doubt about both the "scientific respectability" and the "moral legitimacy" of their methods.[2]

Where once the great masters of history were Gibbon, Macaulay, and Ranke, today they more often are Weber, Freud, and Lévi-Strauss. Where history was once primarily (often entirely) narrative, now it is primarily (often entirely) analytic. The old questions "What happened?" and "How did it happen?" have given way to the question "Why did it happen?" And among the methods used to answer that question are psychoanalysis and quantification—psychohistory and quantohistory, as they have been inelegantly called.* If these methods are less hotly debated today than they were a decade or two ago, it is because they have become so familiar and so well established in the profession that it seems churlish to raise once again the old issues. The required course in Historical Method ("method" in the singular), which was once the staple of every graduate history program, has gone the way of all requirements. Instead the student may elect a course in Historical Methods (in the plural) or a "workshop" in Computer Science or Psychoanalysis for the Historian; and Computer Literacy may be substituted for the language requirement. The presumption is that any method has its own justification, has to be tolerated on its own terms and judged by its own rules.

One of the first and most incisive critiques of the new methods is Jacques Barzun's *Clio and the Doctors*.[3] Never one to shirk a good fight, Barzun takes on two formidable adversaries, quantohistory and psychohistory. An attack on either alone would have been provocative enough; it might even have earned him the good will of the other. But Barzun is not interested in minor skirmishes or easy victories. He is intent not only upon destroying both flanks of the "new history" but in implicating each in the defeat of the other. His book contains few examples of the absurdities that psychohistory and quantohistory abound in and that would have been easy game for his keen wit. Preferring to elucidate principles rather than score points, he does not engage in ridicule. Nor does he take refuge in the kind of latitudinarianism that passes for principle in the profession today. He does not propose to legitimate the new historians if only they behave themselves, if they give up their excessive claims to truth and dissociate themselves from their more egregious cohorts. He does not say that

---

*In the United States quantitative history sometimes goes by the name Cliometrics, although Robert Fogel, the master Cliometrician, defines this term more comprehensively to include social-science models as well as quantification. In France the more common term among the Annalistes is "serial history," to emphasize the series of homogeneous units which supposedly gives coherence and precision to *la longue durée*.

every historian can "do his thing" as long as he extends the same courtesy to others. He knows that this kind of tolerance trivializes their "thing" as it does his own. He does his opponents the honor of taking them seriously. If he has principles, so, he assumes, do they. And it is their principles that he finds incompatible with the traditional principles of the historian.

Psychohistory, Barzun insists, is not merely the use of psychological explanations in historical contexts. There would be nothing new in that. Historians have always used such explanations when they were appropriate to a particular problem and when there was sufficient evidence for them. But this kind of eclectic, pragmatic use of psychology is not at all what the psychohistorian intends. He is committed to a particular theory of psychology—psychoanalysis—and a particular school of psychoanalysis at that—Freudianism or neo-Freudianism. And this commitment, Barzun argues, precludes a commitment to history as historians have always understood it. Psychohistory derives its "facts" not from history but from psychoanalysis, and deduces its theories not from this or that instance but from a view of human nature that transcends history. It denies the basic criterion of historical evidence: that the evidence be publicly accessible to, and therefore assessable by, all historians. And it violates the basic tenet of historical method: that the historian be alert to the negative instances that would refute his thesis and to alternative explanations that would be more plausible than his own. The psychohistorian, convinced of the absolute rightness of his own theory, is also convinced that his is the "deepest" explanation of any event, that any other explanation falls short of the truth.

Above all, what Barzun objects to is that psychohistory, not content to violate history (in the sense of the proper mode of studying and writing about the past), also violates the past itself. It denies to the past an integrity and will of its own, in which people acted out of a variety of motives and in which events had a multiplicity of causes and effects. It imposes upon the past the same determinism that it imposes upon the present, thus robbing people of their individuality and events of their complexity. Instead of respecting the actions and professed beliefs of contemporaries, it presumes to expose the real impulses that lay behind those actions and the real feelings that conditioned those beliefs.

It is this lack of respect for the individuality and complexity of history that Barzun takes to be the common characteristic—and the common fallacy—of psychohistory and quantohistory. Where the psychohistorian looks for the psychic mechanisms that account for historical phenomena, the quantohistorian looks for the behavioral patterns—expressed in figures, charts, tables, and graphs—that reduce the multiplicity of instances into their common denominators. Again the fallacy is that of a simplistic, mechanistic determinism. If people and events can be described and explained quantitatively, it can only be because they are conceived as homogeneous, hence quantifiable, units. The population of a country, the number of books produced, the tons of corn exported—these can be counted because the units, for these purposes, are identifiable and identical. But violence, revolution, slavery—the subjects to which quantifiers have tried to apply their techniques—are not homogeneous. They can be added up, measured, charted, only by violating the particularity of each episode (each outbreak of violence, for example), by ignoring the dissimilarities and attending only to the superficial similarities, by arbitrarily focusing on some one characteristic that is specifiable and measurable—and for which, moreover, we happen to have quantitative evidence. The medium, Barzun suggests, has become the message. A mechanistic approach to history implies a mechanistic view of man.

Against both factions of the new history, Barzun unhesitatingly aligns himself with traditional history. It is a measure of the distance we have come that "traditional" should so often be used pejoratively. And it is a measure of Barzun's integrity that he should apply that word to himself. Traditional history, as he conceives it, is not the exclusively political history that its detractors make of it. It draws upon a variety of techniques, disciplines, and sources; it counts, psychologizes, analyzes, compares, reflects, and judges. Above all it narrates. Without that narrative we may have a worthy biography or economic treatise or psychological study, but we do not have history. We may have, as Le Roy Ladurie so memorably put it, a "history that stands still," or a "history without people."[4] But for Barzun, that is not history at all.*

---

*In a footnote on Macaulay (p. 110), Barzun illustrates what he takes to be the proper relationship of the narrative and analytic components in history. He commends Macaulay for the famous third chapter of the *History of England,* the chapter describing the social condition of England in 1685. What he especially likes is the fact that Macaulay deliberately placed it

One cannot repeat often enough that psychohistory is not the occasional use of psychology to illuminate a particular historical situation. It is not, for example, an exercise in psychohistory to say that Hitler had a personal obsession with Jews and that this was an important fact in the history of Nazism. Few historians would dispute this proposition, for which there is ample evidence. It takes the psychohistorian, however, to go on to explain the precise psychic mechanism that caused that obsession and to make this psychic mechanism responsible for the precise nature of the historical events resulting from the obsession.

Thus, an article on Hitler traces not only the Holocaust but the specific use of gas chambers to the treatment administered to Hitler's mother by a Jewish doctor. A Dr. Bloch had operated on her for breast cancer, removing the breast, and then, when the cancer recurred, had vainly tried to arrest its progress by the use of an iodine compound called iodoform. Hitler, who had "loved Bloch like a kind father," unconsciously blamed him for his mother's death, as well as for the "huge terminal bill paid on Christmas eve"—hence his later rage against "the Jewish cancer, the Jewish poison, the Jewish profiteer." When Hitler himself was hospitalized for gas poisoning in 1918, the gas burned through his skin "just like iodoform," and he naturally "associated" his own condition with his mother's. Shortly afterward, in a hysterical relapse, he experienced the hallucination in which he was called upon to undo Germany's defeat, the Germany he was going to avenge being "transparently his mother." The gas chambers of World War II, similarly "associated" with the iodoform episode and his own gas poisoning, completed Hitler's "psychological continuum": "the futile surgery performed on his mother's cancer (the expulsion program), yielding to the representation of her death as a mercy killing (the Euthanasia program), and this in turn to his retaliation against Bloch (the Final Solution)."[5]

The correspondence that is being asserted between the psychic experience and the historical events may also be seen in that part of Binion's article which purports to explain the concept of *Lebensraum*. In appealing for living space for Germany, Hitler is said to have been reex-

---

not at the opening of his work (where any modern historian would have put it) but after two chapters of "rapid storytelling." Those narrative chapters, Barzun says, built up the momentum and suspense that carried the work safely past the "necessarily static" third chapter.

periencing his mother's trauma, a trauma induced by the death of three infants before Hitler was born and communicated to the infant Hitler literally at his mother's breast:

> That is, even as he spoke to Germany's emergent need to relive a traumatic experience, his message was shaped by his oral-aggressive fixation and by the traumatic experience that his mother was reliving as she fixated him. His major premise was strictly oral-aggressive: that all history was a fight for feeding ground. His minor premise, that Germany could not feed her children adequately, expressed his mother's maternal trauma as it had come through to him in her compensatory overfeeding of him. And his conclusion, the eastern land-grab, pointed beyond itself toward world conquest, which points back to that satiety at the breast when self and world were one.[6]

That this article is typical of the genre may be demonstrated by any issue of the journal in which it appeared. The genre should, however, be judged not by the typical but by its best example. And the classic of the form is generally agreed to be Erik Erikson's *Young Man Luther*. Erikson traces Luther's rebellion against the pope (equated with a rebellion against God) to his initial rebellion against his father and the "identity crisis" of his youth. The best-known part of Erikson's analysis is the role assigned to toilet training and "anal defiance" in this momentous rebellion:

> We must conclude that Luther's use of repudiative and anal patterns was an attempt to find a safety-valve when unrelenting inner pressure threatened to make devotion unbearable and sublimity hateful—that is, when he was again about to repudiate God in supreme rebellion, and himself in malignant melancholy. The regressive aspects of this pressure, and the resulting obsessive and paranoid focus on single figures such as the Pope and the Devil, leave little doubt that a transference had taken place from a parent figure to universal personages, and that a central theme in this transference was anal defiance.[7]

The boldness of Erikson's thesis is matched by a methodological audacity that leaves the traditional historian breathless. Only certain minimal conditions have to be met for non-facts to acquire the same status as facts. "We are thus obliged," Erikson says, "to accept half-legend as half-history, provided only that a reported episode does not contradict other well-established facts; persists in having a ring of truth; and yields a meaning consistent with psychological theory."[8] Moreover, the stock of facts and non-facts can come from any time or place in history, from any observer or experience, so that a theory about Jesus or an event in the life of Freud are as much the data of Luther's life as those facts (or legends or hypotheses) deriving from Luther's own childhood or career. A typical chapter of Erikson's book contains half a dozen pages on Hitler (an account itself based on various and conflicting sources); references to city gangs and Zen Buddhism; quotations from such diverse authorities as Crane Brinton, Friedrich Nietzsche, William James, and Thomas Wolfe; and lengthy disquisitions on psychoanalytic theory and practice. And all of this is assumed to have an immediate bearing on the case of Luther. The facts are few, Erikson concedes. "But a clinician's training permits, and in fact forces, him to recognize major trends even where the facts are not all available." The analyst, he assures us, has learned to make "meaningful predictions as to what will prove to have happened," and to "sift even questionable sources" in order to produce those predictions. "The proof of the validity of this approach," he writes, "lies in everyday psychoanalytic work."[9] The most critical historian could not have made the point better. Whatever validity psychohistory may claim comes from psychoanalysis, not from history.*

It has been said that Erikson's books (on Gandhi as well as Luther) are contributions to psychobiography rather than psychohistory, that psychohistory, properly speaking, concerns itself with collective entities—groups, classes, societies—rather than individuals. But Erikson himself subtitled his book on Luther, *A Study in Psychoanalysis and History*. He draws freely (very freely) upon historical materials. And he purports to explain a historical event of the greatest magnitude—a Reformation not only of religion but also of the political structure of Europe and of the "ethical and psychological awareness" of all man-

---

*Rudolph Binion, replying to the comments on his article on Hitler, suggests an additional test of validity—"subjective assent" or "empathy": "We cannot empathize with prices in sixteenth-century Europe to feel whether the influx of bullion from America really did cause their rise; we can empathize with Hitler to feel whether Dr. Bloch really was 'the Jew' for him. A right reading in psychohistory is like a dead language deciphered or a code broken: it not only checks, but you *know* it is right" ("Hitler's Concept, p. 249).

I do not know whether other psychohistorians subscribe to Binion's test of truth, or even whether cryptographers and paleographers do. But certainly other historians do not "know"—empathetically or otherwise—what Binion so confidently knows.

kind.[10] It is surely a semantic quibble to deny to this work, and to the host of others for which it has served as inspiration and model, the character of psychohistory.

It has also been suggested that the term psychohistory should be reserved for subjects that have an obviously large psychological component—the history of childhood or the family, for example. But this is to confuse subject with method. As a subject, the history of childhood can be dealt with in the historian's usual eclectic, pragmatic manner. The traditional historian might cite changes in technology and industry bringing about new patterns of work and family life, philosophical theories positing a novel view of human nature and therefore of socialization and education, the rise of the middle class, the development of political democracy—as well, of course, as changes in breast feeding, toilet training, or any other psychological data for which there is historical evidence, but for which he would claim no necessary primacy or determinacy. The psychohistorian, by contrast, approaches the subject with a prior psychoanalytic commitment. He knows in advance what to look for. His "facts" are psychoanalytic constants. All he need do is to scour history—or "half-history," as Erikson put it so well—for manifestations of those facts.

Most conventional historians, priding themselves on being enlightened, progressive, broadminded, are disposed to be sympathetic to psychohistory. Even if they do not themselves feel competent to engage in it, they would like to be appreciative of the efforts of others. They would like to see psychoanalysis inform history as it has informed their own understanding of human nature and behavior—as it has, for many, intimately affected their own lives. But even those historians who come to it with the best of will and the highest of hopes may harbor grave doubts. They may question whether a method devised for a patient on the couch—and which requires, even in that situation, great subtlety and skill to elicit truths—can be applied to someone not personally available for analysis. The difficulty is obviously compounded when it is not a single person but a group or entire society that is being analyzed. And it is compounded still more as the psychohistorian attempts to go further back in time, as he reaches a period when knowledge of the simplest objective facts becomes sparse, let alone of the feelings and emotions that are at the same time most obscure and most essential to his case. At some point one is moved to wonder whether it is more presumptuous to profess to understand the most intimate secrets of the dead, or to profess to understand—and reveal—the most intimate secrets of the living.

Short of these ultimate questions, the traditional historian is apt to become querulous when confronted with the typical products of psychohistory. Why, he asks, cannot psychohistory observe the rules of the historical craft? If the psychohistorian wants to analyze a politician (Nixon, for example),[11] on the basis of his writings and speeches, why does he not perform the preliminary chores the rest of us do: determine the authorship of the relevant passages and cite them accordingly (was it the politician or his ghostwriter who wrote them?), take account of the occasion for which they were intended (was the politician saying what he thought his audience wanted to hear?), establish the reliability of the secondary sources in which they appear, find out whether other politicians do not on similar occasions express similar sentiments, and so on? It seems little enough to ask of a scholar who is advancing a theory of some consequence.

That psychohistorians—not only the worst but also the best of them—repeatedly fail to observe these elementary rules of evidence should give the sympathetic reader pause. If an intelligent scholar flouts these conventions, it can only be because he is operating on a level that makes such mundane procedures irrelevant. The sociologist will recognize the phenomenon of the ideologue whose ideology is so total and compelling that it imposes itself on the most recalcitrant data. The theologian might see a resemblance to the gnostic in possession of truths not accessible to the ordinary man and not amenable to the ordinary canons of evidence. The conventional historian will simply conclude that the psychohistorian, however brilliant as a psychoanalyst, cannot be held responsible as a historian because he has transcended the realm of history.

If psychohistory appeals to some "deeper" level of explanation that goes beyond the empirical evidence of the traditional historian, quantohistory appeals to a more "scientific" mode of explanation. But this too poses problems that are as much substantive as methodological. A typical example of this genre examines the "salient question" of the literacy of the English people in the period of their greatest political upheaval, the Cromwellian revolution. By the end of the first paragraph, that salient question is reduced to "the capacity to sign names"—for the simple reason that this is "nearly all we now know or indeed are ever likely to know in the future." From an examination of the hearth-tax returns, which required signatures, the author arrives at one deduction that is as unexceptional as it is predictable: "ability to sign was positively correlated with wealth"; and at another conclusion that is seriously questionable: "many ordinary workers and artisans must have had an ability to read fluently and write." It is not clear how the evidence of signatures can warrant any assertions about reading fluency. Nor is it clear how the author arrives at his final comment about the "submerged one-third" who probably could not read or write: "Perhaps it is no wonder that this latter group took so little interest in the fortunes of the Civil War."[12] Even the most "impressionistic" historian (as the quantohistorian is apt to characterize his more conventional colleague) might be moved to wonder whether the French and Russian peasants, who supposedly took a more lively interest in their respective civil wars, had a higher literacy rate.

Again, however, one should consider not only the typical example of this method but one of the best examples. For all the controversy it has provoked, *Time on the Cross,* by Robert Fogel and Stanley Engerman, is a serious and ambitious attempt to apply the quantitative method to one of the most important problems in American history, the problem of slavery.[13] The subtitle, *The Economics of American Negro Slavery,* suggests a more limited subject than is evident in the work itself, which is concerned as much with the social and psychological as with the economic character of slavery. And by relegating most of the supporting data to a separate volume, the authors avoid the conspicuous, visual evidence of their method. Yet that method is the basis for generalizations of the largest import about the quality of life as well as the material conditions of slaves in the South. From data on the number of slaves bought and sold in the slave market, the number of families broken up by such sales, the average age of black women at the birth of their first child, and the like, the authors arrive at conclusions about such matters as the prevailing sexual mores of both blacks and whites, the stability of the black family, the dominance of the male within the black family, and the social ties between the races—to say nothing of the economic issues of the profitability of slavery and its viability as an economic system.

Time on the Cross has been criticized by some historians for being insufficiently rigorous in its use of quantitative data, by others for ignoring the literary evidence that might have made for a less agreeable picture of slavery. But most of the critics, one suspects, were provoked less by methodological scruples than by the authors' conclusions: that slavery was an economically viable system, that the material and moral conditions of the slaves were better than has been thought, and that many of the more shocking abuses attributed to slavery (the "stud farms," for example, where slaves were supposedly bred for the market) were myths. Yet the real problem posed by the book lies in its method. And not in the particular methodological lapses that critics have fastened upon—imprecise and insufficient data, lack of analytic rigor—but in the assumption that quantitative data, however precise, adequate, and rigorous, can supply the answers to the larger questions raised. Had the authors confined themselves to the subject described in their subtitle, the economics of slavery, that assumption might have been justified. But the vital, and vulnerable, point of the book is suggested by the title. *Time on the Cross* has a religious, at the very least a moral, dimension that defies measurement, however subtle or sophisticated the instruments. The difficulty is not, as some critics have said, the authors' failure to pass judgment on slavery or their deficiency in moral fervor; Fogel and Engerman are as implacably opposed to slavery, as morally outraged by it, as any of their critics. What is at issue is the moral as well as the economic impact of slavery upon the slaves themselves and upon the entire society. Here no amount of statistical ingenuity will suffice. Here the historian must call upon every resource available to him, whether or not it can be fed into a computer.

To Barzun quantohistory is as insidious as psychohistory, and for much the same reason—because it is deterministic and mechanistic, seeing only one dimension of reality and reducing all reality to that level. One may agree with him that this is a very real tendency in quantohistory. But one may also question whether it is an irresistible tendency, whether it is as inherent in the method as it is, Barzun would also say, in psychohistory. The latter posits a basic human nature that determines the behavior of man and thus reduces history to the status of "epiphenomena," the superficial expression or manifestation of reality. (The parallel to Marxism, with its "infrastructure" and "superstructure," is striking.) Quantohistory, however, need not be—although it often is—deterministic in the same way. Quantitative evidence can be used selectively, eclectically, to illuminate only one part of the historical reality. Barzun might retort that just as psychohistory is not merely the occasional psychologizing about history, so quantohistory, in any serious sense, is not merely the occasional use of figures; it is the systematic, comprehensive use of figures in such a way as to exclude or belittle all other kinds of data. The point is well taken; this is, in fact, what many influential quantitative historians do. But there are others who do not make an ideology of the method. Although they use figures, charts, and models more extensively and systematically than the traditional historian, they also draw upon whatever other sources are available, including literary sources. And if they do not themselves use these other sources, they leave room for them; they invite others to complement and supplement their work. For them quantification is a means rather than an end, an instrument of analysis rather than a theory about human behavior, or social action, or even the writing of history.[14]

In this more modest sense, quantohistory may be seen as monographic history rather than history per se. In an age when history, like everything else, has been democratized, this distinction may seem invidious. But if we can restore to the monograph the respect it once enjoyed, we might find that many works of quantohistory fall into this category. They are concerned not with the whole of a historical situation but with a part of it, a particular aspect or problem. Eventually their quantitative findings will be absorbed into a larger context in which they will appear in proper proportion and perspective. It is significant that some extremely valuable studies in quantohistory are entirely negative in their implications; they have the effect of disproving received opinion rather than advancing a new theory.[15] David Landes' comment on economic history is even more applicable to quantohistory: "Much of economic history, with its abstraction from complex reality, its suiting of behavior to theory rather than theory to behavior . . . is an exercise in tidying up rather than an effort to see people whole."[16] Such an exercise in tidying up is no mean accomplishment, for it may bring about a reinterpretation of a crucial event. Yet however consequential, it is essentially monographic in character. And as such it may be accommodated in traditional history, subjected to the ordinary rules of evidence, and made part of a larger historical enterprise.

The traditional historian, witnessing the proliferation of "new methods," may take comfort in the thought that fashions come and go and that these too will pass. He may be heartened, for example, by the appearance in the same year of English translations of two books by one of the best known of the Annalistes, Emmanuel Le Roy Ladurie. The first is a collection of essays containing such choice specimens of the quantohistorical credo as "Tomorrow's historian will have to be able to programme a computer in order to survive" and "History that is not quantifiable cannot claim to be scientific."[17] The second, *Montaillou,* hailed as a brilliant exemplar of *mentalité* or "structuralist" history, has more in common with a historical novel or anthropological field study than with "scientific" history.[18] Only half a dozen years separated the original publication of the essays eulogizing quantohistory and the book that so dramatically belies that creed. If Le Roy Ladurie could so rapidly make that transition, so, one might think, could we all.

Unfortunately, disciples (to say nothing of epigones) are less versatile than their masters. Committed to one mode of history, and trained only in that mode, they cannot so readily adopt another. They may, indeed, be incapacitated from doing so. The "quantitative literacy" they pride themselves on, and find deplorably lacking in other historians, is all too often acquired at the expense of ordinary literacy—indeed, often requires the suspension of verbal discourse. So too "psychoanalytic literacy" depends on a set of concepts and a structure of reasoning that may be alien to the layman (and offensive to his ear) even when they are couched in ordinary language. This is not a matter of "mere" style—although that would be serious enough. It goes to the very substance of history; it determines how the historian thinks about, as well as writes about, the human beings, human affairs, and human events that constitute the subject of history.

The special literacy required by these disciplines has its own attraction. It not only establishes a community of the faithful, discoursing in a recondite language, prescribing its own rites and rituals, communing with each other in its own journals and conferences. It also appeals to the gnostic instinct, the yearning for a deeper, more certain truth than is available to the ordinary historian—a truth different from mere appearance, from the ephemera of events that Braudel in a memorable passage compared to the flickering of fireflies: "I remember a night near Bahia, when I was enveloped in a firework display of phosphorescent fireflies; their pale lights glowed, went out, shone again, all without piercing the night with any true illumination. So it is with events; beyond their glow, darkness prevails."[19]

In their different ways the quantohistorian and the psychohistorian promise to illuminate that darkness—the former by means of the hard, measurable, certain facts elicited by "scientific" methods; the latter by means of the eternal verities of human nature as revealed by "depth" psychology. "Social science," Braudel says, "has almost what amounts to a horror of the event."[20] So too does psychoanalysis, the "event" in this case being the conscious, manifest level of behavior. The traditional historian has no such disdain for the ephemeral or the existential. He lays no claim to certitude, has no blinding revelation, no arcane knowledge (no "gnosis") that penetrates to the "underlying realities" beyond the "capricious," "delusive," "contingent," "provisional" realm of events.[21] Indeed, it is just this mundane realm that he prefers to dwell in, that he accepts as reality. And his explanations of these events are as contingent and provisional as the events themselves. Having no grand theory or methodology to unite all of history, to create a "total history," he is content to try to understand the past as best—and as imperfectly—as it can be known. This may be a modest aspiration, but not an unworthy one.

Whatever the fate of the new history in *la longue durée,* as the Annaliste would say, in the short run it has taken a human as well as intellectual toll. In some circles it has generated cynicism and opportunism, a transparent desire to cash in on a good thing. Even more deplorable is the behavior of some of the true believers. I do not know which is more distressing: the sight of young (or not so young) historians callowly psychoanalyzing great thinkers and consigning great historians to the ash heap of history, or the sight of mature scholars "retooling" themselves (as one put it to me) to avoid obsolescence. There is, of course, nothing wrong with taking courses in computer science, any more than with studying Greek or any other subject in which one may be deficient. There is something terribly amiss, however, when a serious historian feels that he can no longer do the kind of work he has done so admirably—and that perhaps today, more than ever, needs doing.

Two Nations or Five Classes: $\cdot 3 \cdot$
The Historian as Sociologist

I n 1969, when the "new history" was sufficiently novel to spawn symposia on "New Trends in History," one such meeting was enlivened by the suggestion that what the history profession needed was "a little anarchy." This, Frank Manuel said, was the great merit of the new history—its variety, openness, and pluralism. If Charles Tilly chose to study the French working class by counting the incidence of strikes, while he, Manuel, did so by dramatizing the personalities of the strikers, that was all to the good. There was no meeting ground between them, and there need not be. All that was necessary was the tolerance to permit "different people doing different kinds of things in different ways." Lawrence Stone, himself a practitioner of the new history, was moved to protest: "If this is true, I think it is tragic. It is appalling if two men studying a single phenomenon just walk past each other and have nothing to say to each other."[1]

Stone was describing an experience that has become all too familiar in recent years. For all of the brave talk about interdisciplinary studies, scholarship has never been as factional and parochial as it is today. Two historians working on the same subject are apt to produce books so disparate that they might be dealing with different events centuries and continents apart. This has come about not, as was once feared, because of a fragmentation of learning, a division of labor with each scholar intensively cultivating his own small piece of the turf. Nor is it because the "two cultures" have created disciplines so specialized and recondite that their practitioners can no longer understand each other. In spite of the technical apparatus of the "new" methods, the quantohistorians and the psychohistorians can still understand each other, and the traditional historian can understand them both. In one respect they understand one another all too well. This, indeed, is the difficulty. For what they understand is that each school is staking out for itself the largest part, if not the whole of the subject; each is laying claim to the deepest level of understanding; each thinks it has the most direct access to the truth. If they agree to tolerate each other, as Manuel suggests, it is out of sheer civility. But they do not really communicate with each other, because they insist upon speaking different languages, with different vocabularies, different rules of syntax, different intonations and gestures—all reflecting profoundly different interpretations of reality.

The situation would be harmless if it affected only such relatively limited topics as strikes in nineteenth-century France. What makes it serious, and what Stone was properly exercised about, is the fact that the most comprehensive and most crucial themes are treated in the same disparate manner. Take, for example, a subject that has been said to be at the heart of all history, that to some degree impinges upon most human activities—the subject of class. There are periods and events in history that are unintelligible without reference to the phenomenon of class, centuries of literature and entire genres (the novel, most notably) that have drawn sustenance from it, philosophies and ideologies of the greatest practical as well as theoretical import that make of it the central fact of life. When this subject is treated as diversely as it has been in recent years, to the point where serious scholars "walk past each other and have nothing to say to each other," we may well be disturbed.

There was a time when not only historians but all humanists spoke the same language and found much to say to each other. In 1950, when Lionel Trilling's *Liberal Imagination* was published, the historian, no less than the literary critic, could read that book as a testament of his own faith. When Trilling spoke of the social reality that was the substance of the novel, when he deplored the misguided liberalism that thought it enlightened to ignore the fact of class—as if that fact was a philistine intrusion upon the literary imagination, demeaning to the critic and novelist alike—the historian was heartened, recognizing that social reality as the very stuff of history. And when Trilling admonished the critic to avoid the opposite extreme, the fallacy of supposing that the fact of class had nothing to do with ideas, that the social reality stood apart from and independent of the exercise of mind, the historian took that too to heart. In Trilling's concept of the "moral imagination" the historian, as much as the literary critic, could find his own mission: to examine the assumptions and preconceptions, the attitudes, beliefs, and ideas that are as much the facts of history as of culture.[2] And the facts of history in both senses of "history"; if the moral imagination shaped the past, it must to the same degree shape our thinking and writing about the past.

But that was before the new history itself reshaped the very idea of history. Today a school of historians is being trained to write a kind of history that is as nearly devoid of moral imagination as the computer can make it. It was one of Trilling's heroes, Matthew Arnold, who characterized as "barbarians" and "philistines" those in his own day who were inaccessible to ideas and therefore obsessively concerned with the "machinery" of life.[3] But neither Arnold nor Trilling could have anticipated the mechanization of ideas, which is more insidious than the mere use of computers.

In place of the moral imagination, we are more and more confronted with something that might be called the sociological imagination. The sociologist cum historian assimilates history to the social sciences. He prides himself on using only hard data, precise and unambiguous, the kind that can be counted, sorted and weighed, arranged in tables, charts, and graphs. In a more sophisticated variant of this method, he goes beyond the empirical, quantitative method and constructs models intended to represent the abstract essence of the data.

Model-building has recently emerged as the ne plus ultra of the sociological imagination. The model seems to have all the advantages of the quantitative method and more. It is abstract as well as precise; it lends itself readily to comparative analysis; it is scientific, objective, and "value free"; it makes explicit what might otherwise remain implicit; it evokes the largest statements, generalizations, and theories. As one disciple of the method has said, it liberates history from the conventional, undisciplined, "impressionistic" historian who takes refuge in "literary grace," in "paradox, antithesis, innuendo, and gratuitous irony."[4]

Although any aspect of history is amenable to quantification and model-building (it has become a measure of the ingenuity of the sociological historian to apply his methods to political, diplomatic, military, even religious history), social history is the special province of the sociological historian. And within social history, the subject he has staked out for himself is that of class. Reading the recent literature on this subject, one can easily get the impression that the sociological historian invented, or at the very least discovered, the phenomenon of class. One is tempted to forget that the consciousness of class is as old as class itself, and that in some periods—in nineteenth-century England most notably—contemporaries spoke of class with a candor and clarity that may come as a shock to some latter-day historians.

The most ambitious attempt to build a class model for early-nineteenth-century England may be found in an article by R. S. Neale originally published in 1968 and reprinted in 1972.[5] In place of the conventional three classes, Neale proposes a five-part division: upper class, middle class, middling class, working class A, and working class B. To the unsophisticated eye, this may look like the familiar distinctions of upper, upper-middle, lower-middle, upper-lower, and lower-lower. But Neale has something much more ambitious in mind. His classes are based not only on the distinctive sources of their income, their professions or occupations, but also on their attitudes toward themselves and their relations with each other.

So far, Neale concedes, his five-class model is essentially static and therefore inappropriate for an England where the only certainty was the fact of change. To convey the dynamic nature of the model, the classes are visualized not as separate boxes in the usual manner, but as pools of water:

> Think of the five classes, each embracing a number of social strata, as separate pools of water linked together by streams of water and located on a convex but asymmetrical hill with the Middling Class on the summit exposed to all the elements. The Upper and Middle Class pools lie on the sheltered sunny side of the hill and both Working Class pools lie on the higher and more exposed northern slope. The stream linking the summit or Middling Class pool to the Middle and Upper Class pools is controlled by traditional sluices between each pool. The two Working Class pools are linked to each other and the Middling Class pool by more sluggish streams but there are no obstacles to the downward flow of water although eddies will result in water moving backwards and forwards between any two pools.[6]

Even this verbal account cannot describe the model in all its precision, abstraction, and complexity. Only a diagram can do justice to it (Figure 1).

Neale has taken us far from an old-fashioned "impressionism" or even an old-fashioned mode of quantification. The language of the model suggests a high order of sociological abstraction: "authority" and "deferential" levels, "social stratification," "status" and "behavior" barriers, "ascribed" status and "privatized" behavior. These concepts are presented in such a manner as to connote a correspondingly high degree of precision: lines are solid or broken, of varying thicknesses, graduated on a scale, pointing in one direction or another. The model even contains something resembling a formula: "Interaction of growth and 'n' achievement." And a note appears to give instructions for calculating the "probability" of movement from one class to another: "Probabilities will vary with rate of growth, 'n' achievement, time, population growth, and the strength of barriers."

It may seem carping to complain that one does not know what this elaborate diagram means or what it contributes to our understanding of the subject. What good is a formula in which some of the variables cannot be quantified because the historian lacks the necessary data (the "rate of growth" at any particular time), and in which other of the variables are by their nature unquantifiable ("the strength of barriers")? If the formula is only intended to point to the presence of these factors, does one need either a formula or a diagram? Is a "guessed probability" indicated by the "thickness of line" a better guess, more exactly "indicated," than that which might be conveyed verbally by such notoriously inexact words as "more" and "less"? Does the diagram really tell us anything more than the admittedly imprecise accounts of the conventional historian?

The diagram does have one important virtue: it offers an alternative to the traditional three-class model. But that alternative emerges earlier in Neale's article without benefit of diagrams, charts, or even statistics. It is on the basis of the usual kinds of literary, impressionistic evidence—excerpts from commission reports, articles, memoirs, letters, buttressed by an occasional reference to a secondary source—that the author is moved to challenge the traditional three-class model. But if he finds three classes insufficient to account for the complexities of the social reality, why stop at five? Would it not be more precise to separate some of the disparate groups lumped together in the middling

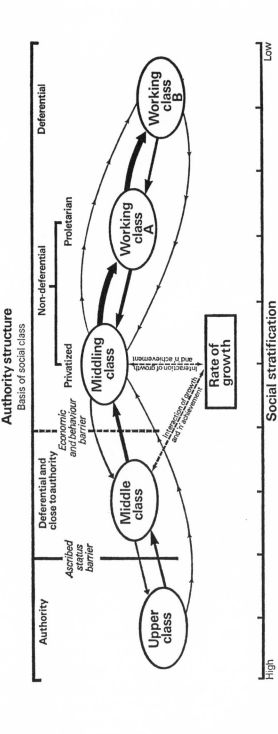

Arrows indicate direction of flow.

Thickness of line indicates guessed probability of moving from one class to another *circa* 1800 (probabilities will vary with rate of growth, 'n' achievement, time, population growth and the strength of barriers). Given sustained growth the probabilities of moving from low to high increase, the probabilities of moving from high to low decrease.

Figure 1   Diagram of the five-class model. From R. S. Neale, "Class-Consciousness in Early Nineteenth-Century England: Three Classes or Five?" *Victorian Studies*, September 1968; reprinted by permission.

class—"petit bourgeois, aspiring professional men, other literates, and artisans"—or the motley assortment comprising working class B— "agricultural laborers, other low-paid nonfactory urban laborers, domestic servants, urban poor, most working-class women whether from Working Class A or B households"?[7] Surely these groups did not share the same attitudes and social relations. Why not, for the sake of greater precision, assign each of these groups a pool of its own, with its own streams, sluices, barriers, and all the rest?

Neale is undoubtedly right to be dissatisfied with the conventional class trinity, especially with the category of the middle class. (George Kitson Clark put the matter well when he said that the concept of the middle class has "done more to stultify thought about Victorian England than anything else.")[8] And there is much in Neale's article that is suggestive and valuable. The question is whether the model helps or hurts his case—whether it does not, for all its curves rather than straight lines and arrows pointing in both directions, make for new crudities and rigidities. It also raises the question of whether a misplaced or spurious precision is better than an unabashed and avowed imprecision. A five-class (or seven- or eight- or *n*-class) pool-model is not, after all, the only alternative to a three-class box-model. Another alternative is a well-reasoned, well-documented argument in which the nuances of language, rather than the direction and thickness of lines, bear the burden of conveying the complexities and subtleties of the social reality.

To the sociological historian, however, language is a "burden" in the worst sense. Having made a great virtue of precise and explicit definitions, he often proceeds to formulate definitions that are either so obtuse as to be incomprehensible or so tautological as to be useless. For the sociologist, there may be some meaning or utility in the definition of social classes as "conflict groups arising out of the authority structure of imperatively coordinated associations";[9] its abstractness may be appropriate to his purpose, which is to describe the phenomenon of class in its most general, universal, abstract sense. For the historian, interested in the particularity of a historical situation, such a definition can hardly be helpful. At best it plays no part in his research. At worst it distracts him from attending to the "actualities" of the historical situation by promoting the illusion that by virtue of some such definition, he has "objectively identified" the concept of class.[10] It is this illusion, this claim of objectivity, that is the driving force behind the enterprise of sociological history.

The historian—any historian—may properly be accused of hubris, of professing to know more about a historical event, to understand it better or more objectively, than those contemporaries who lived through it. It is an inescapable occupational hazard. For all the historian's wariness of the fallacy of hindsight, for all his attempts to avoid that fallacy by immersing himself in contemporary sources, it remains his eternal temptation and besetting sin. But where the traditional historian is disturbed by his presumptuousness, the sociological historian flaunts it; it is his pride and distinction. He invents a language that he claims conveys the social reality better than the language of contemporaries. He freely reorders and remodels the experiences of contemporaries. He abstracts, generalizes, theorizes for whatever purposes he deems proper, to elicit whatever categories or postulates he deems important. At every point he is asserting his independence of and his superiority over those contemporaries who provide his material. In the currently fashionable phrase, they are his "objects"; he alone can see them "objectively," scientifically; he can "construct" or "deconstruct" them at will.

Yet even as objects, contemporaries have a limited interest for the sociological historian, whole dimensions of their experience being denied or belittled by him. The only parts of their experience he can recognize, because they are the only parts he can use, are those that manifest themselves externally, that are visible, measurable, quantifiable. Their ideas, attitudes, beliefs, perceptions enter into his tables and models only when they express themselves behaviorally—in riots, or elections, or church attendance, or production and consumption.

It is often said that this kind of sociological history is the only democratic form of history; it is the history of "anonymous" masses instead of "great men"—the politicians, writers, leaders of one sort or another who emerged in their own time as identifiable individuals. Sociological history has indeed had the effect of suppressing these notable individuals. The question is whether it has succeeded in bringing to life the anonymous masses, whether it has not "upstaged" the masses just as it has the leaders, whether it does not display toward the masses the same condescension, the same sense of superiority, it does toward all contemporaries.

It is true, of course, that individual contemporaries, contemporaries who distinguished themselves in one fashion or another, cannot be presumed to speak for the anonymous masses. But if distinguished contemporaries are thus disqualified, surely a historian, generations removed from those masses, familiar with them only through certain kinds of records that happen to have been preserved, must be immodest indeed to think that he can understand them better than the wisest men of their time. Surely he cannot afford to ignore the considered judgments of these contemporaries. Nor can he afford to confine himself to their private letters and memoirs in preference to their essays and books, on the assumption that truth is best revealed—exposed, "given away"—at the level of least consciousness, that greater consciousness brings with it more of the delusions of "false consciousness." There is something slanderous about this assumption. It implies that a great contemporary, precisely when he is at his greatest, expressing himself most carefully and deliberately, is least to be trusted to tell the truth. And if the great men of the time are thus defamed, so also are all the anonymous people who bought their books, listened to their speeches, and otherwise accorded them the title of greatness. What purports to be democratic history may well prove to be the most insidious kind of elitist history.

When the discussion of class is returned to contemporaries, one discovers quite different conceptions from those found in the tables and models of sociological historians. One also discovers why these historians cannot readily incorporate the contemporary concepts into their own models. Contemporaries, it appears, were not only acutely class-conscious; their class consciousness was a highly charged moral affair. Over and above all the economic, legal, and social distinctions that can be quantified and diagrammed, there is an order of facts that defies the sociological imagination: men's perceptions of themselves in relation to others, and their conceptions of what was proper and improper, just and unjust, right and wrong about those relations. The most ingenious sociologist cannot translate these perceptions and conceptions into the language—the models, abstractions, and quantifications—of sociology. They were rendered at the time, and are still only intelligible, in literary language, the discourse of ordinary people as well as the learned, of the anonymous masses as well as notable individuals. And that language is thoroughly, ineradicably penetrated by moral nuances.

If we refuse to indulge the current prejudice against greatness, we may choose to consult, on the subject of class, one of the great commentators on Victorian England, Thomas Carlyle. Carlyle was great not only in himself but in his influence, and in his influence not only upon readers of all classes but also upon some of the greatest and most influential of his own contemporaries—Mill, Arnold, Dickens, Eliot, Disraeli, Kingsley, Ruskin, Swinburne, Thackeray. Some of these (Mill particularly) were eventually put off by the blatantly undemocratic tone of Carlyle's later writings. But the younger Carlyle helped shape the moral, intellectual, and social consciousness of early Victorian England as perhaps no other single figure did. Even when he provoked criticism, he confronted his critics with an alternative vision of society they could not ignore. George Eliot, herself a formidable moralist, explained that even those who shared few of Carlyle's opinions found the reading of *Sartor Resartus* an "epoch in the history of their minds."

> It is an idle question to ask whether his books will be read a century hence: if they were all burnt as the grandest suttees on his funeral pyre, it would only be like cutting down an oak after its acorns have sown a forest. For there is hardly a superior or active mind of this generation that has not been modified by Carlyle's writings; there has hardly been an English book written for the last ten or twelve years that would not have been different if Carlyle had not lived.[11]

What is remarkable is that Carlyle had the effect he did in spite of a rhetoric so extraordinary that today it tends to repel all but the staunchest devotee. We think of the nineteenth century as an age of intolerable conformity, repressive of all individuality, enthusiasm, passion. We also think of it as an age of complacency and hypocrisy, in which the realities of life were obscured by polite euphemisms and a mindless adherence to convention. If anything could put such myths to rest, a reading of Carlyle would do so.

He was the most individualistic, indeed eccentric, of writers—and the most outspoken. He denounced the false "gospels" of the age, the "foul and vile and soul-murdering Mud-gods," with all the fervor of a Jeremiah.[12] His invectives are famous: utilitarianism was "pig philosophy"; laissez-faireism was the freedom of apes; parliamentary reform was "constitution-mongering"; material progress was "mammonism"; rationalism was "dilettantism." The more he denounced these false idols, and the more intemperately and idiosyncratically he did so, using elaborate metaphors and obscure references, presenting his ideas in the guise of a newly published work of German philosophy or the chronicle of a twelfth-century monk, the more attentively he was read. It is perhaps just as well that much of his audience did not understand all his allusions; Professor Teufelsdröckh, the hero (or antihero) of *Sartor Resartus,* translates in its most refined version as Professor Devil's Dung. But those who did know German, including Mill and Arnold, were not disconcerted by his pungent language, perhaps because they respected the moral passion inspiring it.

It is ironic—but only because of what historians have since made of it—that Carlyle should have coined the phrase "condition-of-England question." Today this is generally interpreted as the "standard-of-living question," which is taken as an invitation to quantification, the amassing of statistics relating to wages and prices, production and consumption. Carlyle understood it quite otherwise. Having opened his essay "Chartism" with the "condition-of-England question," he followed it with an extremely skeptical chapter on "Statistics."

> Tables are like cobwebs, like the sieve of the Danaides; beautifully reticulated, orderly to look upon, but which will hold no conclusion. Tables are abstractions, and the object a most concrete one, so difficult to read the essence of. There are innumerable circumstances; and one circumstance left out may be the vital one on which all turned. Statistics is a science which ought to be honourable, the basis of many most important sciences; but it is not to be carried on by steam, this science, any more than others are; a wise head is requisite for carrying it on. Conclusive facts are inseparable from inconclusive except by a head that already understands and knows.[13]

To "understand" and to "know," Carlyle said, was to ask the right questions, questions that could not be answered with the most comprehensive figures and charts. The first sentence of his essay defined the condition-of-England question as the "condition and disposition" of the working classes. If we are inclined to forget the second of these terms, Carlyle never was. What gave Chartism its enduring strength, he explained, was the fact that it was only a new name for an age-old phenomenon: it meant "the bitter discontent grown fierce and mad, the wrong condition therefore, or the wrong disposition, of the Working Classes of England." The question "What is the condition of the working classes?" had as its corollary, "Is the condition of the English working people wrong; so wrong that rational working men cannot, will not, and even should not rest quiet under it?" And this raised the further questions: "Is the discontent itself mad, like the shape it took? Not the condition of the working people that is wrong; but their disposition, their own thoughts, beliefs and feelings that are wrong?" The answers to these questions were not quantifiable because the condition of people depended not on their material goods but on their moral disposition. "It is not what a man outwardly has or wants that constitutes the happiness or misery of him. Nakedness, hunger, distress of all kinds, death itself have been cheerfully suffered, when the heart was right. It is the feeling of *injustice* that is insupportable to all men."[14]

Carlyle's other famous invention, the phrase "cash payment the sole nexus," derived from the same moral impulse.[15] He attributed to the economists the deplorable idea that men were subject to the principle of supply and demand as surely as material goods were, that human relations were best left to the impersonal forces of the marketplace, that cash payment was the sole nexus between man and man. What outraged him was not only that men were reduced to this inhuman condition—although that would be outrage enough—but that this condition should be represented as perfectly natural, a God-given law of nature. This was blasphemous as well as inhuman, a mockery of God and of man.

If the relations of individual men were tainted by this modern heresy, so were the relations of classes. Like most of his contemporaries, Carlyle had a simple view of the class structure of England: there was an upper class and a lower class, a class of the rich and a class of the poor. Generally, again like most of his contemporaries, he pluralized both of these, making them the "upper classes" and "lower classes"; sometimes he gave them a special Carlylean twist, as when he spoke of the "under class." But his special contribution to the nomenclature—and to the conception—of classes was his distinction between the "toiling classes" and the "untoiling."[16] It was here that the two classes, so far from being simple descriptive terms, became morally charged.

And it was here that Carlyle parted company with Marx and Engels, who borrowed his aphorism about the cash nexus and quoted him on the condition of the working classes. What Carlyle meant by the toiling classes and the untoiling classes was not at all what might seem to be their Marxist equivalents: labor and capital. The toiling classes included those members of the upper classes who did in fact work, and the untoiling classes those of the lower classes who did not work. So too there were rich "master-workers" as well as "master-idlers" (or "master-unworkers"), and poor "unworkers" who spent their days in poorhouses euphemistically known as "workhouses."[17]

The implications of Carlyle's distinctions are momentous, for they mean that he was not at all the cryptosocialist that some present-day socialists would make of him. Socialists can share Carlyle's outrage at the condition of the poor, his condemnation of the idle rich, his detestation of laissez-faire economics. They can find in him premonitions of the dehumanization, desocialization, and alienation they attribute to capitalism. They can even share his respect for work, under certain ideal conditions. The young Marx might have said, as Carlyle did, "Labour is not a devil, even while encased in Mammonism; Labour is ever an imprisoned god, writhing unconsciously or consciously to escape out of Mammonism!"[18]

What the Marxist cannot do, however, and what Carlyle insisted upon doing, was to give work an ennobling quality for the capitalist as well as the laborer—provided only that the capitalist was a master-worker rather than a master-idler. *Laborare est orare:* this was the gospel according to Carlyle.[19] "All work . . . is noble; work is alone noble."[20] And this dictum redeemed the capitalist, the working capitalist (the "Mill-ocracy," as Carlyle put it), as much as the workingman. Just as in the Marxist schema the concept of surplus value, or exploitation, illegitimized, so to speak, the capitalist, making him the villain of that morality play, so the concept of work legitimized him for Carlyle—made of him a "captain of industry," a natural leader and a true hero.

This is why the struggle between rich and poor, between the upper and lower classes, was not for Carlyle the same inexorable, fatal war-to-the-death it was for Marx. Indeed, for Carlyle a symptom and also a cause of the prevailing misery and discontent was the fact that there was such a struggle. The idle aristocracy, abdicating its natural political role, made the process of government seem artificial, the fortuitous product of competition and struggle. This was the true perversion of political economy. Denying the proper function of government, the laissez-faireists subverted the proper relationship of the governed and the governors. And in the absence of such a relationship, cash payment became the sole nexus connecting the rich and the poor.

After reading the reviews of "Chartism," Carlyle remarked: "The people are beginning to discover that I am not a Tory. Ah, no! but one of the deepest, though perhaps the quietest, of all the Radicals now extant in the world."[21] Carlyle's radicalism may not be ours. Nor was it that of all radicals in his own time.* But it was a form of radicalism that most of his contemporaries recognized as such. One reader of *Past and Present* quipped that the book would be very dangerous if it were ever "turned into the vernacular."[22]

Carlyle's radicalism consisted not in the answers he gave to the condition-of-England question but in putting the question itself, and in putting it in such a form that it raised the most fundamental doubts about the legitimacy of prevailing doctrines and class relations. Nothing is more banal than the idea that England, or any country, is divided into an upper and a lower class, into rich and poor. What Carlyle did was to raise the idea of class to a new level of consciousness by giving it a moral urgency. In Victorian England the idea of work was a powerful moral concept, a cogent instrument of legitimization and illegitimization. By associating it with the idea of class, Carlyle made problematic—"dangerous," as one reader said—what had previously been the most natural and innocent of propositions, that England was divided into two classes.

In *Sartor Resartus* Carlyle described the extremes to which those two classes were being pushed. The book is an elaborate play upon a treatise, *Die Kleider, ihr Werden und Wirken,* by the ubiquitous Herr Teufelsdröckh, Professor of Allerlei Wissenschaft at the University of Weissnichtwo. The clothes metaphor inspired Carlyle to invent two

---

*Nor of radicals abroad, although they too testified to its radicalism. Marx and Engels paid Carlyle the high tribute of borrowing and publicizing his phrase about "cash payment" constituting the "sole nexus of man to man." And Engels, reviewing *Past and Present,* said it was the only book published in England that year "worth reading." Although he rebuked Carlyle for not realizing that the cause of the social evil was private property, his much lengthier criticism was directed at Carlyle's "pantheism," which he took to be as outmoded and pernicious as conventional religion. Echoing Feuerbach, Engels insisted that the old question "What is God?" had finally been answered by German philosophy: "God is Man." (Karl Marx and Friedrich Engels, *Collected Works* [New York, 1975–], III, 463–466.)

sects, Dandies and Drudges, the first worshipping money and the trappings of gentlemanliness, the second slaving to keep barely clothed and fed.

> Such are the two Sects which, at this moment, divide the more unsettled portion of the British People, and agitate that ever-vexed country . . . In their roots and subterranean ramifications, they extend through the entire structure of Society, and work unweariedly in the secret depths of English national Existence, striving to separate and isolate it into two contradictory, uncommunicating masses . . . To me it seems probable that the two Sects will one day part England between them, each recruiting itself from the intermediate ranks, till there be none left to enlist on either side.[23]

If Carlyle's final words remind us of Marx, with his predictions of the polarization of classes—the increasing concentration of wealth on the one hand, the increasing proletarianization and pauperization on the other—the rest of the passage recalls Disraeli's famous phrase "the two nations." One need not go so far as some historians who claim that Disraeli made of that expression a "household word."[24] Nor need one make too much of the fact that others used it before him.[25] It is enough to say that Disraeli dramatized and popularized a concept that was "in the air."

Disraeli also dramatized, perhaps romanticized as well, the condition-of-England question. In *Coningsby,* published in 1844, five years after Carlyle's "Chartism," Disraeli referred to the "Condition-of-England Question of which our generation hears so much."[26] A few months later, in an address to his constituents, he claimed some priority for that concept: "Long before what is called the 'condition of the people question' was discussed in the House of Commons, I had employed my pen on the subject."[27] He had already begun writing *Sybil* and was evidently anticipating a criticism that was to be leveled against that book: that parts of it sound like a transcript of Royal Commission reports and parliamentary debates. Having listened to those debates (a Factory Bill had been introduced in that very session of parliament) and having actually inserted verbatim into his novel portions of one of those reports (the second report of the Children's Employment Commission, released in 1842), Disraeli had reason to be sensitive on this account.[28]

The message of *Sybil* is perfectly clear and explicit. Unlike Carlyle, with his extended metaphors and heavy irony, Disraeli, even when writing fiction, was engaged in a not very subtle form of political indoctrination. If parts of *Sybil* read like transcripts of the blue books (which they were), other parts sound like extracts from a *Short Course in the History of England, by a Young Englander,* or from penny pamphlets on "the social problem." In the novel the crucial passages announce themselves, so to speak, by the device of capitals. Thus the first mention of the two-nations theme appears in a dialogue between Egremont, the good aristocrat (one is tempted to capitalize these identifications, as in a morality play), and "the stranger," later identified as Stephen Morley, an Owenite who has joined forces with the Chartists.

> "Say what you like, our Queen reigns over the greatest nation that ever existed."
>
> "Which nation?" asked the younger stranger, "for she reigns over two."
>
> The stranger paused; Egremont was silent, but looked inquiringly.
>
> "Yes," resumed the stranger. "Two nations; between whom there is no intercourse and no sympathy; who are as ignorant of each other's habits, thoughts, and feelings, as if they were dwellers in different zones, or inhabitants of different planets; who are as formed by a different breeding, are fed by a different food, are ordered by different manners, and are not governed by the same laws."
>
> "You speak of—" said Egremont, hesitatingly.
>
> "THE RICH AND THE POOR."[29]

This final line of capitals is followed by a fade-out scene worthy of a grade C movie: the gray ruins are suffused by a "sudden flush of rosy light," and the voice of Sybil is heard singing the evening hymn to the Virgin—"a single voice; but tones of almost supernatural sweetness; tender and solemn, yet flexible and thrilling."[30]

This is Disraeli prose at its worst, blatantly tendentious and mawkishly romantic. Most of it is very much better—tendentious, to be sure, but cleverly so—sharp, acerbic, witty, and surprisingly often conveying some provocative thought. And even the romantic interludes are redeemed by a latent irony that makes for a slightly offbeat, campy effect. *Sybil* is, in fact, an eminently readable book, and although the literary strategy is obvious enough—the contrast between high society and the lowliest poor, between parliamentary intrigue and Chartist conspiracy—there are memorable episodes satirizing the upper classes and dramatizing the lower. The opening scene in the fashionable club finds a group of rich, blasé, and rather effete young men chatting idly about the forthcoming Derby races, with one man confessing that he rather likes bad wine because, you know, "one gets so bored with good wine."[31] In the same mood are scenes featuring the ladies of the great houses, who think they are wielding political power (perhaps they are—the novel is ambiguous at this point) by extending or withholding invitations to their dinner parties; they vainly attempt to extract information from dim-witted lords who do not know they are being pumped, for the very good reason that they know nothing at all.

On the other side of the social spectrum is the reality that these fashionable men and women are so abysmally ignorant of: the reality of THE PEOPLE, or THE POOR—terms that Disraeli uses interchangeably. Disraeli has been criticized, and properly so, for overdramatizing the condition of England in the nineteenth century and overidealizing the condition of England in the good old days. As if she were recalling her own youth in pre-Reformation times, Sybil reflects:

> When I remember what this English people once was; the truest, the freest, and the bravest, the best-natured and the best-looking, the happiest and most religious race upon the surface of this globe; and think of them now, with all their crimes and all their slavish sufferings, their soured spirits and their stunted forms; their lives without enjoyment, and their deaths without hope; I may well feel for them, even if I were not the daughter of their blood.[32]

Even if the extravagant rhetoric, with all those superlatives—the truest, the freest, the bravest—do not forewarn us that Disraeli intends the passage to be read mythically and allegorically, the last sentence should surely alert us to that possibility; for at this point in the story we know that Sybil is not, in fact, "the daughter of their blood," that far from being of "the people," she is the descendant of one of the oldest and noblest families.

Apart from such mythicized representations of past and present (intentionally mythicized, as I read Disraeli), there are scenes that, however exaggerated, reveal important and frequently ignored aspects of social reality. For all his fantasies and extravagances, Disraeli had a clear perception of different conditions and kinds of poverty. He distinguished, for example, between rural and industrial poverty, between manufacturing and mining towns, between the ordinary working poor and an underclass that was almost a race apart, brutalized, uncivilized, living in a virtual state of nature. There is a precision in these distinctions that the historian may well respect.

The historian may also profitably read the exchange between the good aristocrat Egremont and the Chartist Gerard in which each cites statistics about the condition of England, the one proving that it is much better, the other much worse, than ever before, with Gerard concluding (like Carlyle before him) that in any event it is not so much material conditions that are at issue as the relations of men with one another. The Owenite Morley makes the same point: "There is no community in England; there is aggregation, but aggregation under circumstances which make it rather a dissociating than a uniting principle."[33] It is only when he goes so far as to denounce the home as "obsolete" that Gerard balks. "Home is a barbarous idea," Morley says, "the method of a rude age; home is isolation; therefore antisocial. What we want is Community." "I daresay you are right," Gerard replies, "but I like stretching my feet on my own hearth."[34]

When sociologists distinguish between "community" and "aggregation," under the labels of *Gemeinschaft* and *Gesellschaft,* historians listen respectfully. When Disraeli does it, he is dismissed as a medievalist and romantic. Yet Disraeli is careful to assign this speech about community not to Sybil, who *is* a medievalist and romantic, but to the Owenite, who believes that "the railways will do as much for mankind as the monasteries ever did."[35] Neither Morley nor Gerard has any hankering for a preindustrial age; both want only to humanize and socialize relations under the conditions of industrialism. The one character in the novel whose occupation it is to exalt and perpetuate the past is a fraud, if a kindly one; this is the antiquarian Hatton, who made his fortune by tracing—inventing, if need be—the lineage of noble and would-be noble families, and who himself turns out to be the brother of the vilest and lowest of the rabble.

If Disraeli's cast of characters includes good aristocrats as well as bad, it also includes good factory owners as well as bad. To be sure, the best of these factory owners happens to be the younger son of an old, impoverished landed family. And it is this heritage that makes him so exemplary a character: "With gentle blood in his veins, and old English feelings, he imbibed, at an early period of his career, a correct conception of the relations which should subsist between the employer and the employed. He felt that between them there should be other ties than the payment and the receipt of wages."[36] (If the last sentence is not a conscious echo of Carlyle's "cash nexus," it testifies to the prevalence of that sentiment at the time.) Disraeli's account of this model factory town is more than a little idyllic; everyone is happy, healthy, moral, and content. But it is also noteworthy that what Disraeli is idealizing, contrary to the conventional impression, is a *factory* town. (In the same spirit, in his earlier novel *Coningsby,* he has Sidonia interrupt Coningsby's reveries about the glories of Athens. "The Age of Ruins is past," Sidonia reminds him. "Have you seen Manchester?")[37]

Disraeli's two nations, like Carlyle's two classes, are more complicated than they appear at first sight—again, because they are moral as well as descriptive categories. Just as Carlyle's upper class contains a toiling and an idle class, so Disraeli's rich contains a responsible and an irresponsible element. For the indolent club-lounger titillated by the idea of drinking bad wine, or the ladies of the salons who look on politics as a game devised for the exercise of their female wiles, Disraeli has nothing but contempt. Riches, position, power are said to have "only one duty—to secure the social welfare of the PEOPLE."[38]

Just as work was the legitimizing principle for Carlyle, so duty was the legitimizing principle for Disraeli. Where Carlyle, putting a premium on work, found most of his heroes among the "Mill-ocracy," the captains of industry, Disraeli looked primarily to the landed aristocracy who in his mythical rendition of English history traditionally functioned in this responsible, moral fashion. Although Carlyle and Disraeli chose to eulogize and mythicize different groups among the upper classes, they agreed that it was the responsibility of the upper classes to rule—humanely, justly, compassionately, but rule—and the obligation of the lower classes to be ruled. The main plot of *Sybil* centers on the attempt of the lower classes to find salvation in and by themselves, to try to cure their condition with their own resources, to develop leaders of their own and seek power on their own behalf. This was the aspiration of the Chartists, represented by Gerard, the purest and noblest of men, who dies in the course of a wild, bloody, pointless rampage. Only after his death is Sybil disabused of her "phantoms," as Egremont delicately puts it—her illusion that the people are wise and good, that the poor can do no wrong and the rich no right, and that between the two "the gulf is impassable."[39]

Sybil is generally taken to be the heroine of the book. As such, she is a distinctly flawed character—the heroine, perhaps, but not the hero. The unequivocal hero is Egremont, the good and wise aristocrat, who wants to obtain, as he says, "the results of the Charter without the intervention of its machinery." That cryptic statement bewilders some characters in the novel and is interpreted by others as "sheer Radicalism"—"the most really democratic speech that I ever read."[40] What Egremont means, of course, is that the welfare of the people can best be ensured not by transferring power to them, as the Chartists advise, but by exercising power on their behalf. Elsewhere, less cryptically, Egremont declares that "the rights of labour were as sacred as those of property; that if a difference were to be established, the interests of the living wealth ought to be preferred; . . . that the social happiness of the millions should be the first object of a statesman, and that, if this were not achieved, thrones and dominions, the pomp and power of courts and empires, were alike worthless."[41]

Contemporaries did not always know what to make of Disraeli, and historians know still less. The distinguished historian G. M. Young, who was old-fashioned enough (and old enough) to draw upon his own memories and those of his acquaintances, asked one elderly Gladstonian why his generation was so profoundly distrustful of Disraeli. The answer surprised Young. It was, the old man said, because of "his early Radicalism."[42] Whatever one may think of the practicality of Disraeli's kind of radicalism, or of its desirability, or whether it was radical at all, or even whether Disraeli was entirely serious in propounding it, one cannot deny that it did color his own thinking and that of contemporaries about him.

More important than Disraeli's solution of the social problem—the nation unified under the direction of a "natural" aristocracy dedicated to the "social welfare"—was his conception of the problem itself: a society in which the two classes were diverging so rapidly that they were perilously close to becoming "two nations." Many contemporaries who did not subscribe to his ideology, who found him either too radical or insufficiently radical, shared his view of the social condition. And it was this view—this model, so to speak—that was enormously influential, that made the "two nations" a graphic image of the social reality and a powerful symbol of discontent.

Disraeli and Carlyle are only two of the many Victorians whose vision of the social reality helped shape that reality as well as reflect it. If one is looking for class models, surely their two-nation and two-sect models are as worthy of consideration as any the historian may devise. Or one might contemplate the three-class model reluctantly advanced by James Mill—reluctantly because utilitarianism was a profoundly individualistic theory loath to assign any reality to such "fictions" as society or class. Yet even Mill could not entirely dispense with some idea of class, although he did shun the word. In his schema the people were divided into an "aristocratical body," a "democratical body," and a "middle rank," the latter being the repository of virtue, intelligence, and leadership. Matthew Arnold's three classes were substantively the same as Mill's, but his characterizations of them made for a radically different conception of society. Positing an aristocracy of "barbarians," a middle class of "philistines," and a populace combining the worst features of both, he obviously had to look elsewhere for virtue, intelligence, and leadership—to a state capable of transcending these classes. Without this image of the classes one cannot begin to comprehend either his idea of the state or his analysis of the social reality.

There are obviously other ways of drawing upon the contemporary consciousness of class, not only by inquiring into all the eminent and less eminent men who had occasion, in books, articles, speeches, or memoirs, to reflect upon their times and experiences, but also by consulting a variety of other sources that dealt with the same issue more obliquely, less self-consciously: novels, tracts, newspaper accounts, parliamentary debates, Royal Commission reports, legislative acts, and administrative measures. A few obvious models emerge from these sources—two or three classes, for the most part, often with each class pluralized ("working classes," for example), suggesting an acute sense of the fluidity and complexity of social relations. Whatever the model, it almost invariably contained a strong moral component. The classes themselves were described in moral terms, and the relations among them were presumed to have a moral character (or were criticized for failing to exhibit the proper moral character, which was itself a moral judgment). Just as we would not today (or most of us would not, even today) define familial relations in purely behavioral terms—age, sex, habitat, financial ties—so the Victorians would have found inadequate any purely behavioral description of social relations that did not take into account such moral facts as duty and obligation, propriety and responsibility.

This is where much of sociological history goes grievously astray. Even those works that avoid the more egregious fallacies of misplaced precision, excessive abstraction, and obfuscatory language tend to be insufficiently attentive to the quality of mind that permeated nineteenth-century England. It may seem odd that historians should fail to avail themselves of such obvious sources of evidence as the ideas and beliefs of contemporaries—of the great men of the time as well as the ordinary men—until one realizes that to take seriously that evidence would be to jeopardize the enterprise of sociological history as it is generally conceived. Intent upon creating a scientific, objective history, these historians think it necessary to purge the social reality of the values that interfere with this "value-free" history.

It is not only this ideal of positivist history that is inimical to the moral imagination. It is also a distaste for the particular kind of moral imagination that prevailed in nineteenth-century England. Today all moral concepts are to some degree suspect; they strike the modern ear as condescending, subjective, arbitrary. And they are all the more disagreeable when applied to class—when the poor were described (as they habitually were in the nineteenth century) as "deserving" or "undeserving," or when the working classes were divided into the "respectable" and the "unrespectable," or when reformers announced their intention of fostering among the lower classes the virtues of thrift, temperance, cleanliness, and good character.

To the latter-day historian this moral temper suggests a failure of understanding as well as of compassion. One author has characterized it as an ideological "deformation" produced by the "distorting lens" of the middle class, a deformation so pervasive it even affected the consciousness of the working classes themselves.[43] From this perspective the moral imagination of the Victorians is not something to be understood and described as an essential part of the social reality, but something to be exposed and criticized from the vantage point of the historian's superior understanding of that reality. And the reality itself is assumed to be best understood in "objective"—which is to say, economic—terms, without reference to such "subjective" ideas as moral character.

To call for a restoration of moral imagination in the writing of history—in the writing of all history, but it is in sociological history that it is most sadly lacking—is not to give license to the historian to impose his own moral conceptions on history. This has been the impulse behind yet another fashionable school of thought, that of the "engaged" or "committed" historian. In this view, all pretensions of objectivity are suspect, the only honest history being that which candidly expresses the political and moral beliefs of the historian. At the opposite pole, in one sense, from the sociological mode, this kind of "engaged" history shares with sociological history a contempt for the experiences and beliefs of contemporaries and an overweening regard for the wisdom and judgment of the historian.

What is wanted is not so much the exercise of the historian's moral imagination as a proper respect for the moral imagination of those contemporaries he is professing to describe. This, to be sure, takes an exercise of imagination on the historian's part—a sensitivity to ideas, a tolerance for beliefs that may not be his own, above all a respect for moral principles as such, so that he will not dismiss them too readily as rationalizations of interest, or deformations of vision, or evidence of an intellectual obtuseness that conceals from contemporaries those economic and social facts that are so obvious to the historian.

It is a modest undertaking that is called for, indeed an exercise in modesty. It asks nothing more than that moral data—the ideas, beliefs, principles, perceptions, and opinions of contemporaries—be taken as seriously, be assigned the same reality, as facts about production and consumption, income and education, status and mobility. The historian is in the fortunate position of being able to do what the sociologist cannot do; he can transcend the fact-value dichotomy that has plagued sociological thought. The values of the past are the historian's facts. He should make the most of them, as the great Victorians did.

The "Group":
 British Marxist Historians   ·*4*·

"Why was there no Marxism in Great Britain?" A recent issue of the *English Historical Review* poses yet again one of the perennial problems in English history.[1] Why, in the first country to meet all the conditions for a mass Marxist movement, was there no such movement? Why, in the country that gave birth to the industrial revolution, was there no social revolution? Why, in the first country to create a proletariat worthy of the name, was the very word "proletariat" alien and exotic? These questions have been the staple of historical inquiry at least since Elie Halévy early in the century tried to explain the "miracle of modern England": the ability of England, by virtue of its unique institutions and traditions, to accommodate change, conciliate interests, and mitigate conflict.[2]

There is another question, however, that has not often been asked. Why, in a country so resistant to Marxist socialism, have there been so many eminent Marxist historians? And not as mavericks but as members of a respectable and influential (although not, to be sure, dominant) school. And influential precisely in the field of English history, offering Marxist interpretations of a history that has been notably inhospitable to Marxism as a political ideology.

Part of the answer lies in a fascinating and little-known episode in English intellectual history. It is only recently that we have come to learn something of the origins of English Marxist historiography and to appreciate how well organized and consciously ideological it has been. The story of the "Communist Party Historians' Group" (or "collective," as it has also been called)[3] is all the more interesting because it comes from the principals themselves and their disciples—from memoirs, interviews, essays, and, most recently, a full-length book.

In 1983 one of the most influential historical journals in England opened its one-hundredth issue by recalling its founding in 1952: "The history of *Past and Present* begins in the years of the cold war with a group of young Marxist historians, at that time all members of the British Communist Party and enthusiastic participants in the activities of the 'C. P. Historians' Group' which flourished notably in the years 1946 to 1956." Those young historians were, in fact, old "friends and comrades":

> They thus had the quadruple bond of a common past (most had known each other since the late 1930s), a common political commitment, a passion for history, and regular, indeed intensive, contact at the meetings of the Historians' Group at which they debated the Marxist interpreta-tion of historical problems and did their best, in the military jargon then favoured in Bolshevik circles, to 'wage the battle of ideas' on the 'front' most suitable to historians.[4]

This account comes to us with the authority of three distinguished historians who were founders both of the Communist Party Histo-rians' Group and of *Past and Present*—Christopher Hill, R. H. Hilton, and E. J. Hobsbawm—and who are still active in the affairs of the journal. (Today Hill is president of the Past and Present Society, and Hilton and Hobsbawm are chairman and vice-chairman of the editorial board. The fourth founder of the journal and the oldest member of the Historians' Group, Maurice Dobb, died in 1976.)

A memoir by Hobsbawm, "The Historians' Group of the Commu-nist Party," describes the organization that played "a major part in the development of Marxist historiography" and thus in "British historiog-raphy in general."* The Historians' Group, he reports, was one of many professional and cultural groups operating under the aegis of the

---

*It is fitting that this memoir should have been published in a Festschrift for A. L. Morton, one of the founders of the Group and (in 1978 when the volume was published) still the chairman. Morton had a special role in the founding, since one of the initial purposes of the Group was the revision of his *People's History of England,* a popular but embarrassingly unscholarly book. Published by the Left Book Club just before the war, it went through a dozen printings in England and as many translations and editions abroad. The Group was soon diverted into other tasks and never completed the revision.

National Cultural Committee of the party—"from the Party's point of view, the most flourishing and satisfactory" of them, attracting not only professional historians but also party leaders and union organizers.[5] The founding of *Past and Present* was only one episode in the "battle of ideas" (the "B of I," as it was familiarly known) that was the mission of the Group.[6] It also organized conferences and celebrated anniversaries (1848 was commemorated by a dramatized version of the *Communist Manifesto* in Albert Hall); arranged for translations (of Marx and Engels, Lenin and Stalin, and such latter-day Marxist luminaries as Gramsci); assigned historical projects to be carried out by individual members; and published, among other works, a four-volume collection of historical documents and a volume of essays, *Democracy and the Labour Movement,* that foreshadowed many of the themes now identified with Marxist history.

The Group included some of the best-known historians in Britain today: E. P. Thompson, Eric Hobsbawm, Christopher Hill, Rodney Hilton, George Rudé, Dorothy Thompson, Royden Harrison, John Saville, Victor Kiernan, George Thomson, Raphael Samuel. (Among those no longer alive, and remembered fondly and respectfully by the others, are Maurice Dobb and Dona Torr, whose membership in the party went back almost to its origin.) Hobsbawm comments on the curious fact that so many talented Communist intellectuals chose to become historians.* Just as curious is the fact that so many talented historians chose to be Communists—not only in the thirties, when the depression, the Spanish Civil War, and the rise of Nazism made Communism seem, to many intellectuals, the last hope of civilization, but after the war, when they found the Western democracies more menacing than the Soviet Union and Stalinism more congenial and sympathetic than capitalism.

In its early years, Hobsbawm recalls, the members of the Group "segregated themselves strictly from schismatics and heretics," even from Marxists and Marxist sympathizers who had no party credentials.[7] With the advent of the Popular Front in 1951, they became less sectarian. (The founding of *Past and Present* reflected this turn in the

*In fact, in the 1930s there was an equally prominent group of Communist scientists. Cambridge alone boasted J. D. Bernal, J. B. S. Haldane, Lancelot Hogben, Hyman Levy, and Joseph Needham. When the *Modern Quarterly,* the organ of the Communist Party, was founded in 1938, more than half of the editorial board were scientists.

party line.) In 1956, after Khrushchev's speech to the Twentieth Congress denouncing Stalin, and the Soviet invasion of Hungary later that year, many historians left the party. They retained their personal associations, however, as well as their commitment to Marxism—unlike their confreres in France, Hobsbawm observes, where the break from the party generally resulted in a disaffection with Marxism. Hobsbawm himself has remained in the party, and the Historians' Group continues to this day.

During the whole of that time (including the period described by Hobsbawm as the "Stalin-Zhdanov-Lysenko years" of "ultra-rigid Stalinism"),[8] the members of the Group saw no conflict between their roles as historians and as Communists.

> Our work as historians was therefore embedded in our work as Marxists, which we believed to imply membership of the Communist Party. It was inseparable from our political commitment and activity . . . We were as loyal, active and committed a group of Communists as any, if only because we felt that Marxism implied membership of the Party. To criticize Marxism was to criticize the Party, and the other way round.[9]

Indeed, their loyalty to both Marxism and the party was such that even Hobsbawm, in retrospect, finds them excessively zealous. "There is no doubt that we ourselves were apt to fall into the stern and wooden style of the disciplined Bolshevik cadres, since we regarded ourselves as such." Thus their arguments on specific historical subjects such as the English Revolution were "sometimes designed *a posteriori* to confirm what we already knew to be necessarily 'correct'." If their work did not suffer more from the "contemporary dogmatism," he explains, it was because the authorized Marxist versions of history dealt with real problems and could be discussed seriously ("except where the political authority of the Bolshevik Party and similar matters were involved"); because there was no party line on most of British history and the work of Soviet historians was largely unknown to them;* because "our loyalty and militancy were not in any doubt prior to 1956" so that party officials were well disposed to them; and because a "certain old-

---

*Hobsbawm himself mentions Soviet historians who were translated and were known to the Group. Both Hill and Hilton were familiar with Soviet scholarship on their subjects and were much influenced by it.

fashioned realism" in the party made it possible to criticize and modify some of the orthodox doctrines.[10]

It was in this milieu that some of the distinctive theories of British Marxist history were first formulated: about the nature of feudalism and absolutism, the development of capitalism, the character of the English Civil War, the relation of science and Puritanism to capitalism, the effect of industrialism on the standard of living of the working classes, the nature and role of the "labor aristocracy." The Group also contributed to the new social history—history from below, the history of the common people—which became, as it were, a fellow traveler of Marxist history.

To a young American radical historian looking back on that time, it must seem a heroic age, when radical history had a coherent doctrine, a cohesive community, and a political purposiveness he might well envy. This is certainly the impression one gets from *The British Marxist Historians* by Harvey J. Kaye.[11] The five historians who are the subjects of this study, all members of the original Group, are meant to suggest the range and diversity of Marxist scholarship, their shared concerns and themes, and above all their commitment to a kind of history that is of "scholarly *and* political consequence."[12]

Maurice Dobb is generally regarded as the founding father of the Group. "The major historical work which was to influence us crucially," Hobsbawm has said, "was Maurice Dobb's *Studies in the Development of Capitalism* which formulated our main and central problem."[13] Published in 1946, the *Studies* coincided with the formation of the Group, but long before then Dobb had established himself as a leading Marxist "theoretician." He had joined the British Communist Party in 1922, shortly after it was founded, and made the first of many visits to the Soviet Union three years later. From 1924 until his retirement in 1967 he was a Lecturer and then a Reader in Economics at Cambridge, where he became the mentor of generations of Communists and Communist sympathizers. (It is curious now to read of the debate in 1932 in which he argued for the motion, "This house sees more hope in Moscow than Detroit"; his opponent on that occasion was G. Kitson Clark, who later became one of the most eminent of non-Marxist English historians.)[14]

Dobb described his *Studies* as a work in "historical economics,"[15] and it is this historical dimension, the application of Marxist economic theory to the development of capitalism, that made it so influential among the Marxist historians. Describing the emergence of capitalism in England, Dobb identified the two "decisive moments" in its development: the "bourgeois revolution" of the seventeenth century, and the "industrial revolution" of the late eighteenth and early nineteenth centuries. As a prelude to these moments, he posited another: the "crisis" of feudalism in the fourteenth century, which set the stage for the transition to capitalism.[16] In retrospect one can see in this schema something like an agenda for the historians in the Group, with Hilton taking up feudalism, Hill the English Revolution, and Hobsbawm and Thompson industrialism. Dobb relieved the others of the need to work out details of the Marxist analysis, such as the primitive accumulation of capital and the concept of surplus value, and provided them with a more sophisticated and respectable version of Marxist economics.

From the perspective of a non-Marxist, or even of a later generation of neo-Marxists, Dobb represents a stringent mode of economic determinism ("economism," as Marxists now call it). Yet this was not the way it seemed at the time to members of the Group. In a famous controversy between Dobb and the American Marxist Paul Sweezy, it was Sweezy who appeared to be taking the more narrowly economic view. He criticized Dobb, among other things, for equating feudalism with serfdom rather than defining it as a particular mode of production, and for failing to recognize that the expansion of trade had undermined the feudal system of production-for-use and prepared the way for the capitalist system of production-for-exchange. In his reply Dobb argued that the dissolution of feudalism resulted from the internal contradictions of the social relations of production rather than from the growth of commerce and towns, and that Sweezy's was a static conception of feudalism which neglected the class struggle.[17] Kaye sees in this debate a conscious attempt on the part of Dobb (and of Hilton, Hill, and Hobsbawm, all of whom came to his defense) to move away from "a narrow economism to a broader politico-economic perspective" and to redefine class as a "historical phenomenon, as opposed to merely an economic or sociological category."[18]

Rodney Hilton, a generation younger than Dobb, joined the Communist Party while a student at Oxford before the war. He spent most of his professional career at the University of Birmingham and was an active member of the Group until he left the party in 1956, after which he remained closely associated with his former comrades. He has explained how he came to take feudalism as his subject:

> As a communist I was interested in the potentialities for resistance to exploitation of the subordinated classes. It seemed sensible to begin with medieval peasants and craftsmen—of course within the general economic and social context of the time. I expected to move forward to modern times, but found myself too much involved in the study of medieval society as a whole.[19]

The radical nature of his enterprise (radical in both senses of that word) can be appreciated only by comparison with the prevailing theories of English feudalism. For his thesis requires not only the injection of the class struggle into a period more often thought of as relatively stable, but a redefinition of the very concept of feudalism. The conventional non-Marxist view—to oversimplify a vastly complicated subject—sees feudalism as essentially a relationship between the lord and his vassals, with a social structure reflecting values and functions that were not necessarily, certainly not primarily, economic. By shifting the focus to the lord and his peasants, Hilton creates a feudal system that was an "exploitative relationship between landowners and subordinated peasants, in which the surplus beyond subsistence of the latter, whether in direct labour or in rent in kind or in money, is transferred under coercive sanction to the former."[20] The peasants, far from being passive victims of this process, were active agents of their own history; and the social order, far from being static and stable, was ridden by class struggle. It was this struggle, punctuated by recurrent peasant uprisings, that was the "motor," or "prime mover," of medieval society and the principal cause of the "crisis" of feudalism.[21]

This would seem to be an obvious Marxist interpretation of feudalism. Yet it was not Marx's own interpretation; thus Hilton was, in effect, engaged in a doubly revisionist enterprise. The class struggle Marx focused on in feudalism was the struggle between the landowning aristocracy and the nascent bourgeoisie, not that between the aristocracy and peasantry. Indeed, Marx doubted whether the peasants even in modern times (and a fortiori in the Middle Ages) constituted a class. In a famous passage in *The Eighteenth Brumaire of Louis*

Bonaparte, he defined a class as formed by those who "live under economic conditions of existence that separate their mode of life, their interests and their culture from those of the other classes, and put them in hostile opposition to the latter." By that definition the peasants "do not form a class," for they live in similar conditions "but without entering into manifold relations with one another," acquire their subsistence "through exchange with nature rather than in intercourse with society," and beget "no community, no national bond and no political organization." Instead of attributing to them the character of a class, Marx saw them as the "simple addition of homologous magnitudes, much as potatoes in a sack form a sack of potatoes."[22]

Nor was Engels, contrary to common opinion, more appreciative of the class character of the peasantry. In his *Condition of the Working Class in England* he described the preindustrial workers—agricultural laborers as well as handloom weavers—as intellectually and socially inert. "Comfortable in their silent vegetation," enjoying a "patriarchal relation" with the squirearchy, aware only of their petty, private concerns, they were not a class. Indeed, "in truth, they were not human beings." They became truly human only when the industrial and agricultural revolutions drew them into the "whirl of history" and thus into the class of the "proletariat."[23] Engels did later speak of a "peasant war in Germany." But his book of that title deals with the Reformation, not the medieval period; and the "peasant war," led by the religious "chiliast" (as Engels describes him) Thomas Münzer, is said to foreshadow not a proletarian revolution but a bourgeois one: "The social upheaval that so horrified its Protestant burgher contemporaries actually never went beyond a feeble, unconscious and premature attempt to establish the bourgeois society of a later period."[24]

Hilton, by engaging the feudal peasants in a class struggle, endowed them with the essential historical attribute of a class, thus bringing them into the forefront of history and making them worthy of sympathy and respect. He also gave them a measure of "class consciousness." It was an imperfect class consciousness, to be sure, only intermittently achieved and all too often negative (expressing itself in hatred of the landlord) and conservative (reflecting the "dominant ideology" of the ruling class). But it was also informed by a "memory" of ancient rights and customs, and this gave the struggle of the peasantry both dignity and historical meaning.

The next historical "moment" was appropriated by Christopher Hill. Hill preceded Hilton at Balliol by several years and upon his graduation gained a coveted Fellowship at All Souls. He spent a year studying in the Soviet Union and joined the British Communist Party in 1936. After a brief teaching stint at Cardiff, he returned to Balliol in 1938 as Fellow and Tutor. During the war he was transferred from the army to the Foreign Office, presumably because of his knowledge of Russian and of the Soviet Union. While at the Foreign Office he wrote *Two Commonwealths,* a comparison of the United Kingdom and the Soviet Union; it was published under the pseudonym K. E. Holme, the Russian equivalent of his own name.[25] He resumed his lectureship at Oxford after the war and served as Master of Balliol from 1965 until his retirement in 1978.

Hill's studies in the Soviet Union had focused on Soviet interpretations of the English Civil War, and his first important essay, *The English Revolution,* was written under the influence of the Russian historian E. A. Kosminsky (to whom Hilton too was much indebted). The title suggests the theme: the English Civil War was a revolution, "a great social movement like the French Revolution of 1789."[26] The revolutionary nature of this thesis can be seen by comparison with the classic Whig interpretation, in which the Civil War appears primarily as a struggle for constitutional and religious liberty, and in which the "excesses" of the period make it an "interregnum" in the history of England. For Hill the Civil War was a "class war" between a despotic king representing the "reactionary forces" of landlords and the Church, and Parliament representing the commercial and industrial classes in the towns, the yeomanry and "progressive gentry" in the countryside, and the enlightened elements among the masses. As a result of that class struggle, "an old order that was essentially feudal was destroyed by violence, and a new and capitalist social order was created in its place."[27]

This thesis provoked controversy not only among non-Marxist historians but also among those Marxists who had located the beginnings of capitalism in the sixteenth century. Debated for years within the Historians' Group, the issue was resolved in 1948 when the Group officially endorsed Dobb's interpretation of the Civil War, which was a modified version of Hill's. Hill then incorporated that version in a new edition of *The English Revolution* published the following year. A third, slightly amended edition appeared in 1955; reprinted half a dozen times, it is still in print. In the current version (and in essays written since), Hill makes it clear that while the revolution may not have been consciously willed by the bourgeoisie, its effect was nonetheless to promote the interests of the bourgeoisie.[28] Similarly, Puritanism is now given a religious as well as economic and social dimension; but in the revised essay, as in the original one, the "religious squabbles" are set in the context of the class struggle.[29]

While Hill's later writings on cultural and intellectual subjects are far more erudite and subtle than that early essay, they remain within the framework of Marxism as he understands it. *The World Turned Upside Down* views the English Revolution as not only a successful bourgeois revolution but also a failed democratic revolution, an abortive revolution of the common people to subvert the bourgeois supremacy. Masked in the language of religion, the Levellers espoused political equality, the Diggers communism, and the Ranters, although lacking any political or economic agenda, preached and practiced a doctrine of free love that was truly revolutionary: "a negative reaction to nascent capitalism, a cry for human brotherhood, freedom and unity against the divisive forces of a harsh ethic."[30]

So too the *Intellectual Origins of the English Revolution* exposes the economic and social functions of the scientific, legal, and historical ideas that constituted the "intellectual origins" of the revolution. Thus Walter Raleigh prepared the way for the revolution in "the optimism and forward look of his belief in private enterprise, in empire, in Parliament"; Edward Coke contributed to the "confidence of the men of property in themselves and in private enterprise"; and Francis Bacon caught "the optimism of the merchants and craftsmen, confident in their new-found ability to control their environment, including the social and political environment."[31] This view of Bacon is a much muted version of Hill's earlier account of him, in which he appears as a "progressive" thinker foreshadowing that other notable progressive, Lysenko. In 1951 Hill wrote:

> Bacon inaugurated the bourgeois epoch in science as Lysenko and his colleagues are inaugurating the new epoch today. In the Soviet Union the obstructive dogmas of bourgeois science have to be brushed aside, to the indignation of the logic-choppers, if socialist science is to devote itself whole-heartedly to the relief of man's estate: so Bacon was fighting

against the prejudices and dogmas of an effete civilisation, dogmas which a priestly academic caste continued to preach although they manifestly impeded the development of industrial science. Bacon's conception of science, in striking contrast with that of the high priests of bourgeois science in its decadence, was materialistic, utilitarian and profoundly humane.[32]

Although Hill left the Communist Party in 1957, he still looks back on the discussions in the Historians' Group as "the greatest stimulus I have ever known."[33] Others pay tribute to him as the greatest stimulus of them all. Recalling the influence Hill had on him in those early years, E. P. Thompson describes him as a "formidable theoretical practitioner [who] restructured whole areas of historical consciousness in England."[34] And Hobsbawm credits him with turning the attention of the Historians' Group to "the social history of *ideas*"[35]—thus giving a new dimension to the B of I.

Eric Hobsbawm has been called the "premier" Marxist historian in England[36]—in part because of his continuing relationship with the Communist Party (he is still a member of the Historians' Group and on the editorial board of *Marxism Today,* the official organ of the party), in part because of his far-ranging scholarship and far-flung activities. He himself has attributed his political views and cosmopolitan interests to his personal history, which makes it all the more regrettable that he has given us so tantalizingly few details about that history.[37] We are told that his grandfather, a Russian Jew, emigrated to England in the 1870s, but not when or why his father and Austrian mother moved to Alexandria, where Hobsbawm was born in 1917. Two years later the family settled in Vienna; in 1931 Hobsbawm moved to Berlin and in 1933 to London. Having joined a Communist youth organization in Berlin, he associated himself with the party as a schoolboy in London, selling Communist Party pamphlets and improving his English (and his Marxism) by reading a popular book by Dobb, *On Marxism Today*. At the university he found himself in a congenial political atmosphere. "We were all Marxists as students at Cambridge," he later recalled;[38] and like many of them, he was an active member of the Communist Party. After serving in the education corps during the war, he returned to Cambridge to complete his studies, then took a position at the University of London where he remained until his retirement in 1982.

Hobsbawm's main area of research is nineteenth-century English labor history. Impatient with institutional history, he has devoted himself to such subjects as the effect of the Industrial Revolution on the standard of living of workers, the relationship between the working classes and Methodism, and the nature of the "labor aristocracy." In each case he has brought new empirical evidence to bear on the conventional Marxist view, or has given orthodox Marxism a somewhat different reading. Thus where Marx, and Lenin even more, attributed the "reformism" of the English labor movement to the strength of the labor aristocracy, Hobsbawm emphasized the role of the labor aristocracy in the organization and radicalization of the labor movement.[39] His theses are still the subject of controversy among Marxist as well as non-Marxist historians, but they have reinvigorated some well-worn topics and have given Marxism itself a new lease on life.

Hobsbawm also opened up new frontiers for Marxism with the concept of "primitive rebels," a term that he takes to comprise "social bandits" of the Robin Hood type, "secret societies" like the Mafia, peasant millenarian movements, urban mobs, and religious labor sects.[40] To the orthodox Marxist, the continued existence of these primitive or "archaic" groups is an anomaly. Hobsbawm, by giving them the status of rebels and bringing them together as a "social movement," has legitimized them and made them part of the Marxist schema. Instead of being aberrations, even counterrevolutionary deviations, they are represented as the "adaptation of popular agitations to a modern capitalist economy"—"pre-political" movements, which do not themselves aspire to political power but do promote a "political consciousness" that has made this century "the most revolutionary in history."[41] It is this work that has endeared Hobsbawm to a generation of radical historians committed to "history from below," the history of the "anonymous masses," who are seen as leading lives of quiet (sometimes not so quiet) desperation and who express their alienation and rebellion by means of criminality and other forms of "social deviancy." Many of these historians are attracted by the nonpolitical (at least not overtly political) nature of this rebellion. For a leading American Marxist historian, however, the great achievement of Hobsbawm is that he has kept faith with the political mission of Marxism. "To be 'Hobsbawmian' means to be Marxist," Eugene Genovese has said— that is, to make the "politics of class struggle" central to history, and to make "historical materialism" central to Marxism.[42]

Hobsbawm himself, describing *Primitive Rebels* as "a political as well as a historical" work, has explained the conjunction of circumstances that first brought this subject to his attention in the 1950s: his extensive acquaintance with Italian Communists who were familiar with the Mafia; his reading of Antonio Gramsci, a founder of the Italian Communist Party, who made much of this kind of "nonpolitical protest movement"; an invitation to speak on the European precedents for the Mau Mau uprisings in Kenya; and the Twentieth Congress of the Communist Party in 1956, which inspired a reevaluation of the role of the party and the "bases of revolutionary activity." All of these events, Hobsbawm says, are reflected in the implicit message of the book, that a "strongly organized party" is necessary, although there is no "one railroad" leading to the desired goal.[43]

The reference to 1956 prompts Hobsbawm to observe that the chief effect of that momentous year was to "set us free to do more history, because before '56 we'd spent an enormous amount of our time on political activity."[44] Yet he himself has continued to be politically active, both within the British Communist Party and abroad (in Latin America as well as Europe)—which makes it all the more remarkable that he has been so productive as a historian, a journalist, even (under the pseudonym of Francis Newton) a commentator on jazz.[45]

The best known and, in America at any rate, the most influential of this group is E. P. Thompson. The youngest of them (he was born in 1924), he had joined the party and barely begun his studies at Cambridge when he was called into service. The war itself was more traumatic for him than for the others, his older brother (who had also been a Communist at Cambridge) having been executed by the Nazis while fighting with the Bulgarian partisans. Thompson himself was an officer during the war and afterward spent some months as a railroad construction worker in Yugoslavia and Bulgaria. Returning to Cambridge to complete his degree, he met and married another historian who was also a Communist—indeed, a more active member of the Historians' Group than he. As an extramural lecturer at the University of Leeds, he devoted half his time, by his own estimate, to political activities; his chief responsibility, as a member of the Yorkshire district committee of the Communist Party, was to organize opposition to the Korean War. In 1956 he emerged as one of the leading "dissident

Communists," a founder of the *New Reasoner* and of its more influential successor, the *New Left Review.* He was forced off the board of the *Review* in 1962 when it came under the control of the faction led by Perry Anderson and Tom Nairn. At Warwick University in the sixties, he became involved in the radical causes that convulsed that highly politicized university; he later resigned to devote himself to scholarship and politics.

In retrospect it may appear that even in his years as a loyal party member, Thompson displayed "deviationist" tendencies. Yet this may be more a matter of style than substance, the expression of a literary and poetic sensibility (he had originally intended to be a poet) that distinguished him from the more prosaic historians in the Group. It is no accident (as a Marxist might say) that his first book was a biography of William Morris, who had the double virtue of being a poet and a Marxist. Thompson himself claims to see in this book a "muffled 'revisionism'."[46] When it was published, however, in 1955, it was entirely consistent with the party line. As far back as 1934, even before the turn to the Popular Front, the party had tried to appropriate Morris as its spiritual and political ancestor by redeeming him from the "myth" of romantic medievalism and establishing him as an indigenous Marxist Communist.* In 1976, shortly before the appearance of the second edition of his biography, Thompson commented on the "Morris/Marx argument" that still looms so large in his thinking. "To defend the tradition of Morris (as I still do) entailed unqualified resistance to Stalinism. But it did *not* entail opposition to Marxism; rather, it entailed rehabilitating lost categories and a lost vocabulary in the Marxist tradition."[47]

In fact there is nothing in the first edition of that book to suggest any "resistance to Stalinism." Indeed, the deletions made in the second edition highlight what Thompson himself calls the "Stalinist pieties" of the earlier edition:[48] the endorsement of the cliché "All roads lead to Communism";[49] the posthumous induction of Morris into the Communist Party ("Were Morris alive today, he would not look far to find the party of his choice");[50] the assurance that Morris' utopian vision of

---

* After World War II the struggle for Morris' soul was fought on the floor of the House of Commons in a heated exchange between Clement Attlee, leader of the Labour Party, and Willie Gallacher, Communist member of Parliament, each of whom claimed Morris for his party and ideology.

"A Factory as It Might Be" had already been realized in the Soviet Union ("Today visitors return from the Soviet Union with stories of the poet's dream already fulfilled");[51] the long quotation from Stalin that supposedly confirmed Morris' views by providing a "blue-print of the advance to Communism";[52] the suggestion that Morris envisaged "the 'party of a new type' of Lenin—a party of militant *cadres* educated in Socialist theory, the vanguard of the working class, the spearhead 'which is to pierce the armour of Capitalism'."[53] Yet even the Morris of the revised edition, shorn of these "Stalinist pieties," is still a staunch Marxist revolutionary, committed to "scientific Socialism" and repelled by Fabianism, reformism, and "semi-demi-Socialism."[54] (The revised edition was also shorn of some of the philistinism characteristic of Morris in his militant socialist period: "Poetry is tommy-rot," and "Modern tragedy, including Shakespeare, is not fit to be put upon the modern stage.")[55]

In his account of Thompson, Kaye inexplicably omits any discussion of the book on Morris. Yet without it one cannot truly understand Thompson's most celebrated work, *The Making of the English Working Class*. Published in 1963, it is still the most influential book produced by any member of the Group. Kaye echoes the opinion of many radical historians when he says that it is probably "the most important work of social history written since the Second World War."[56] If its tone owes much to Morris, its thesis is more boldly Marxist than anything proposed by previous generations of radical and socialist historians. For it maintains that by 1832, even before the rise of Chartism, England had witnessed the emergence of a single "working class" (in contrast to the "working classes" of common usage)—a class that was fully developed, fully conscious of its class identity and class interests, consciously committed to the class struggle, politically organized to carry out that struggle, and ideologically receptive to an alternative economic and social system. There was no actual revolution in England, the argument goes, only because the counterrevolutionary forces succeeded in repressing or suppressing it. But the revolution was a latent historical reality, even if it was only intermittently manifest.

Put so baldly, the thesis is all too easily disputed. But Thompson does not put it so baldly; indeed, it is not the thesis itself that has made the book so influential. What has caught the imagination of a younger generation of radical historians is the passionate tone of the book, the variety of sources, and the latitude given to the crucial concepts. Thus the "working class" is taken to include "the Sunderland sailor, the Irish navvy, the Jewish costermonger, the inmate of an East Anglian village workhouse, the compositor on *The Times*"[57]—and many others who, by social status or occupation, would not normally be consigned to a single "working class." Similarly, expressions of working-class consciousness are found in William Blake's poems as well as in folk ballads; the class struggle is deduced from abortive uprisings, sporadic rick-burnings, Irish nationalist conspiracies, and clandestine plots; political organization is attributed to Luddite machine-breakers, secret societies, and trade unions; and a revolutionary alternative to capitalism is seen in any hostility to industrialism, any nostalgia for an old "moral economy" or yearning for a new moral order. In this long, eloquent, richly documented work, these anomalies and contradictions have the perverse effect of appearing to validate a thesis that seems all the more persuasive precisely because it can contain all those anomalies and contradictions. What finally unites these disparate elements is the moral passion of the author, his overt, personal commitment to the working class as he conceives it and to the revolutionary cause with which he identifies it. A sentence from his preface has been so often quoted that it has become the rallying cry of the cause: "I am seeking to rescue the poor stockinger, the Luddite cropper, the 'obsolete' hand-loomer, the 'utopian' artisan, and even the deluded follower of Joanna Southcott, from the enormous condescension of posterity."[58]

More than any other part of his thesis, it is the concept of class consciousness that has attracted a host of disciples and emulators. All of the historians in this group (with the exception of Dobb) have departed, to one degree or another, from the more rigorous classic Marxist model, which relegates consciousness to the superstructure and which sees the superstructure as derived from and determined by the mode of production and class relations reflecting that mode. But none of the others has made consciousness so integral a part of the concept of class—while at the same time insisting upon the material base of consciousness itself and the materialistic nature of the historical process. And none has been so polemical in defending this version of Marxism against both the conventional historian who finds it excessively materialistic and deterministic, and the Athusserian or Leninist Marxist who finds it excessively empirical and moralistic.

Thompson's great appeal is to the currently fashionable "humanistic" Marxism, the Marxism (or "neo-Marxism," as is sometimes said) supposedly deriving from the young, or early, Marx. Yet Thompson himself, while sometimes referring to the early Marx, does not make much of him, perhaps suspecting that the real young Marx was not quite what he has been made out to be. Instead, Thompson claims to be recovering a "lost vocabulary" in the Marxist tradition, a vocabulary that in Marx himself "was partly a silence—unarticulated assumptions and unrealized mediations."[59] One wonders what Marx would have made of Thompson's vocabulary or of his intention to "rescue" the "deluded follower" of Joanna Southcott, the religious mystic and millenarian who inveighed against the "Whore of Babylon" and prophesied an apocalypse of destruction and salvation. In one of the most memorable sections of the book Thompson describes the "psychic processes of counter-revolution," the "chiliasm of despair" and "psychic blackmail" that characterized this period of "emotional disequilibrium."[60] Yet for all its psychoanalytic overtones, his account is only a more sophisticated version of the "opium of the masses" theme. So too his description of Methodism—the "psychic ordeal" by means of which "the character-structure of the rebellious pre-industrial labourer or artisan was violently recast into that of the submissive industrial worker"[61]—is a modish rendition of the familiar view of Puritanism as an instrument of capitalism.

Since *The Making* (as it is familiarly known to admirers), Thompson's historical research has taken him back into the eighteenth century, where he finds the "plebians" trying to restore an older "moral economy."[62] But more of his energies have gone into political activities, especially the nuclear disarmament movement, and into lengthy and heated polemics. In a hundred-page "Open Letter to Leszek Kolakowski" (complete with seventy-five footnotes), he berated the distinguished Polish philosopher for abandoning Marxism and Communism. And in a series of essays amounting to a good-sized volume, he charged Perry Anderson and the other English "acolytes" of Louis Althusser with a moral obtuseness and "intellectual agoraphobia" reminiscent of Stalinism.[63] To some readers these polemics, in their intensity and turgidity, may recall those of Marx and Engels against the "Holy Family" (the Bauer brothers) and the "Sainted Max" (Stirner). (*The Poverty of Theory,* the title of Thompson's volume, is obviously meant to evoke *The Poverty of Philosophy,* Marx's attack on Proudhon.) Thompson and Anderson have since been partially reconciled, brought together under the umbrella of nuclear disarmament. Anderson praises Thompson as "our finest socialist writer today," while Thompson, who now contributes to the *New Left Review,* calls Anderson a "comrade" and partially absolves him of the sin of Althusserianism.[64]

The controversy between Thompson and Anderson, both claiming to be Marxists, raises once more the old questions about Marxist history. What does it mean to be a Marxist historian? How "revisionist" can Marxist historians be—about the materialist conception of history, for example—and still remain Marxist? To what extent must Marxism be taken into account in understanding and evaluating their work? What, in short, is the relevance of their Marxism?

To address all of these questions adequately would require nothing less than a treatise on Marxism and historiography. But some of them have been implicitly, sometimes explicitly, answered by the Marxist historians themselves, who insist that their Marxism is indeed relevant, that they are not merely historians but Marxist historians. A non-Marxist, believing that every work of history must be evaluated on its own merits rather than by reference to some external theory or philosophy, may choose to disregard such assertions. Indeed, some of the most severe critiques of Marxist histories have been scrupulously empirical, analyzing specific facts and sources, assumptions and generalizations.[65] Some have gone so far as to disallow any consideration of Marxism, as if that would be improper and invidious, rather like an ad hominem argument.

J. H. Hexter, reprinting a long and devastating critique of Hill's *Change and Continuity in Seventeenth-Century England,* removed the single parenthetical reference to Marxism on the ground that it was "irrelevant" and "ungracious," and that the critique stood or fell quite independently of Hill's "substantive philosophy of history." The flaws in the book, he says, can be ascribed to something like a faulty "filing system," which has files for the categories and facts that support the thesis but none for those that might confute it. Yet a few pages later Hexter explains, "We have here not a casual error, misquotation, misunderstanding, the sort of thing that happens to all of us, but systematic error and symptomatic error, error that suggests a systematic flaw in a man's *habit* of looking at evidence."[66] Surely an error so systematic and habitual is a reflection of a system and habit of thought—an ideology—rather than a system of files. And surely it is neither irrelevant nor ungracious to invoke Marxism in a serious analysis of a book in which the author himself says that he finds the "Marxist conception of a bourgeois revolution . . . the most helpful model for understanding the English Revolution."[67]

The idea that it is invidious to consider the "substantive philosophy" of a Marxist historian is itself invidious, for it refuses to take seriously what the Marxist historian takes most seriously. Does it really do justice to the historian to ignore the theories and philosophy he himself invokes in support of his thesis? (Each of these historians has quoted, sometimes copiously, from Marx, Engels, Lenin, and, in their earlier works, Stalin.) One of the happy by-products of the recently published memoirs is to release us from the convention that holds it improper to allude to these historians as Marxists. If they find Marxism so central to their work, if they think it important to identify themselves as Marxists, surely we can do no less.

There is one other subject that can be explored more candidly, now that the Marxist historians have taken the lead in doing so. That is the intimate (dialectical, a Marxist would say) relationship between history and politics—between writing about the past and acting in the present. Whatever differences Thompson has with Anderson, it is not likely that he would dispute Anderson's comment that each of Thompson's historical works is "a militant intervention in the present, as well as a professional recovery of the past."[68] Nor would he or any of the other Marxist historians take issue with the editors of *Visions of History* (a volume of interviews with Thompson, Hobsbawm, and other radical historians), who commend these historians for the way "their politics inform their practice as historians" and for their commitment to Marx's dictum that the task is "not only to interpret the world but to change it."[69] Marxist history, it would appear, is a continuation of politics by other means.

It is this idea of history more than anything else—more than any specific ideas about class and class struggle, consciousness and culture, mode of production and social relations—that is the common denominator of Marxist history. Marxist historians can be revisionist about almost everything else in the Marxist canon, but they cannot separate politics from history. They cannot abandon, or even hold in abeyance, their political agenda of changing the world while engaged in the historical task of interpreting it.

The Marxist would say, and quite rightly, that all historians reflect in their work a political bias of some sort, that the ideas, interests, and experiences of the historian inevitably intrude upon the writing of history, that the very process of selecting sources, presenting facts, and writing a coherent account necessarily presumes some conception of reality, some order of values, that precludes objectivity. He might also go on to say that the Marxist, in being candid about his bias (unlike the "bourgeois" historian who would conceal it, possibly even be ignorant of it), is giving the reader the opportunity to judge it and make allowance for it. But this is to shift the burden of responsibility from the writer to the reader. The issue is not whether the reader can make the proper discriminations and judgments (he is generally not in a position to do so), but whether the historian has done so—whether he has made an effort to control and correct his bias, to look for the evidence that might confute his thesis, and, no less important, to construct a thesis capable of confutation. The Marxist, on the other hand, is so assured of the truth of his thesis—its political as well as historical truth—that the temptation, as Hobsbawm says, is to invoke arguments "designed *a posteriori* to confirm what we already knew to be necessarily 'correct'."[70] By the same token (Hobsbawm elsewhere admits) the Marxist is inclined to avoid arguments and facts that he knows to be true lest they undermine the orthodox doctrine or divert him from his polemical task.*

The Marxist theory of history, moreover, is so comprehensive—its great appeal is that it makes sense not of this or that part of history but of the whole of history—that the historian committed to it has to find it confirmed at every decisive "moment" of history. Any significant exception would be a denial of the whole, since the theory itself is a

---

* In reconsidering his earlier essays on the labor aristocracy, Hobsbawm explains that he had deliberately obscured his disagreements with the Leninist thesis "both because he was, for reasons which seemed good at the times of writing, reluctant to stress views which were then heterodox among Marxists, and because he preferred to engage in polemics against those who, on anti-Marxist grounds, denied the existence or analytical value of the concept of a labour aristocracy in nineteenth-century Britain" (*Workers,* p. 249n).

whole. Where the "eclectic" or "empirical" historian (pejorative words in the Marxist vocabulary) tries to understand each subject in whatever terms seem appropriate to it, finding evidence of a class struggle in one event but not in another, giving priority to economics in one period and to religion in another, the Marxist historian is bound by a predetermined schema that applies to all periods and events. That schema may be modified, qualified, "revised," but in some basic sense it has to be retained if Marxism itself is to be a meaningful part of his enterprise—and to be meaningful for the present as well as the past, for politics as well as history. It is a formidable burden that the Marxist historian carries.

In addition to the burden of ideology, the Marxist is saddled with the burden—the incubus, some would come to think of it—of party. The editors of the interviews explain that one of their questions could be put only to the older generation of historians: "How did the political repression of the cold war era affect you and your work?"[71] But they did not think to put the corollary question: "How did the intellectual repression of the Communist Party affect you and your work?" Hobsbawm himself has said that for "obvious reasons" they felt "very constrained about twentieth-century history" and shied away from writing about it. One reason he was a nineteenth-century historian, he confessed, was because one could not be an orthodox Communist and write about the period after the founding of the Communist Party. And he also explained that the Group had to abandon one project to which it had given much thought in 1952 and 1953—a history of the British labor movement—because the period since the founding of the British Communist Party "raised some notoriously tricky problems"; the book that was eventually published, in 1956, terminated in 1920, the year the party was founded.[72] (This inhibition seems to have affected *Past and Present* as well. A reviewer of the hundredth anniversary issue pointed out that in the thirty years since its founding there had been no "overt discussion of communism," and that the first article on Stalin appeared only in 1979.)[73]

If admirers of the Group are reluctant to confront the question of what loyalty to the Communist Party entails by way of discipline and conformity, they are even more loath to confront the question of what loyalty to the Soviet Union entails—which is, after all, the sine qua non of membership in the party. Kaye carefully notes the dates when each of the historians joined the party and when most of them left it. But apart from passing references to the events of 1956 that led to the break, there is little or no discussion of what was happening in the world or in the Soviet Union during the period of their membership. Dobb was a party member for more than half a century, from the early twenties until his death in 1976; Hobsbawm's membership covers a different half-century, from the early thirties to the present; Hill and Hilton were members for about twenty years, and Thompson for about fifteen. A good deal of history is contained within those dates.

In his memoir Hobsbawm observes that "it was among the historians that the dissatisfaction with the Party's reactions to the Khrushchev speech at the Twentieth Congress of the CPSU first came into the open."[74] This makes it all the more remarkable that the historians had to wait for Khrushchev to tell them what the informed public had long since known. Both as historians and as party members during the thirties and forties, they had more reason than most to be aware of the highly publicized purges and trials, the executions and mass imprisonments, the precipitous changes in the party line requiring comrades to be Bolsheviks one week and Popular Fronters another, pro-war and anti-Fascist one day and anti-war and pro-German the next. For almost two years while their country was at war with Germany, they had to defend the Hitler-Stalin pact. Asked in a recent interview how he felt about the pact, Hobsbawm replied, "Oh, like most people I was absolutely loyal to the Party line."[75]

That absolute loyalty persisted for a decade after the war. The heyday of the Historians' Group from 1946 to 1956, a period some of them still recall with much satisfaction, was also the era that Thompson calls "High Stalinism." It was a time when intellectuals, scientists, and artists, to say nothing of politicians and political dissidents, were the victims of systematic purges; when Lysenkoism was the official doctrine of state, and when not only Darwinism but other manifestations of "bourgeois science," such as the theory of relativity, were proscribed; when the apotheosis of Stalin took bizarre forms long before Khrushchev exposed the "personality cult"; when the trials in Hungary, Bulgaria, and Czechoslovakia recalled the Moscow trials of the thirties; and when the "Doctor's Plot" of 1952–1953 was accompanied by an anti-Semitic campaign in the course of which a hundred or more Jewish intellectuals were shot. These were, after all, historians, not naive scientists and artists, who lived through these events. As party members they tacitly sanctioned them, and even now, Hobsbawm says, they "look back without regret on their years in the Group."[76]

In describing the meeting of the Group after Khrushchev's speech, Hobsbawm remarks upon the special sense of responsibility felt by the historians qua historians: "The fact is that historians were inevitably forced to confront the situation not only as private persons and communist militants but, as it were, in their professional capacity, since the crucial issue of Stalin was literally one of history: what had happened and why it had been concealed." He quotes one member who protested that they had "stopped being historians" when they accepted the Soviet interpretation of current affairs, and that they "must become historians in respect of present too." In retrospect Hobsbawm endorses that judgment. "Historical analysis," he reflects, "was at the core of Marxist politics."[77]

Yet no member of the Group has undertaken that historical analysis. One can understand why Hobsbawm, who has chosen to remain in the party, has not done so. It is more difficult to understand the reticence of those historians who have left the party. "I commenced to reason," Thompson prefaces a volume of essays, "in my thirty-third year [1956, when he left the party], and despite my best efforts, I have never been able to shake the habit off."[78] But even now he seems reluctant to give his reason free rein lest it give comfort to the enemy. Although he has been more vigorous than the others in denouncing Stalinism, he has done so only in a polemical context. What he has not done is bring his considerable historical talent to bear upon such momentous subjects as the relationship between Stalinism and Leninism, or Leninism and Marxism, or Marxism and the "Libertarian Communism" he now professes. In his "Open Letter" to Kolakowski he prides himself on not following the "well-worn paths of apostasy," on not becoming a "Public Confessor and Renegade"[79]—as if it would be disreputable to write a scholarly work on twentieth-century Communism or even a candid memoir of his experiences in the party.

Kaye concludes his account of the British Marxist historians by reaffirming the intimate relationship between politics and history which is their guiding principle. In this respect, he says, they go beyond Marx—at least beyond the Marx who wrote that "the social revolution of the nineteenth century cannot draw its poetry from the past, but only from the future," that the revolution "must let the dead bury their dead."[80] More than Marx, they believe that the past is a "well of conclusions from which we draw in order to act," and that action itself requires a "historical education." "We must educate those for whom struggle is a determined necessity today with the historical experiences of those for whom struggle was a determined necessity yesterday."[81] The same lesson is drawn by the editors of *Visions of History,* who tell us that the radical historians "have much to teach us about the past and its bearing on the work of liberating the present."[82]

We still await that "historical education." It is thirty years since most of the members of the Group left the party. Yet there is no scholarly study of Marxism or Communism by the historians who were personally, actively committed to those ideologies. Nor has there been any serious reevaluation by them of the histories inspired by those doctrines—or, indeed, of the philosophy of history that posits an intimate relationship between "praxis" and theory, politics and history. This omission is all the more conspicuous in the light of developments in France, where eminent historians have confronted, seriously and candidly, both their experiences in the Communist Party and the implications of Marxist history.[83] For their English confreres, it would seem, Marxism is still a forbidden zone. "Here lie dragons . . ."

Social History in Retrospect · 5 ·

Twenty-one years after the publication of the *Origin of Species*, T. H. Huxley reflected on the "coming of age" of that momentous work.

> History warns us . . . that it is the customary fate of new truths to begin as heresies and to end as superstitions; and, as matters now stand, it is hardly rash to anticipate that, in another twenty years, the new generation, educated under the influences of the present day, will be in danger of accepting the main doctrines of the *Origin of Species*, with as little reflection, and it may be with as little justification, as so many of our contemporaries, twenty years ago, rejected them.[1]

Because Huxley was one of Darwin's most ardent disciples, his warning about the fate of "new truths" has a special poignancy. Practitioners of the new social history may well ponder his words as they contemplate their own coming of age. The year 1965 was a good one for social history; it was then that two influential and controversial books were published, Lawrence Stone's *The Crisis of the Aristocracy* and Peter Laslett's *The World We Have Lost*. Both authors have since had occasion to reconsider the genre of history so eminently represented by these books and by their own careers.

*   *   *

94

Reflections of a Chastened Father

In *The Past and the Present* Lawrence Stone, a founding father of the new history, takes stock of his progeny. The book, a collection of essays and reviews, turns out to be less a celebration of a coming of age than a memorial to a golden age, a "heroic phase," that is already in the past.[2] If the memorial sometimes sounds more like a dirge than a eulogy, it is because Stone, like Huxley, seems to suspect that the brave heresy of his youth has degenerated into a mindless orthodoxy, and that some of his precocious children have grown into swaggering, blustering adults. Yet Stone, again like Huxley, does not despair of his wayward offspring. His mission is to separate them from their undesirable comrades, to rescue the doctrine from the doctrinaires, to remove its excesses and excrescences, and to restore the "cutting edge of innovation" that was the pride of the new history in one of the most creative periods in the history of the profession.[3]

For all his reaffirmations and protestations, Stone may well be suspected by his colleagues of giving comfort to the enemy. Certainly no traditional historian has so effectively exposed the fallacies, pretensions, and assumptions of quantohistory, or been so curtly dismissive of the "disaster area" of psychohistory.[4] This is not to say that Stone rejects quantification or psychoanalysis—in the appropriate place and to the appropriate degree. But he does insist upon their limitations and dangers. Above all, he warns of the reductivism inherent in the attempt to make of history a social science. Contemplating the sad state of the social sciences these days, he suggests that "it might be time for the historical rats to leave rather than to scramble aboard the social scientific ship which seems to be leaking and undergoing major repair."[5]

In counseling these rats to leave the sinking ship of social science, Stone is not urging them to return to the old history, but rather to board the newest ship in the armada of the new history, the flagship sailing under the banner of *mentalité collective*.[6] Dedicated to the study of popular beliefs, attitudes, customs, sentiments, and modes of behavior, *mentalité* history models itself on a humanistic anthropology. Stone himself has enlisted in this enterprise. His book *The Family, Sex and Marriage in England* has an epigraph from Clifford Geertz, the anthropologist who is the guru of this school: "The problems, being existential, are universal; their solutions, being human, are diverse . . . The road to the grand abstractions of science winds through a thicket of singular facts."[7] The more famous phrase of Geertz (quoted so often and so inappropriately that he must be heartily sick of it) is "thick description": the technique of bringing to bear upon a single episode or situation a mass of facts of every kind and subjecting them to intensive analysis so as to elicit every possible cultural implication.[8]

In espousing this kind of cultural-social-anthropological history, Stone repudiates both the pseudoscientific methodology and the deterministic ideology of much of the new history. He is critical of the economic and social determinism of the Marxists, the materialistic determinism (economic, geographic, demographic) of some of the Annalistes, and the econometric and sociological determinism of the Cliometricians. "The culture of the group," he asserts, "and even the will of the individual, are potentially at least as important causal agents of change as the impersonal forces of material output and demographic growth."[9] They might even, on occasion, be the primary and determinant causes of change. Contraception, for example, is "as much a product of a state of mind as it is of economic circumstances or technological inventions." So too the Puritan ethic was a "by-product of an unworldly religious movement" long before there was any economic need for a new work ethic.[10] Moreover, in this cultural realm, elites and even individuals are often more influential than the masses in shaping history, and shaping it in political ways as well as social. "Civilizations have risen and fallen due to fluctuations in political authority and shifts in the fortunes of war"—an obvious fact overlooked, Stone observes, by those who preen themselves on being in the vanguard of the historical profession.[11]

Stone goes so far as to suggest that there is under way, among some new historians, a "revival of narrative," a prime example being Emmanuel Le Roy Ladurie's *Montaillou,* an account of life in a village in the Pyrenees in the early fourteenth century.[12] (Among his other examples of the new narrative mode are Eric Hobsbawm's *Primitive Rebels* and E. P. Thompson's *Whigs and Hunters.*) But here Stone seems to be playing with words, the "narration of a single event" being more analytic or structural than narrative; at most it can be described as episodic or microscopic.[13] Certainly it is not what Gibbon, Macaulay, or Ranke would have understood by narration—a story developed chronologically over the course of years, so that the end of the period is significantly different from the beginning. In *Montaillou* we have exactly the opposite, not so much a story as a "moment" in the Hegelian sense, in which the course of history is stopped in order to capture its essence, as in a still photograph.

If Stone, who normally chooses his words carefully, seems to be violating the obvious meaning of "narrative," it is to dramatize the break, as he sees it, between *mentalité* history and "scientific" history. "Narrative," he explains, is a "shorthand code-word."[14] It signifies a rejection of the analytic methodology, the scientific pretensions, and the economic and materialistic determinism of the new history. And it marks "the end of an era"—the end of the revolution.[15] As in many a revolution, the end is being heralded not by some malcontent of the old regime but by one of the original revolutionaries. In Stone's other works—*The Crisis of the Aristocracy; The Causes of the English Revolution; Family and Fortune; The Family, Sex and Marriage*—he has established himself as a skillful practitioner of the new history. In *The Past and the Present* he emerges as one of its most severe critics.

The long methodological essays in the first part of that book will attract the most attention, and deservedly so. Yet in some respects the shorter reviews that make up the second part are even more revealing. Dating from the 1960s and 1970s, they deal with books that Stone regarded at the time as exemplars of the new history. Rereading these reviews today, one is impressed by the rigor of his criticism from the beginning. Even in the first flush of revolution, his zeal was tempered by a vigilant skepticism. ("Tempered" is perhaps not quite the right word to describe some of his reviews, not reprinted here, which are notably intemperate in tone and almost vigilante in pursuit of error.)[16]

It is curious to find the same pattern repeating itself in one review after another. The book is first placed in its largest framework and pronounced a major contribution to a most important subject. The reviewer then professes to be overwhelmed by the imaginativeness and boldness of the thesis, the number of facts and variety of sources brought to bear upon it, and the ingenuity of the author in weaving them all together. Before long that glowing tribute gives way to a detailed critique of thesis, facts, sources, and reasoning, by the end of which little is left of the "flawed masterpiece" or "seminal work."[17]

Some of Stone's most devastating critiques, moreover, are not of the social-science type of history but of the *mentalité* genre. In the case of Philippe Ariès' *History of Childhood* and David Fischer's *Growing Old in America,* it is the methodology and data that Stone finds inadequate or faulty. In E. P. Thompson's *Whigs and Hunters* and Christopher Hill's *Society and Puritanism in Pre-Revolutionary England,* it is the Marxist or neo-Marxist ideology that selects and distorts the evidence to fit the preconceived thesis. In Barrington Moore's *Social Origins of Dictatorship and Democracy,* it is the wrong questions that are asked. In J. Bossy's *English Catholic Community,* it is the absence of all the "external events" of the old history, which can be ignored by the new only at the risk of throwing out the baby with the bathwater.

One does not want to leave the impression that Stone is unduly harsh. Indeed, he seems often to go out of the way to be generous, to give each book, at least at the outset, the benefit of the doubt, to credit it with serious intentions. It may be that his own expectations are an invitation to disillusionment. In any case, his criticisms are usually justified. Again and again, toward the end of his reviews, Stone puts the question his reader must be asking: Where are we now? And all too often he regretfully concludes that we are not all that much farther along than we were before—except, and here Stone reaffirms his original faith, that an important subject has been raised, one that would not have been raised by the traditional historian and that some day may be dealt with more satisfactorily than it has been so far.

Stone has raised so many issues and has dealt with them so candidly that it may be churlish to ask still more of him. He has made a large point, for example, of the role in the new history of ideology in general and of Marxism in particular. This is all the more noteworthy because he himself is not only a new historian but a man of the left; his heart, he makes it clear, is still with his mentor, the socialist historian R. H. Tawney, even though he can no longer subscribe to most of Tawney's historical theses. It is also noteworthy that in spite of his socialist sympathies, Stone has not been cowed by the animus against elitist history. *Crisis of the Aristocracy* is largely devoted to one such elite, 382 noblemen by his count. *Family, Sex and Marriage* deals mainly with the gentry and upper-middle classes, on the assumption that modern feelings about the family ("affective individualism," as Stone calls it) originated with them and filtered down to the lower classes—a thesis that has been predictably attacked as paternalistic, elitist and "culture-bound."[18] And *An Open Elite?* defines that elite so narrowly (in terms of a country house of a size that excludes most of the gentry and some of the aristocracy) that it is questionable whether such a definition can sustain any significant conclusions about social mobility.

Yet more should be said about the ideological impulse behind the new history. If, as Stone admits, it tends to ignore or belittle political, constitutional, and diplomatic history (or attend to them only by as-similating them into the categories and methods of social history), it also ignores and belittles intellectual history. And here, unfortunately, Stone joins the pack, deriding "traditional intellectual history" as a "kind of paper-chase of ideas back through the ages (which usually ends up with either Aristotle or Plato)," and complaining that "great books" (in quotation marks) are studied in a "historical vacuum."[19] This is a bit of philistinism unworthy (and untypical) of Stone. But it is all too typical of the historian who is suspicious of "elitist" ideas that may indeed trace their lineage to Plato or Aristotle, and of a discipline that does presume to characterize some books as great books (without the invidious quotation marks).

In this respect *mentalité* history is one of the worst offenders. Not content to establish itself as an independent discipline devoted to the study of "mental structures"—"feelings, emotions, behavior patterns, values, and states of mind"[20]—it feels obliged to denigrate those other mental structures known as ideas, especially ideas that emanated from the best minds of the time. Stone complains of the "hubris" of the new historian.[21] But surely it is the grossest kind of hubris for the historian to be dismissive of great books and great thinkers, to think that reality is better reflected in second-rate and third-rate thinkers than in first-rate ones. And it is surely a peculiar sense of historical relevance to think that everything about a book is worth studying—the technology of printing, the economics of publishing, the means of distribution, the composition of the reading public—everything, that is, except the ideas in the book itself. This cavalier attitude toward ideas, which sometimes verges on a positive animus against them, derives from the same populist or Marxist ideology that elsewhere Stone deplores (and that others have used to discredit his own work).

Stone points out that the tendency of quantitative history to let the data dictate the subject all too often produces subjects that are trivial or trite. The *mentalité* historian falls into the opposite trap of choosing a subject regardless of the availability or reliability of the data. It takes no great imagination, even for the traditional historian, to formulate wonderful questions to which he would dearly love to have answers. The historical record, unfortunately, like the geological record, is notoriously inadequate, full of gaps and flaws, infuriatingly lacking in the missing links we are always seeking. This is a problem for all historians, old and new. The old historian minimizes it by deliberately focusing on those subjects—political, institutional, diplomatic, intellectual—which do have more or less adequate records, and which can be subjected to what was once called (the very expression now seems archaic) "canons of evidence." The new history, especially *mentalité* history, has a penchant for subjects that, by definition, produce few such records; the "states of mind" of the "inarticulate masses" are too subtle and private to lend themselves to the kind of evidence that survives the ages.

It is a challenging task that confronts the new history, and one can understand why the brightest and most ambitious are attracted to it. It is an exciting game to ferret out whatever facts one can, however and wherever one can, and to make of them whatever one can, by way of deduction, generalization, extrapolation, supposition, intuition, imagination. Only a crotchety old historian would throw a damper on the festivities by pointing out that the results, more often than not, are thoroughly speculative and problematic—"impressionistic," as the quantitative historian would say. Yet even among the new historians there is evidence that the game is turning sour. Where the largest theses can be contrived out of the smallest facts (and the most tenuous of facts), there is obviously much room for controversy, and it is no wonder that the new historians are even more contentious than the old.

As Stone would say at this point in one of his reviews, Where does this leave us? He thinks it leaves us with a chastened new history, less arrogant about what it can accomplish, less intolerant of the old history, more rigorous methodologically, and more pluralistic ideologically. He also predicts that with the revolution over, the new history will consolidate its gains and make some overtures to the opposition. The rest of us, mindful of the course of other revolutions, **may be less** sanguine. Several generations of historians (as generations go in the university) have a stake in the new history as they have come to know it. What others may criticize as methodological laxity, they regard as creativity; what others look upon as ideological indulgence, they take pride in as an act of moral commitment. Stone may think that the new historians have captured the commanding heights of the profession and carried out the basic objectives of their revolution. Like all successful revolutionaries, however, they still see themselves as embattled and besieged, having to fend off the forces of darkness and reaction. It will take many more voices like Stone's, voices from within their own ranks, to convince them that the new history is not necessarily admirable simply because it is new, nor the old contemptible simply because it is old.

Recovering a Lost World

When *The World We Have Lost* was first published in 1965, it received the kind of review in the *Times Literary Supplement* that would have driven a less stalwart author to despair. The lead review (anonymous, as all reviews in the journal then were), it consisted of two pages of detailed, relentless criticism.[22] That review, and others no less severe, may have contributed, paradoxically, to the *éclat* enjoyed by the book in academic circles; surely only an important work could be worthy of such extensive criticism. In any event the book throve on controversy. It was reprinted and translated, reissued in a new edition in 1971, and, almost twenty years after its original publication, Peter Laslett has prepared yet another edition.

The latest edition, with *Further Explored* added as a subtitle, is a revised but unrepentant version of the first.[23] It has been emended to remove some of the mistakes pointed out by critics, and amplified by references to new evidence and documentation culled from the abundant literature on the subject in the past two decades. In all essential respects, however, the original theses are reaffirmed. The book's (and the author's) resilience may be explained by the fact that it (and he) are part of a collective enterprise, the Cambridge Group for the History of Population and Social Structure, which prides itself on being on the "cutting edge" of the discipline. This may also account for the severity of the initial response, which was directed not only against this particular book but against the mode of history it represented—demographic, sociological, quantitative, "scientific."

By now the new history has become so well established in the profession that it is in the mainstream rather than on the cutting edge. Yet its practitioners retain a defensive spirit, as if they were a beleaguered minority. Thus one passage in the original edition of *The World We Have Lost* appears in the present edition, but now in the form of a quotation:

> Why is it that we know so much about the building of the British Empire, the growth of Parliament, and its practices, the public and private lives of English kings, statesmen, generals, writers, thinkers and yet do not know whether all our ancestors had enough to eat? . . . Why has almost nothing been done to discover how long those earlier Englishmen lived and how confident most of them could be of having any posterity at all? Not only do we not know the answers to these questions, until now we never seem to have bothered to ask them?[24]

"Not one of these plaintive queries," Laslett comments, "is as appropriate now," and some of them (about the length of life, for example) are "entirely inappropriate"—presumably because they have been answered. Lest this be taken as cause for complacency, he hastens to add that the situation is far from satisfactory. We are still not always asking the right questions and are only beginning to appreciate their implications for "human association altogether" rather than just for preindustrial England.[25]

In this passage and the subsequent comment may be found the strengths and weaknesses of the book: a boldness that makes excessive claims to originality (some of these questions had in fact been asked before); a confidence that is not always warranted (some of the answers are notably inadequate); an ambitiousness that gives rise to questions that are unanswerable (about "human association altogether"). It is also apparent that much of the controversy generated by the book comes not from these kinds of questions—about longevity, fertility, or diet in preindustrial England—but from another order of questions, the answers to which cannot be found in the extensive files of parish registers assembled by the Cambridge Group or in the sophisticated statistical techniques it has devised.

Of those questions that are amenable to quantitative analysis, some are so complicated that the answers remain mired in formulas and distinctions that defy easy generalization; for these Laslett refers us to the more detailed studies of his colleagues, E. A. Wrigley and R. S. Schofield. Others are more readily summarized, and here Laslett takes the opportunity to correct some prevalent "misbeliefs" that derive from literary sources.[26] The idea, for example, that people in preindustrial England married at an early age comes to us with the authority of Shakespeare, who had Juliet marry at fourteen and her mother at twelve. The statistical evidence, however, shows that the average age of marriage for the gentry and nobility was close to twenty, and for the population as a whole nearer the midtwenties. Similarly, the vision of the peasantry disporting themselves in the hay, as in *A Midsummer Night's Dream,* is not borne out by statistics of births in the ninth month following these revelries. (But it was in May rather than June, as Laslett says, that Shakespeare had them disporting themselves, which suggests that Laslett may have been looking at birth statistics for the wrong month.) Nor was the illegitimacy rate higher in the late seventeenth century, as Restoration dramatists would have us believe. Nor was starvation (actual starvation as distinct from malnutrition) nearly so common as has been supposed; indeed, it was extremely rare. Nor was infant mortality, even among the poorest families, nearly so high. Nor was the "extended household" the norm in preindustrial times; except for some of the aristocracy, the one-generation nuclear family was as typical then as it is today. Nor was the family so large as has been thought; late marriage and prolonged breast-feeding effectively limited the number of children. Nor were there factories in Tudor times, as a much-quoted but entirely fanciful contemporary poem suggests; nor, for that matter, were there any until the eighteenth century.

These and other findings are of great importance, and all historians are indebted to Laslett and the Cambridge Group for the enormous labor that went into them. But they are not what made the book so controversial initially or what sustained interest in it over the years. Much more provocative have been its theses about the "one-class society" and the "English Revolution."[27] When Laslett characterizes preindustrial England as a "one-class society," he does not mean, as some of his critics have suggested, that it was an egalitarian or classless society, but rather that there was only one *effective* class, the landowning class. Within this class, ranging from the upper aristocracy to the lower gentry, were considerable differences of status, wealth, and power, but also considerable mobility; outside it were the great bulk of the people who were too heterogeneous and powerless to qualify as a class. By putting the nobility and the gentry in the same class, Laslett has challenged the prevailing views of this period—not only the Marxist theory of an emergent capitalist class in conflict with the feudal aristocracy, but those non-Marxist theories that posit something like a class struggle between the "rising" and "falling" gentry.

The concept of a one-class society also rules out the familiar idea of the "English Revolution," a term Laslett would like erased from the vocabulary of historians (together with that other misnomer, the "rise of the middle class"). The English Revolution, as Marxists and neo-Marxists understand it, applies primarily to the Civil War, which is regarded as the beginning of the revolution of the middle class against the aristocracy, a revolution that culminated in the Whig Revolution of 1688. Laslett is here denying two distinct propositions: that there was a social revolution which pitted the aristocracy against the gentry (or middle, or capitalist, or bourgeois class); and that a political revolution necessarily involves a major change of economic and social power. During the whole of this period of supposed revolution, Laslett argues with great plausibility, the social structure remained essentially intact and the solidarity of nobility and gentry gave them a virtual monopoly of "political society."[28]

If Laslett finds no evidence of a social revolution in the seventeenth century, he finds ample evidence of one in the late eighteenth and the nineteenth centuries. And this revolution, the Industrial Revolution, was far more cataclysmic than any kind of "English Revolution."* By totally altering the scale of life, by removing work from the domain of the family and transferring it to a huge, impersonal structure, by destroying the rural community together with the bonds that sustained it, by subverting religious faith and traditional authorities, by democratizing the polity and transforming society, industrialism brought

---

*In refuting the idea of an "English Revolution," Laslett also proposes to dispense with such other revolutions as the "Puritan Revolution," the "Scientific Revolution," the "Revolution in Government," and the like. He retains the "Industrial Revolution," although he is not entirely happy with it.

about the demise of the old world, "the world we have lost." The penultimate chapter, "After the Transformation," describes the new world as it took shape in England in the early twentieth century. Recalling the most dismal pictures drawn by the most pessimistic historians of early-industrial England, Laslett has the English proletariat, a century or more after the Industrial Revolution, seeming to confirm the Marxist law of "immiseration." Working-class children, for example, are described as "scrawny, dirty, hungry, ragged, verminous," and their parents as "perpetually liable to social and material degradation."[29] Laslett concedes that this picture may be overdrawn. If, as a contemporary study showed, almost half the workers were below the poverty line, over half must have been above it. Moreover (as that study also suggested), a large item in bringing them below that line was the six shillings a week (one-sixth of their income) spent by the average family on beer (thirty-one pints). But Laslett does not permit these facts to detract from his portrait of a pauperized and degraded working class, whose condition, he claims, did not materially improve until the advent of the welfare state after World War II.

It is curious that Laslett should accept so readily the kinds of stereotypes about the "new world" he is properly suspicious of in the case of the "old world." Industrialism did, obviously, transform society in myriad ways—but not totally and not cataclysmically. By the early twentieth century poverty was far less degrading, materially and morally, than it had been in the early industrial period; and social and economic mobility, the opportunity to escape from poverty, was far greater than it had been in the preindustrial period. In this sense a two-class or three-class society (or five-class, as other historians would have it) was a happier world for the poor than a "one-class" society, in which the poor were too poor and too powerless to constitute a class at all. Moreover Laslett himself, correcting some misbeliefs about preindustrial England, suggests that in crucial respects—the nuclear family, the size of the household, the age at marriage, the incidence of illegitimacy—the world we have lost was not entirely lost, that it was more like our own world than many "literary" historians have led us to believe. He reminds us, for instance, that aged parents in preindustrial times did not normally die in the bosom of their family, as a romantic view of that world might suggest, but alone in their cottage or in the poorhouse.

These examples of continuity between the old and new worlds may be more persuasive than Laslett's examples of change. Thus he cites, as a crucial feature of the old world in contrast to the new, the "human life-span" that once characterized all "temporal" matters—the death of the master-baker, for example, resulting in the end of the bakery.[30] Yet other temporal affairs exhibited a longer than human life-span, indeed a far longer span than is customary today; land tenure and material goods (even modest ones, such as quilts and furnishings) were passed on from generation to generation, in contrast to the mobile, disposable, and consumable habits of our own time. So too Laslett's description of the "minuscule" scale of life in the old world must be qualified by his claim that urbanization grew more rapidly in England in the "five generations of pre-industrial times" than in any European country at any time.[31] London itself doubled its population in the first half of the seventeenth century and almost tripled it by the end of the century. Nor was the metropolis as alien from the rest of the country as may be supposed; by the early eighteenth century, Wrigley estimates, one adult in six had had some direct experience of London life by living there for at least a short time.[32]

In spite of much evidence to the contrary, the effect of *The World We Have Lost*—indeed, of its very title—is to induce a nostalgia for that lost world. "Time was when the whole of life went forward in the family, in a circle of loved, familiar faces, known and fondled objects, all to human size. That time has gone for ever. It makes us very different from our ancestors."[33] Laslett insists that this is not the familiar paean to a Golden Age, that the loving family circle might well have comprised tyrannical fathers, resentful mothers, and exploited children. But even here he lapses into nostalgia. "Who could love the name of a limited company or of a government department as an apprentice could love his superbly satisfactory father-figure master, even if he were a bully and a beater, a usurer and a hypocrite?"[34]

These are not the kinds of observations one expects from a quantitative historian. Yet they may help explain the appeal of the book over the years. And not only of this book but of this genre of history, which invokes the authority of science while indulging in the rhetoric of nostalgia. Social history, when it is not a dismal science, can easily become a sentimental one.

Case Studies in Psychohistory   ·6·

The critic of psychohistory is at some peril. His motives can be impugned, his criticisms can be "psychoanalyzed away." A panoply of psychoanalytic concepts can be invoked to explain his obtuseness: denial, repression, resistance, evasion, anxiety, rage. One eminent psychohistorian professes to find this tactic "tempting but illicit." But in the course of disclaiming any such intention, Peter Gay insinuates precisely this: it is the historians' "emotion-laden acts of rejection," he says, that the psychohistorian must refrain from interpreting as "resistances." In the preceding sentence he has the "overwhelming majority of historians" confronting Freud with "reasoned skepticism, ill-concealed anxiety, or cold rage."[1] Earlier still, that skepticism is depicted as a series of "aggressive defenses" or "defensive maneuvers" set up by the fearful historian: "If he is obliged to surrender the outermost wall to the enemy, he can fall back on the second set of bulwarks to offer further resistance; if the second falls, the third remains, and so forth, right down to the fortress in which the historian nervously awaits the invader."[2]

The military metaphor recalls the hoary image of the "warfare of science and religion" once used to describe the forces of light battling the forces of darkness. The psychohistorian may find, like the historian of science before him, that scholarship is not well served by such images. He may also find that two can play at that Freudian game: if the historian is portrayed as nervously, defensively resisting the truths of psychohistory, so the psychohistorian may be portrayed as nervously, aggressively psychoanalyzing history for private reasons of his own. It is a "zero-sum game," profiting neither party to this dispute, and profiting history least of all.

The following case studies are offered in a spirit of "reasoned skepticism," on the assumption that psychohistory is prepared to be judged by the canons of historical evidence and proof.

*   *   *

Edmund Burke: An Ambivalent Conservative

Edmund Burke is usually thought of as the archetypical conservative. And with some cause. An uncompromising enemy of the French Revolution in particular and of revolution in principle, an unregenerate defender of the established order in England and of establishments in general, a brilliant rhetorician who deliberately clothed his ideas in what were even then the most provocative of words—prescription, presumption, prejudice, and superstition—Burke would seem to have impeccable conservative credentials. Yet some liberals, and radicals as well, cannot leave it at that. They keep trying to rehabilitate him. And if they cannot quite claim him as one of their own, they impugn his conservatism, suggesting that he did not mean what he said or that he only said what he did in response to the exigencies of the moment.

These attempts to revise and reclaim Burke (to *übersetzen und verbesseren* him, as German translators of Shakespeare are said to have boasted) is no new thing. A century ago John Morley, himself an unexceptionable liberal, wrote not one but two appreciative studies of Burke, and such eminent rationalists and positivists as Henry Buckle and William Lecky praised him lavishly. In our generation we have been presented with several portraits of Burke that depart even more from the conventional image. Introducing a new edition of the *Reflections on the Revolution in France,* Conor Cruise O'Brien gives us a Burke who is nothing less than a cryptorevolutionist, whose arguments in favor of the Whig Revolution were an implicit argument for an Irish revolution to overthrow the Protestant ascendancy, and whose passionate opposition to the French Revolution liberated a "suppressed revolutionary part of his own personality."[3] Another kind of revolutionist appears in Ruth Bevan's *Marx and Burke: A Revisionist View,* where the protagonists are said to share a similarity in the structure of their thought that is far more significant than their obvious "stereo-typed" differences.[4]

A still more revisionist work is Isaac Kramnick's *The Rage of Edmund Burke*.[5] It is doubly revisionist, for it reinterprets Burke psychologically as well as politically. The subtitle informs us that this is the "Portrait of an Ambivalent Conservative." But the text more often presents him as an "ambivalent radical," which has a somewhat different implication.[6] Burke was politically ambivalent, Kramnick argues, because he was sexually ambivalent. There were, he says, "two Burkes," one identifying with the aristocratic, privileged order, the other with the bourgeois, radical class, the first deriving from the feminine, passive side of his nature, the other from the masculine, aggressive side.[7] The tension and conflict between these two Burkes originated in an unresolved oedipal situation and resulted in an identity crisis that "corresponds perfectly," we are assured, to the Eriksonian paradigm.[8]

Each of the political and intellectual issues confronting Burke is made to fit this paradigm. As the first major theorist of the modern political party, he raised issues that are still a matter of serious debate, not the least of which concerns his own commitment to party. For Kramnick all of this is "beside the point." "The more important issue at stake is the role that party played in the working out of Burke's personal crisis." And about that role Kramnick has no doubt. Party was "an extremely useful mechanism for dealing with the tension inherent in Burke's servile relationship to the great, the tension between the dependency of the agent and the independence of the ambitious man."[9] It represented the "affective male bonding," and at the same time the "beautiful feminine social ideals" of friendship, affection, and attachment; it provided the platform for masculine ambition and the drive for power and also the "warm emotional embrace" of friends and family. It was, in fact, the principal expression of his "homophilic instincts."[10]

So too with the other great issues about which Burke had much to say. In the dispute over the American colonies the Americans represented the bourgeois principle, the English the aristocratic. In defending the Americans, Burke was responding to their "bold and youthful masculinity" as against the "passive feminine" English. "But there is much more," we are told, "to Burke's championship of the Americans than this."[11] The "much more" turns out to be another aspect of his ambivalence—his desire, like that of the Americans, to be independent, "his own master, his own man." On a still deeper level he was responding to a familial situation not unlike his own. He was asking England to be a "nonrepressive parent," so that he (and by projection America) would be able to respond with "love and affection."[12]

India and France brought out the other side of Burke's ambivalence. Warren Hastings, like the French revolutionists, exhibited the aggressive masculine sexuality that characterized the bourgeois spirit. In these cases Burke assumed the feminine role. Repelled by the "unleashed and unrepressed sexuality" of Hastings and by the "violated femininity" of the French aristocracy and monarchy, Burke gave vent to his "rage-filled indictment of bourgeois radicalism."[13] At the same time, however, he was acting as the "spokesman for bourgeois interests." An enthusiastic disciple of Adam Smith, he was as much committed to the principles of laissez-faire and to the Protestant ethic as any "bourgeois manufacturer."[14] Thus once again Burke was torn between the "active/bourgeois/masculine principle" and the "passive/aristocratic/feminine principle."[15]

The concept of ambivalence serves the double function of first creating a multitude of contradictions in Burke's life and thought and then resolving those contradictions—all this without the need to engage in any laborious analysis of texts. At strategic points of the argument we are reminded of the source of Burke's ambivalence: "Guilt over his own apparent oedipal conquest and the subsequent reactive identification with the mother led Burke to doubt his own sexual identity and to repress sexuality in general."[16] Whether that repression took the form of an overt or a latent homosexuality Kramnick finds "far from certain," but "what little evidence there is" suggests to him that Burke had problems in "the area of sexual object choice." At this point psychoanalytic theory provides the evidence lacking in our knowledge of Burke himself. "Psychoanalytic theory hypothesizes that such difficulty is rooted in oedipal and preoedipal experience and Burke's sexual ambivalence seems no exception."[17] The young boy's "incestuous designs on the mother" could only be resolved by identification with the father, and unfortunately, just when that identification should have taken place, Burke's father was absent.[18]

The oedipal theme is referred to again and again. Yet Burke's childhood occupies only a few pages of the book, and the decisive evidence turns upon a single fact: "The most crucial event in his early years was his separation from his father from the age of six to eleven."[19] His ambivalence toward his father, thus his own sexual ambivalence—and thus too his political ambivalence—derived from his sense of being "deserted" by his father, while his mother, whom he adored, remained close to him.[20] Unfortunately, that "crucial event," so far as one can reconstruct it, seems to have been undramatic and commonplace—involving, moreover, a separation for long periods from his mother as well as from his father. Burke was a sickly child prone to lung ailments, and his parents' house in Dublin, located on a canal, was so damp as to exacerbate his condition. For this reason he was sent, at the age of six, to live with his mother's family in the south of Ireland. Kramnick informs us that his father, because of his legal practice, seldom visited the boy, but that his mother did so often. We are given no indication of how seldom or often those visits took place, perhaps because the sources cited say nothing at all of them, let alone of their frequency. In any event, the episode hardly bears out the contention that the father abandoned or deserted his son; on the contrary, it might be taken as evidence of his solicitude in seeking for the child a more salubrious environment. Nor is there any evidence that the son felt abandoned and deserted by him, in contrast to the closeness he is presumed to have felt for his mother. Again, in the absence of any evidence, one might as reasonably suppose that even if her visits were more frequent, the child's sense of deprivation might be greater, the separation from a mother being at least as traumatic as the separation from a father.

The facts, such as they are, can obviously be made to bear almost any interpretation, all the more because a child's feelings need have no necessary relation to the actual facts. As it happens, we do have some evidence about Burke's feelings. His letters repeatedly refer to those years away from home as an especially happy time in his life, and he always retained the warmest memories of his mother's family. Perhaps the boy was pleased to be away from a father who was notoriously ill-tempered and ill-natured, and not only toward his sons. A psychoanalyst might argue that a child's happiness in the absence of his father could easily translate itself into guilt. But it is precisely the facility of such arguments, the ability to deduce almost anything from anything (or from nothing), that serves to remind us of the precariousness of this kind of analysis.

The combination of inadequate evidence and arbitrary interpretation makes almost every part of this psychological portrait suspect. "There is ample evidence," we are told, "that Burke, in fact, hungered for his father's love and affection. In 1758 he named his first son (and only one to survive) with his father's name, Richard."[21] The familiar psychoanalytic fallacy—attributing great psychological significance to a commonplace convention (the naming of one's son after one's father)—is compounded by the parenthetical phrase that seems to reinforce that psychological significance, as if Burke foresaw that this would be the only son to survive; even the most ardent admirer of Burke might be loath to ascribe to him such omniscience. Nor is one persuaded by the rest of that "ample evidence": the fact that he sent his father a copy of his first book, or that he expressed his appreciation for a generous gift of money.

Occasionally, very occasionally, Kramnick expresses himself more cautiously about both the facts and his interpretation. But these few asides are just that, the argument proceeding apace as if they had not occurred. One crucial chapter, on Burke's "Missing Years," promises to conclude on a refreshingly candid note: "There is no solid evidence that can be produced here which would positively sustain the interpretation of Burke's sexual and psychic life offered in this book." But this is followed by an even more dubious assertion: "What can be said, however, is that it is a reading of Burke which far from seeking to discredit him hopes to enhance and enrich our understanding and appreciation of his life and thought."[22]

The last sentence, and especially that last word, is at the heart of the matter. The problem with this and similar exercises in psychobiography is not only that they fail to respect the conventional canons of evidence and interpretation, but that they do not respect the "life and thought"—most conspicuously the thought—of their subjects. The historian Lewis Namier, who took issue with Burke for being, among other things, overly ideological in his interpretation of eighteenth-century politics, has himself been accused of "taking mind out of politics," denuding politics of ideas, principles, and beliefs. Even Namier, however, was not as insidiously anti-intellectual as is the psychobiographer. Namier only took the mind out of politics; he ignored it, pretended it did not exist, constructed his theory without recourse to it. He did not reinterpret or subvert it. He did not "transfer" or "translate" or "project" ideas into something else. Even Marx was not as reductivist as this; since the "superstructure," like the "infrastructure," existed on the class level, it did not intrude so insistently into the mind of each individual. It remains for the psychobiographer to convert ideas into feelings and thus truly take the mind out of politics.

Far from being enlightening, the concept of ambivalence turns out to be an intrusion and a hindrance. Without it Kramnick might have been moved to examine the substance and logic of Burke's ideas. He might then have discovered that instead of being ambivalent about the bourgeoisie and the aristocracy, the new class and the old, Burke made a conscious and sustained effort to accommodate both and keep them in proper balance. As he eloquently wrote in the *Reflections,* a "due and adequate representation of a state" must take account of "ability" as well as "property." So too the "qualification for government" had to include those who possessed "actual" wisdom and virtue as well as those whose birth and rank gave them "presumptive" wisdom and virtue.[23] And when Burke defended the ideas of presumption and prescription, tradition and heredity, it was as a means of preserving not only ancient liberties and possessions but also newly acquired liberties and possessions.

All of this makes for a complicated and subtle system of thought, but not an ambivalent one—unless one understands intellectual complexity and subtlety as symptoms of psychic and sexual disorder.*

James and John Stuart Mill: Ambivalent Rebels

Bruce Mazlish is the most assiduous of psychohistorians. Whatever reservations one may have about his work, one cannot but admire his energy, dedication, and persistence. And his candor. If he is sometimes an embarrassment to some of his colleagues, it is because he says what they believe but rarely say quite so forthrightly (at least outside their own circles). Thus he has declared himself on the much debated sub-

---

*A later essay by Kramnick, "The Left and Edmund Burke" (*Political Theory,* May 1983), retains a politically ambivalent Burke, torn between bourgeois and aristocratic principles, but does not mention the psychic or sexual source of that ambivalence. The fact that Kramnick could write such an analysis without the psychoanalytic framework is itself a powerful argument against his earlier book, for if the conventional mode of intellectual analysis is sufficient, what is the justification for the psychoanalytic mode?

ject of the relationship of psychoanalysis to history: "Psychoanalysis differs from history in one fundamental way. It claims to have a scientific system of concepts, based on clinical data. This claim I accept."[24] It is this claim that gives him the confidence to psychoanalyze (or psychohistoricize) a formidable array of historical figures—James and John Stuart Mill, Marx, Cromwell, Robespierre, Lenin, Mao— and such contemporaries as Nixon, Carter, and Kissinger. He can feel assured, as no mere historian can, that he has penetrated to the "real" person and elucidated the "real meaning" of his life and thought.[25] And he can do so even in the absence of the kind of data the conventional historian requires. He is not discouraged by the discovery that the "first thing" that strikes the student of Nixon, for example, is the "paucity of information" about him, especially about those periods of his life that are most crucial for the psychohistorian.[26] For Mazlish the paucity of biographical information is compensated by the certitude of psychoanalytic information.

> At present, at least, there is a lack of materials about his [Nixon's] early childhood and adolescence. Yet we can assume that the *way* in which he passed through his Oedipal phase—a necessary phase in the development of all young men, for without it, identification with a model of a mature man would be hampered—was of great importance and affected later relationships in his life. So, too, because of lack of information, we cannot, in fact, tell how typical his experiences were, but we can postulate, in theory, a significant connection with his Quaker religion, his rural, Californian culture, his maturation in twentieth-century American society, and so forth.[27]

In the case of a contemporary figure like Nixon, this mode of reasoning is patently unsatisfying. The assertion that Nixon must have passed through some kind of "Oedipal phase" and that this experience must have had some "significant connection" to his religion, culture, and society is not especially informative. Even an uncritical reader, familiar with the multitude of ways in which young American boys (even rural Californians of Quaker families) grow to manhood and respond to their upbringing and environment, will want something more than bland assumptions and generalizations; and told that there is a notable "lack of materials" and "lack of information" about this particular boy and his particular experiences, he may well be tempted to read no further. In the case of a historical figure, however, the lack of information may not be so evident or seem so egregious. The reader may be more easily satisfied by a historical background that looks specific only because it is dramatically different from his own, but that is actually not at all specific in relation to the particular subject. Indeed, it is likely to be less specific for a historical figure than for a contemporary one, the facts being even more sparse about, for example, a particular rural Scottish child born in 1773 than about a particular rural Californian child born in 1913.

Mazlish's account of one rural Scottish child opens candidly enough: "The facts about James Mill's early life can be briefly stated."[28] He was born in 1773 in a Scottish village called Logie Pert. His father, originally James Milne (the spelling was later changed by his wife), was a shoemaker; his mother, Isabel Fenton, daughter of a farmer, had been a servant girl in Edinburgh before her marriage. The younger James was the oldest of three children; his younger brother was an apprentice shoemaker, and his sister took care of the cow. Recognizing the boy's superior abilities, the mother allotted him one of the three rooms in the house for a study. "At some point" he attended Montrose Academy. At the age of eighteen he came to the notice of Sir John and Lady Jane Stuart who sponsored him at the University of Edinburgh, where he studied for the ministry. After five years he was licensed as a preacher, gave itinerant sermons, but found no permanent post. In 1802 he went to London, traveling in Sir John's carriage.

Those are the hard facts as related by Mazlish in his *James and John Stuart Mill*. The entire account of James Mill's "early life" (which takes him well beyond his childhood and adolescence) covers three and a half pages and testifies as much to the paucity of facts as to the imaginative reconstruction of them. In the first of three paragraphs on James Mill's father, for example, we are told: "Though we have little information about him, we know he was a shoemaker. As such, he was part of an artisan class notorious for being above the average in intelligence and interest in political affairs."[29] The rest of the paragraph locates him, "at least by trade," in the radical tradition stretching from Thomas Hardy's Corresponding Society in the 1790s to George Odger's International Workingmen's Association in the late 1860s, and across the channel to the sansculottes of the French Revolution. The next paragraph, however, nullifies much of this "tradition" with the admission: "We know nothing of what influence he may have had on his son. We do not even know whether he was typical of the shoemakers, as I have described them."[30] The little we do know, Mazlish continues, comes from his son's biographer, Alexander Bain, who described him as industrious, good-natured, pious, and devout (indeed "very strict in all observances of a religious nature")—but not especially intelligent. This might suggest (although Mazlish does not say so) that the father was not at all the type of artisan described earlier, who was notorious for all the opposite traits: intelligence, radicalism, and religious skepticism. Mazlish finally concludes that "the father seems to be nonexistent as a formative influence in James' life."[31] This is not quite accurate either, since it is only the evidence that is nonexistent. (Moreover, the father is later assumed to have had a momentous formative influence, if only in inspiring the rebellion on the part of his son that is the main thesis of the book.)

Perhaps because more is known about the mother, Mazlish sees her as the dominant influence on her son. He cites Bain to this effect: "Clearly, Bain believes her to be the source of her son's intelligence and drive; perhaps Bain's prejudice is at work."[32] But Bain did not "clearly" believe this; on the contrary, he was clearly skeptical of it: "It was the fancy of those that knew her, that she was the source of her son's intellectual energy; but the only proof now attainable is the apparent absence of any unusual force of character in her husband."[33] Undeterred, Mazlish continues, "In any case, she was certainly ambitious for James," lavishing attention on him in a way "calculated to appeal to his narcissistic feelings."[34] She did so, we are told, by means of discipline rather than love, initiating a pattern that was to be repeated by James himself in relation to his own wife and children. This conclusion is obviously of some consequence, not only for the psychobiography of James Mill but also for that of John Stuart Mill. Yet it too is based on the flimsiest of evidence, as Mazlish freely admits. The crucial page is littered with demurrals—"we can surmise," "we can only speculate," "we can conjecture"—culminating in the candid admission: "Yet we must make clear that this is all mere speculation. In truth, we know almost nothing about James' early life and feelings."[35] Far from inhibiting further speculation, this disclaimer only serves to invite and stimulate it.

What is at issue is not only this mode of psychobiography, although that would be serious enough. Mazlish is engaged in the more ambitious enterprise of psychohistory. The subtitle, *Father and Son in the Nineteenth Century,* refers not only to this particular father and son (a highly particular pair, one might add), but to the generic, so to speak, father and son of that time. The work goes beyond psychohistory in the ordinary sense, for in addition to interpreting history in psychoanalytic terms it aspires to understand psychoanalysis itself in historical terms.

Early in the book Mazlish poses the daring question "Was Freud right?"[36] Was he right, that is, about the Oedipus complex, which is at the heart of psychoanalysis and crucial to the father-son relationship? Mazlish's answer is that he was right to posit the Oedipus complex as a "constant" of human nature (a "biological given"), but that that constant manifests itself in different forms of behavior depending upon the social, cultural, and historical conditions in which the individual finds himself. In the nineteenth century, for example, those conditions were determined by major "structural change and ideational change."[37] The ideational change centered on the theory of progress, which Mazlish traces back to the seventeenth-century battle of the Moderns against the Ancients, thence to the Enlightenment, and finally to Darwinism. The structural change he attributes to the "Democratic and Industrial Revolutions," supplemented by the "Demographic Revolution." As a result of these changes, "somewhere between the late eighteenth and early nineteenth centuries" the Oedipus complex began to take on a new form and eventually manifested itself in a "totally new way." What had earlier been a "patterned and secure" relationship became "problematic," erupting into intense "filial rebellion."[38] Mazlish provides no evidence for the earlier supposedly placid relationship; his concern is entirely with the later generational rebellion waged first by James Mill against his father and then by John Stuart Mill against James.

Mazlish's capitalization of these "Revolutions" is, a psychoanalyst might say, significant. He reifies them, quite as he reifies the Oedipal complex. Just as the Oedipal complex is assumed to be true of all young men, so these Revolutions are assumed to have affected all these young men—the young James Mill in Logie Pert in the 1770s and 1780s, his son in London in the 1810s and 1820s, and (making a cameo appearance) the hero of Turgenev's *Fathers and Sons* in Russia in the 1860s. James Mill is said to have satisfied both his psychic and his historic needs by turning against his father, family, and country, and by re-creating himself as a "self-made man." The psychic need was, of course, Oedipal: "The self-made aspect of James Mill begs for an explanation in Oedipal terms, even though we have no direct evidence to sustain our speculation."[39] The historic need was the adjustment to "modernization," having to "bring about and cope with the structural changes of an industrial society."[40] But there is no more specific evidence for this historic "fact" than for the psychic one. Industrialization and modernization were as hypothetical in that Scottish rural hamlet of nine hundred people as the Oedipal complex was in the young boy about whose early life we know so little. (Indeed, more hypothetical: the Oedipal complex might be posited as a constant of human nature, but not even the most ardent proponent of "modernization theory" would make of the Industrial Revolution a constant of history.)

A psychohistory of the Mills is necessarily a psychointellectual history, since their historical importance lies so heavily in the realm of ideas. It is to Mazlish's credit that he fully recognizes this, that he takes their ideas as seriously as their libidos and makes an earnest effort not to reduce the one to the other. To avoid that reductivism, he formulates the relationship between the two as one of "corresponding processes" rather than of "causation." Ideas, he says, are not "caused" by character traits; they only "correspond" to them. In Erikson's terms, "Identity has become intrinsic to Ideology."[41] (Or, as Mazlish put it in his book on Marx, Marxism is "Marx writ large.")[42]

One can appreciate the intent behind this formulation, as well as the difficulties inherent in it. In some respects it is even more problematic than the familiar theory of causation. Causation requires only (a large "only") that a particular character structure (James Mill's "self-made man," for example) give rise to a particular set of ideas (utilitarianism, in this instance); it does not preclude the possibility that a very different character structure (such as Bentham's) might generate the same ideas. Correspondence is an even more ambitious concept. If character and ideas—"identity" and "ideology"—correspond, how does one account for the fact that Bentham's character was so notably different from Mill's? (Although Bentham figures prominently in Mazlish's book, in relation to the son as well as the father, he is not subjected to any kind of psychological analysis, so that the problem is never confronted.) Or if James Mill's "law of human nature"—that men will seek boundless power over others in order to satisfy their own boundless need for pleasure—reflects his own intense need for independence, his fear of the threats to that independence, and at the same time his "latent desire to be 'dependent',"[43] are we to assume that not only Bentham but also Machiavelli, Hobbes, and a host of lesser thinkers who posited a similar law were motivated by the same need, fear, and latent desire? Or that Locke, who did not posit such a law, did not share that need, fear, and desire?

Or, to take an example that Mazlish makes much of, if James Mill's adherence to laissez-faire expresses his ambivalence toward independence and dependence, what is one to make of the fact that he adopted that theory from Ricardo, whose background, personality, position, and almost everything else that defined his identity were conspicuously different from Mill's? In successive sentences Ricardo appears as a loving and indulgent father to Mill, Mill as "mother-as-pedagogue" to Ricardo, and (because in fact both were almost the same age), Ricardo as a "fantasied sibling" to Mill. "Whatever the correct analysis," Mazlish adds, "we need some such speculation as the above to explain the strange bits of quotation cited, and to allow us to understand the loving relation to Ricardo, which appears so out of character for Mill."[44] A few sentences later, after further apologies for the vagueness and difficulties of the explanation, we are assured that the "intellectual collaboration" of Mill and Ricardo, so fateful for the history of economic thought, had a "strong, unconscious emotional foundation," and thus that there is a "psychohistorical basis" even to so abstract a work as James Mill's *Elements of Political Economy*.[45]

One might expect that John Stuart Mill's *Principles of Political Economy* would provide the occasion for further reflections on the theme of identification and rebellion. The son, after all, deliberately intruded into the father's terrain, challenged his authority, and effectively usurped it. Yet Mazlish, while noting the differences between the two books, makes surprisingly little of them in psychoanalytic terms. The most novel part of his analysis centers on one chapter of the *Principles*, "The Probable Futurity of the Labouring Classes." Mill himself (and most commentators since) took this chapter to be an attack on those who wanted to keep the laboring classes in a position of inferiority and dependency, and a defense of higher wages, trade unions, even the kind of socialism that would promote the improvement of the working classes. To Mazlish the real meaning of the chapter is precisely the opposite. The very expressions "labouring" or "lower" classes he finds invidious and elitist. He makes much of the sexual imagery of "lower," signifying the lower part of the body—the scene of "animal" sexuality in contrast to the "higher" regions of mind—and implying that the lower classes are "baser," unable to control their sexual passions, like "savages" who are presumed to be "lower" in the scale of evolution, thus more animalistic. This image reminds him of Freud's analysis of men who can only have sexual relations with prostitutes or women of the lower classes—which, in turn, recalls the familiar Victorian attitudes toward sex and class. All of this leads to the conclusion that Mill, while professing to argue for greater equality, did not mean it on "that 'lower' level," the sexual level, where presumably reality lies.[46] After this elaborate analysis, it may seem anticlimactic to point out that Mill himself, in the course of this forty-five-page chapter, did not use the expression "lower classes," although that term was common even among radicals at the time.*

In his discussion of John Stuart Mill's most influential book, *On Liberty,* Mazlish quotes Isaiah Berlin, who valued its principles "in part because they spring from acute moral crises in a man's life." "What Berlin calls 'moral'," Mazlish comments, "I prefer to call 'psychological'."[47] It is not clear whether Mazlish thinks he is merely translating Berlin's dictum into more congenial language, or whether he is aware of the enormity of the change he is proposing. In any event, the transmutation of "moral" into "psychological" is a telling commentary on psychohistory itself—on its conception of the "real" man and the "real meaning" of his life, ideas, and historical role.

---

* One wonders what Mazlish would make of the word "proletariat," which (as Marx and Engels were well aware at the time) has a much more explicit sexual connotation. It derives from *proles*—offspring—a term originally applied to the lowest class of Roman citizen who served the state only by producing children. Mazlish had an opportunity to discuss the significance of this word in his book on Marx; yet that book is curiously lacking in this kind of interpretation.

Is National History Obsolete?

"Happy is the nation that has no history."[1] That adage, familiar from at least the eighteenth century, is an ambiguous tribute to those small nations that have been spared the sufferings exacted by history as the price of greatness. Today it is not only history that is distrusted; it is the very idea of the nation. For some historians the motto might be revised to read, "Happy is the history that has no nation."

The aversion to national history is part of the aversion to political history, the history that has traditionally defined the nation. As politics has been taken out of history, so attempts are being made to take the nation out of history. Local history has this effect, by emphasizing what is distinctive to the locality rather than what is common to the country as a whole.[2] So does universal history, by emphasizing what is common to the world (or to "civilization") rather than what is distinctive to a particular country.[3] So does social history, by focusing on categories other than the nation—class, race, ethnicity, family, women, children.[4] In some cases the nation remains the tacit framework of study, even though it impinges little or not at all on the substance of the work; in others the rejection of national history is more aggressive, with often equivocal results. Historians who are hostile to Western nations and to the very idea of nationality in the West are often well disposed to the militant nationalism of some of the emerging nations of the Third World.[5] And Marxists are obliged to tolerate a larger measure of nationality than they might like. Almost a century and a half since the *Communist Manifesto* stripped the proletariat of "every trace of national character" and predicted the disappearance of all "national differences and antagonisms,"[6] Marxist historians still find it necessary to retain a national structure in their work, if only to accommodate the class struggle that takes place within each nation.

Even so conservative a thinker as Michael Oakeshott denies nationality as an organizing principle in the writing of history, for the same reason that he denies any other "practical" or "present-minded" mode of understanding the past. "We may be offered 'A History of France',," Oakeshott says, "but only if its author has abandoned the engagement of an historian in favour of that of an ideologue or a mythologist shall we find in it an identity—*La Nation* or *La France*—to which the differences that compose the story are attributed."[7] Yet it may be significant that the example he uses is France rather than England; one wonders whether he would have rejected quite as emphatically the idea of a "History of England."

*   *   *

The Frenchness of France

It is, in fact, the author of a history of France who has boldly called for the elimination of nationality in the writing of history. Theodore Zeldin owes his reputation to highly acclaimed (and explicitly titled) national histories: the two-volume *France 1848–1945* and, more recently, *The French*.[8] One would think he had a stake in the idea of the nation, at least as it applied to France. Yet he has been forthright in rejecting that idea, both as a historical reality and as a meaningful unit in the writing of history. His rejection of nationality is all the more provocative because it goes together with a rejection of the other categories that have traditionally defined history: chronology, causation, and collectivity—the latter including class and society as well as nationality.

The release of social history from the bonds of politics, Zeldin has argued, is only the first step in its liberation. For it is still in thrall to other no less oppressive "tyrannies": the tyranny of time (manifested in the evolutionary as well as the chronological approach to history), the tyranny of social class, and the tyranny of causation.[9] Even those two proud innovations of recent times, comparative history and interdisciplinary history, have the unfortunate effect of strengthening the old tyrannies: comparative history because it perpetuates the category of the nation-state, and interdisciplinary history because its allied disciplines (sociology, economics, geography, and the other social sciences) impose their own restrictive categories and causal relationships. The historian, Zeldin concludes, will be truly liberated only when he adopts the technique of *pointillisme,* breaking down the phenomena of history into the smallest, most elementary units—the individual actors in history—and then connecting those units by means of "juxtapositions" rather than causes. The reader would then be free to make "what links he thinks fit for himself," thus liberating himself, in effect, from the tyranny of the historian. Only this kind of history, Zeldin declares, is worthy of being called "total history."[10]

If the Annalistes may be said to "structuralize" history, Zeldin proposes to "deconstruct" it. He spelled out the implications of his theory in 1976, shortly before the second volume of his *France* appeared. More recently he repeated his indictment of conventional history, focusing on the tyranny of nationality. The occasion was a book with the provocative title *The English World.*[11] "A national perspective," Zeldin assures us, "cannot be sustained in historical study much longer." It has survived thus far only because of inertia and the "difficulty of developing a satisfactory alternative." There is no such thing as "national identity" because nations are not, contrary to the common impression, "distinct entities." "All our instincts tell us that there is something different between a German and an Italian, but then all our instincts tell us that the earth is flat." In the course of disabusing himself of such primitive instincts, the historian will correct the other distortions of traditional history: the emphasis on political rather than social institutions, on formal religious creeds rather than the "hidden beliefs of the masses," on public lives rather than private lives, on high culture rather than popular culture, on men rather than women and adults rather than juveniles, even (at this point Zeldin goes beyond the now familiar critique of the new historian) on classes rather than individuals. A truly liberated history, he insists, must be totally individualistic and atomistic—not national, not economic, not social, but "personal" history. "It is only by reconstructing our picture of society from the bottom upwards, starting with the individuals who are its atoms, that we can grasp the complexity that lies behind the national stereotypes."[12] The individuals he proposes to resurrect, however, are not those familiar in traditional history. Criticizing one essayist for making too much of Shakespeare's contribution to national culture,

Zeldin protests that Shakespeare represents only a "moment" in English history; he was an exceptional rather than a representative figure. "What proportion of English people who have lived since his day have appreciated or even understood him?"[13]

As if to anticipate the obvious objection, Zeldin remarks in passing that although he himself has written national history, he no longer thinks it "a sensible thing to do today."[14] For the sake of his own chef d'oeuvre, one hopes that it was a sensible thing to have done in 1973 and 1977 when the two volumes of that work were published. The title itself, *France 1848–1945,* is conspicuously political as well as national, the dates having a purely political connotation. The subtitles of the volumes, however—*Ambition, Love and Politics,* and *Intellect, Taste and Anxiety*—are distinctively social.

The first volume opens with a series of chapters on various occupations and professions (doctors, notaries, industrialists, bankers, bureaucrats, peasants, workers), using the familiar kinds of statistics, graphs, and "impressionistic" evidence to arrive at the usual kinds of generalizations. The second part, on marriage and morals, children and women, also draws on a mix of literary and statistical material and offers even more sweeping generalizations. ("The family, as organised in France in these years, . . . was a powerful institution which resisted change with remarkable vitality.")[15] And the third is a social analysis of the political groups and tendencies prominent in the period—Republicanism, Bonapartism, Radicalism, Socialism. The volume is an impressive work of research, a mine of information on the most varied subjects. But it is also less comprehensive and systematic than one might expect. It is, for example, notably cavalier about time, a single paragraph often including statistical and anecdotal evidence ranging throughout the whole of the century (and sometimes before and beyond it). This is, indeed, its most conspicuous methodological "innovation," resembling something like the *pointilliste* method Zeldin was later to recommend in order to subvert the tyranny of time.

The book is, however, an unregenerate work of national history, not only in defining its subject as France, but also in finding that subject a significant unit of study. The discussion of political parties, for example, concludes that there is more consensus among them than the party labels might suggest. "There is much to be said," Zeldin interjects, "for writing the history of Frenchmen not in terms of what divides them but of what unites them."[16] The introduction, to be sure, probably written (as is often the case) after the book was finished, does have intimations of Zeldin's later strictures. "One must first get away from the nationalist perspective, which still unconsciously dominates much writing: one should not unquestioningly assume that France was one nation in this period, simply because the French Revolution proclaimed it to be so." The corrective proposed by Zeldin at this point is that France be seen as "composed of a large variety of groups which had lives of their own."[17] (Groups—not, as in his latest manifesto, individuals.) This antinationalist thesis, however, is contradicted in the opening paragraph of the introduction, where Zeldin expresses the hope that his book will show "how the French differed from other nations in this period,"[18] and in the final paragraph, where he looks forward to the discussion in the following volume of how Frenchmen treated foreigners and "how they evolved their sense of national identity in the process."[19]

The second volume begins with a chapter on just this subject, "The National Identity." Although the intent is clearly to cast doubt on the idea of a distinctive French identity, the evidence and the logic of the argument are often equivocal. The book starts with an account of an inspector of education in 1864 visiting a village school in the mountains of the Lozère and putting to the children two questions: "In what country is the Lozère situated?" and "Are you English or Russian?" Not a single child could answer either question. "This," Zeldin comments, "was in one of the remoter parts of France, but the incident illustrates how Frenchmen only gradually became aware of what it was that distinguished them from other men."[20] The reader might be more impressed by the fact that in 1864 in that backward region there were village schools and visiting inspectors than that the children failed to answer those questions. (One wonders whether they would not have responded more intelligently had the questions been differently worded: "Is the Lozère in France?" and "Are you French or English?")*

This first chapter typifies Zeldin's mode of argument as well as his

---

* Similar tales of abysmal ignorance emanate from every country at the time. Engels, in *The Condition of the English Working Class in England*, cites a passage from the Children's Employment Commission Report of 1843 on the education of the poor. Asked who Jesus Christ was, one child identified him as Adam, another as an apostle, and yet another as "a king of London a long time ago." (*Collected Works* [New York, 1975–], IV, 410.)

thesis. The opening anecdote about the schoolchildren contains no proof that this bit of evidence was at all typical; indeed one might suppose that it was not, since this was such a remote part of France. The episode is nevertheless taken to illustrate the fact that Frenchmen only gradually became aware of "what it was that distinguished them from other men." Conceding that they did, if only gradually, arrive at a sense of their nationality, Zeldin goes on to suggest that that identity was artificially contrived. "The French nation had to be created"—by, he implies, the bourgeoisie and the politicians. Even then the French continued to have "profound differences about what communal life involved," and "diversity was an essential part of their society."[21] They also had different theories about the basis of French nationality—civilization, race, culture, language. Each of these factors, moreover, was itself a compound of diversity. The common language was spoken, but in different dialects; the supposedly common heritage was belied by the number of foreigners and naturalized citizens in the country; and among the masses especially, local and regional loyalties were strong.[22]

The intent of the argument is evident, if the logic is less than compelling. Here, as throughout the book, more is implied than is demonstrated. And what is demonstrated—the fact of diversity, for example—does not disprove either the fact or the idea of national identity. To think of oneself as Parisian or provincial does not preclude thinking of oneself as French. Indeed, the first may reinforce the second: one may believe that Paris (or the province, as the case may be) is the "true" France. So too with differences of party, class, religion, education, culture, taste. National identity does not imply national homogeneity. On the contrary, it is precisely the fact that people are heterogeneous in so many other respects that makes their identity in this one respect all the more significant.

Nor does it belie the sense of national identity to say that it was weaker at one time than at another or that it manifested itself differently over the course of time. A sense of national identity, like a sense of religiosity or ethnicity, has a history. But it is precisely this historical dimension that is blurred here. If the children of the Lozère were so defective in their sense of Frenchness in 1864, is it not possible that they became less so as the educational system improved (a powerful national system of education, as it happened), or as social and geographical mobility began to be felt even in that backwater of France, or as nationalism and patriotism affected the young men and their families who were drawn into one and then another world war? And if the French nation was "created," when exactly (or even approximately) did that happen? We are told that the word "nationalism" was first used in France in 1798, although the idea was much older (as was, of course, *la patrie*). But we are not told what significance, if any, to attach to this date or any others, or, for that matter, to the dates in the title. To say that Zeldin is as casual about dates as about statistics does not mean that he gets them wrong—only that he uses them willfully, shifting back and forth in time, picking up one theme here and another there, with little attempt to relate them chronologically or even logically.

It may be that all of this is intentional, since chronological and logical connections are as arbitrary, in Zeldin's scheme of things, as nationality. "What then does French history add up to?" the last chapter opens.[23] Not to very much, it would appear. Thus far, we are told, intellectuals have done the adding, have made sense of the "chaos of daily life" by imposing upon it their categories and concepts—"the glue that makes events hold together." Zeldin proposes to remove that glue.

> The first aim of this book has been to separate the glue from the events, the myths from the reality, to distinguish what was said from what was done, to contrast what actually happened with what people thought was happening. Once the facts are allowed to come loose, it is possible to think again about the patterns into which they might fall.[24]

Some of the glue, Zeldin admits, the myths about reality, are clues to the reality itself. But they are also misleading, he insists, if, like the politician's myths, they give undue importance to political or legislative events in the lives of the people or if, like the historian's myths, they yield to the "tyrannies" of causation, chronology, class, nationality. Again it is the strategy of *pointillisme* that he recommends to eliminate these illusory constructs and connections and to reduce the complexities of history to their most elementary forms, the ineluctable reality of individuals.

In the first volume of *France 1848–1945,* Zeldin liberates himself from the tyranny of traditional history only to fall victim to the tyranny of social history. In the second volume he begins to liberate himself from the tyranny of social history by abandoning the conventional social groups and subjects and wandering more freely from topic to topic, place to place, time to time. The finished canvas, however, turns out to be more impressionistic than *pointilliste*. His more recent book, *The French,* comes closer to the latter. If he does not entirely succeed in creating a "liberation history" (on the model of "liberation theology"), it may be because there is a limit to what history (like theology) can tolerate by way of liberation.

It is ironic, although not altogether surprising, to find on the jacket of *The French* a blurb describing the author as "the world's foremost authority on Frenchness"[25]—ironic because it is not only the political category of "France" but also the social category of "Frenchness" that Zeldin now denies. From his "microscopic" or "post-pluralist" perspective, there are no distinctive national characteristics attributable either to France as a whole or to particular groups of Frenchmen. There are only individuals (one cannot even call them individual Frenchmen), each of whom is unique and unpredictable. "Individuals, like atoms, are made up of masses of particles struggling inside them, and there is more random behaviour and free choice in them than the group stereotypes allow." These individuals, who have so little in common with others of their own nationality or class that any generalization is of the nature of a "stereotype," are nevertheless said to have much in common with individuals the world over, at least in the "western world."[26] The book concludes with the self-portrait of a "French" singer:

> Catholic by my mother
> Moslem by my father
> A little Jewish by my son
> Buddhist on principle
>
> Alcoholic by my uncle
> Neurotic by my grandmother
> Classless by long-felt shame
> Depraved by my grandfather
>
> Royalist by my mother
> Fatalist by my brother
> Communist by my father
> Marxist by imitation . . .
>
> Atheist, O thanks to God
> Atheist, O thanks to God.[27]

Because all Frenchmen are atypical, they can only be described anecdotally and biographically. This is the method now adopted by Zeldin, his anecdotes and biographical sketches appearing under such chapter headings as "How to Love Them," "How to Compete and Negotiate with Them," "How to Appreciate Their Taste." The facetious titles have the effect of mocking the whole enterprise of generalization, as well as avoiding the usual categories of family, sex, class, region, occupation, generation. When statistics do appear, they are undocumented (except for general bibliographical references at the end of the book), belittled ("these figures, for what they are worth . . ."),[28] and discounted on the grounds that averages and generalizations are meaningless because there are always deviations from the average and exceptions to the generalization.

The first part of the book, "Why It Is Hard to Meet an Average French Person," recalls the feeble gag about the American family with 2.7 children, the third child lacking a limb and part of his face. After compiling a statistical composite that has the average Frenchman spending half his time alone, buying a newspaper once every three days, traveling by bus once every eleven days and by train once a month, buying a pair of blue jeans once every two years and a plastic bag every day, spending one day in hospital every six months and going to court once every four years, residing in a town of twenty thousand inhabitants and dying of heart trouble at the age of sixty-nine, Zeldin concludes: "In practice, of course, the perfectly average Frenchman is a rarity."[29] One does not have to be a quantitative historian to protest this parody of the statistical method, and one is embarrassed to point out that the very idea of an average, so far from assuming a single homogeneous type, assumes heterogeneity, with individuals falling above and below the average in one respect or another.

Much of the book is directed against exactly this presumption of homogeneity. "The first aim of this book," the opening paragraph announces, "is to show why people still believe they can sum up the French in a phrase or an epigram, and what absurdities follow."[30] And the final chapter reminds us of the futility of trying "to describe a nation of 54 million, still less one of 220 million, in a single phrase, to attribute to all its inhabitants identical moral qualities."[31] The idea that nationality stands or falls on the ability to characterize a nation in a single phrase or epigram, or to attribute identical qualities, moral or physical, to 54 million or 220 million people, is as much a caricature of the concept of nationality as the caricature of the beret-wearing Frenchman that Zeldin goes to some pains to dispute. Yet even that beret is more suggestive than he admits. Until 1923, he tells us, the beret was worn only by the Basques. It then suddenly became a French fashion, "almost a national uniform," so that within ten years 23 million were being manufactured, virtually one for every Frenchman.[32] In the 1950s the fashion began to decline, and today less than a million a year are sold. One does not want to make too much (as Zeldin himself does) of the beret as the symbol, still less the substance, of nationality. But even this trivial example tells against him, for in refuting the stereotype, he confirms some generalizations that sound suspiciously like stereotypes: first in assigning the beret initially to the Basques, then in making it almost a "national uniform" for several decades, finally in registering a decline of sales that still leaves it a more important commodity in France than in any other country.*

Nor is the evidence of change as compelling an argument against the idea of nationality as Zeldin supposes. Too many of his examples belie his thesis, for they suggest that some generalizations, while no longer true, were once true, or as true as generalizations (or averages) ever are. If everything else has a history—if dynasties, regimes, and political systems rise and fall, if modes of production and consumption, class attitudes and relations, social mores and cultural values change over the course of time—then nationality too, which partakes of all these and much else, must have a history. And changes in the character, spirit, or strength of nationality do not negate the idea and reality of nationality any more than economic changes negate the idea and reality of the economy, or political changes the idea and reality of the polity, or sexual and domestic changes the idea and reality of sexuality and the family.

Zeldin cannot live up to his brave thesis, not only because he has taken as his subject precisely the entity he denies, "the French," but because he repeatedly, if unwittingly, testifies to the reality of that

---

*Richard Cobb, existentialist historian par excellence, suggests that a history of France from 1930 to 1944 could take as its title "L'Age du Béret," the beret becoming in the years under the Vichy regime the "emblem of moral regeneration," the "visible affirmation of *la francité*." (Cobb, *French and Germans, Germans and French: A Personal Interpretation of France under Two Occupations, 1914–1918/1940–1944* [Hanover, N.H., 1984], pp. 174–175.)

entity. Sometimes it is his own informants who betray him by insisting upon their Frenchness. Albert Jacquard, described as a "member of the international scientific community" who has "devoted himself to attacking racial prejudice," declares ("vehemently," according to Zeldin): "I feel very French, very Parisian. I do not feel at home elsewhere." He and his family spent some time at Stanford University, where he was better paid than at home, lived more comfortably, did more interesting work, found American scientists far more generous with their ideas than his French colleagues, and judged France, compared with America, to be "appallingly competitive and unfriendly." Yet he and his family "did nothing but dream of returning to France," and he himself discovered that "he needed to be a Frenchman."[33]

Here, as throughout the book, Zeldin makes the kind of generalizations that he would be quick to criticize in others as evidence of national stereotypes.

> He is, of course, not the typical French worker.[34]

> In France one must not just eat and drink, but talk also.[35]

> No foreigner should ever mock the French language, first because he does not understand it properly, and secondly because it has divine status in France.[36]

> But very few French Jews have emigrated . . . The imprint of French culture, the attractions of French life are too great.[37]

> That is why no life can be full until it has a small French element in it.[38]

Perhaps in Zeldin's next book he will finally be able to carry out his agenda and write a history so thoroughly atomized and personalized that it will be rid of all those tyrannies that have traditionally dominated it. One can imagine what such a liberated work will look like: a collection, perhaps, of vignettes, biographical or autobiographical, in no particular temporal or spatial order, largely if not exclusively concerned with private matters. One can imagine such a work—but it is not easy to think of it as a work of history. Whatever it might be, it would surely deserve to appear under a new name, liberated not only from the old categories and concepts but also from the associations and expectations evoked by the very word "history."

Although few historians subscribe to the whole of Zeldin's agenda, which would eliminate among other things class, cause, and chronology, many sympathize with that part of it having to do with national-ity. And many more, not prepared to abandon that concept entirely, are inclined to be suspicious of it, both because nationality suggests the importance, if not the primacy, of political history and because it raises the even more distasteful specter of nationalism. It is curious that historians, rather than making the kinds of definitions, discriminations, and qualifications that would serve to distinguish between a sense of national identity and an ideology of nationalism, or between a civilized nationalism and a barbarous one, should adopt the unhistorical strat-egy of impeaching the very idea of nationality, and with it the idea of the nation as an organizing principle in the study of history.

It was no benighted political historian, but the father of social his-tory, Marc Bloch, who said, during World War II: "I was born in France. I have drunk of the waters of her culture. I have made her past my own. I breathe freely only in her climate, and I have done my best, with others, to defend her interests."[39]

The Englishness of England

"The Englishness of the English Novel"—under that title Q. D. Leavis shortly before her death summed up a lifetime of study of that genre. In its heyday, she wrote, the English novel reflected (and also contrib-uted to) the "positive moral life" that was the distinctive quality of the "English character" and of "English national life." If the novel was currently in a state of decay, it was not only because of the subversive effect of "Francophile snobs" and "Bloomsbury criticasters," but, more important, because the English character and national life had come under the influence of new institutions of popular culture which could not sustain that high moral commitment.[40]

Literary critics have been so intent on disparaging the literary canon, the "Great Tradition" that supposedly embodied that moral sensibil-ity—indeed, so derisive of the very idea of a literature defined by any moral sensibility—they have paid little attention to another provoca-tive feature of that canon: the assumption that there ever was such a thing as an English character or national life. It has remained for the new historian to challenge this assumption together with all the other elitist, moralistic, consensual assumptions governing traditional history. And to challenge it, moreover, as a relatively recent "historical innovation," an "invented tradition" that arose for ideological reasons and has been perpetuated as an instrument of "social engineering."[41]

Were it not for this latest fashion in historiography, two large, lavishly illustrated volumes, *The Oxford Illustrated History of Britain* and *The English World: History, Character, and People,* might take their place among the more worthy coffee-table books of our time.[42] As it is, they have a special interest for the historian. The editors of these collaborative volumes, themselves distinguished historians, are well aware that the old truisms are the new "problematics," that ideas once so familiar as to require no arguments are now prime subjects for revisionist interpretations.[43] Perhaps only editors so distinguished could have the courage to resist the tyranny of the new, to reaffirm truisms that happen to be true in preference to theories notable chiefly for their novelty. One of these truisms is the idea that there is such a thing as a character, spirit, or tradition that makes of English history something more than a succession of disparate events (as Zeldin's *pointillisme* would have it), and something other than French history, or German history, or any other national history.[44]

The foreword to *The Oxford Illustrated History* opens: "The distinctiveness, even uniqueness, of the British as a people has long been taken for granted by foreign observers and native commentators alike." Kenneth Morgan goes on to cite foreign observers ranging from Venetian ambassadors in the fifteenth century to Voltaire in the eighteenth and Tocqueville in the nineteenth, and native commentators as diverse ideologically as Churchill and Orwell.[45] It is not easy, Morgan concedes, to define that distinctiveness, and some of the older definitions can no longer be accepted uncritically. The idea of a seamless web of history—a peaceful, progressive continuity of parliamentary institutions and rule of law—is as fanciful as the Golden Age attributed at one time or another to some earlier period. It is all the more fanciful when the subject of that history is not England but, as in this volume, Britain, so that the historian is obliged to incorporate into his narrative the disparate, volatile, often violent histories of Wales, Scotland, and Ireland.

Morgan, himself the author of a history of Wales, is more insistent than most historians on the category of "British" history, and more sensitive than most to the difficulties inherent in that category. He is also convinced, however, that it is the "pressing and fascinating" task of the historian to try to understand the "essential reality of the British experience."[46] "And yet," he observes toward the end of his foreword, after remarking on some of the difficulties of this enterprise, "a reading of these chapters may also leave the clear impression that, however elusive in definition, the sense of Britishness always survived in the post-Roman and post-Norman periods."[47] Beneath the surface of each period he sees a continuity that bears out Macaulay's image of a "preserving revolution," a social cohesiveness that has withstood the most dramatic economic and political changes, and a deeply rooted patriotism that has characterized even the great dissenters—the Levellers, Defoe, Cobbett, Morris, Tawney, Orwell—who were profoundly critical of the social and political institutions of their time but who shared "an almost religious sense of the civilized essence of their country and its people, their history and destiny."[48]

"And yet"—this is the repeated refrain of one chapter after another (often of one paragraph after another), as each contributor finds in his particular period the continuity that underlies change, the consensus that survives dissent. These are no Whig historians inspired by some idealized view of progress, but modern, highly professional historians addressing their subjects dispassionately, nonideologically, and emerging with some variant of the same "essential reality." Even that most traumatic event of British history, "1066 and All That," provides evidence of "a much higher degree of continuity in economic, political, and social organization than is often supposed."[49] So it is in each succeeding period. The development of representative institutions in the Middle Ages "has to be set within a framework of underlying social continuity."[50] The political and administrative innovations of the Tudors (the "Tudor Revolution in Government," as G. R. Elton has called it) were in fact a "quest for political stability."[51] Elizabeth's reign represented a striving for the "perpetual preservation of concord," while James I's marked the "growth of political stability" and the "lessening of religious passions."[52] The Civil War was a "period of major experiment . . . yet a remarkable amount was left untouched."[53] The English Revolution was not much of a political and social revolution; the real transformation was in the "intellectual values" of the age as expressed by Locke.[54]

And so on to the early eighteenth century, when Walpole and

Pelham contributed to the "stability of the political scene," and the latter part of the century when Pitt helped dispel the "spectacle of political instability" by enacting major economic and administrative reforms in a context of "political conservatism."[55] Just as the eighteenth-century "plutocracy" was crucial to the "social stability" of that period, so the survival of "pre-industrial elites" in the following century provided a stabilizing element during a time of industrialization.[56] And just as a "tenacious" religion managed to endure through the scientific age, so the "axioms of Blackstone and Burke"—continuity, the division of powers, the "interpenetration" of government, economy, and society—complemented and mitigated the doctrines of classical economics.[57] Late-nineteenth-century Britain (with the exception of Ireland) remained a "society of remarkable order and balance" in spite of the tensions of industrial and social change; and the crisis of the First World War led not, as some expected, to the "dissolution" of liberal democracy but to the dissolution of the "elements of conflict."[58] In 1945, at a "rare moment in its history," Britain appeared to present a "spectacle of discontinuity and disjunction," but "in fact one phase of continuity was to be followed by another."[59] Indeed, the whole of the turbulent twentieth century, with its two world wars, the massive depression of the thirties, and the social turmoil of the seventies, changed the "surface" of Britain but not its "underlying geology," so that today the country remains "an organic, closely-knit society, capable of self-renewal," and the people continue to exhibit "an innate tolerance and gentleness, a respect for individuality and eccentricity, a rejection of coercion and uniformity"—and, most important, a "deep sense of their history." (In film and television that sense of history is transmuted into a "mystique of ancient identity.")[60]

These dicta, selected from six hundred pages of text and strung together in this fashion, sound like an unrelieved paean of praise such as even Macaulay might have found excessive. In the book itself each of these assertions is much qualified. There are, after all, two sides to every "yet" equation, and all of the contributors scrupulously present the evidence of change as well as continuity, of dissent as well as consensus. To be sure, they are able to do so only within severe limitations of space, and this itself is a source of unwitting distortion. The need to compress a century or more into a single chapter necessarily results in a foreshortening of the "yet" equation, an overly simplified view of the "essential reality." The very process of abridgment and generalization inevitably imposes a pattern on history, a sense of unity and meaning that is obscured, perhaps even belied, in a more detailed and complicated account. And yet, and yet—taking all these considerations and qualifications into account, the reader of this volume, like the editor, must be impressed by the theme that emerges from the book as a whole: the historical continuity that betokens something like a national identity or character.

What is less evident is the nationality to which that identity of character pertains. The chapter on the later Middle Ages concludes with a quotation from the English delegation to the Council of Constance (convened in 1414):

> Whether a nation be understood as a people marked off from others by blood relationship and habit of unity, or by peculiarities of language (the most sure and positive sign and essence of a nation in divine and human law) . . . or whether a nation be understood, as it should be, as a territory equal to that of the French nation, England is a real nation.[61]

The author of this chapter comments that the delegates "spoilt their political case by adding that Scotland, Wales, and Ireland were part of the English nation."[62] It is not clear whether he is rebuking them for speaking of the "English nation" rather than the "British nation," or whether he is questioning whether any rubric could, at that time, comprehend such diverse entities as Scotland, Wales, Ireland, and England—whether, in short, there was the "sense of Britishness" that the editor deduces from this history, or only a "sense of Englishness."

The English World has no such problem. The operative word in the title, and throughout most of the book, is "English," and the subject is unambiguous: "The Englishness of England," as the introductory chapter is entitled. Far from making any claims for Britain as a significant historical unit, the book rejects any such idea. The chapter on "The Unity of the Kingdom" has as its main theme the disunity of the kingdom, the partial integration of Scotland and the dramatic failure of unification with Ireland. Only in the chapters on the "First British Empire" (the settlements in the New World) and the "Second British Empire" (India, Africa, and Australia) does Britain come into its own; with the abandonment of those empires, attention reverts to England and the English.

If the book is more modest in this respect, it is bolder in another. Precisely because it is unencumbered by the rest of Britain, it can pursue more energetically the idea of a distinctively "English World" with its own "History, Character, and People." The introduction opens with Churchill's veiled warning to Ribbentrop, the German ambassador, on the eve of the war: "England is a curious country and few foreigners can understand her mind"; and it concludes with the hope that the reader will gain a better understanding of "the nature of English civilization and of its impact upon the rest of the world."[63] Those who are suspicious of the very idea of an English "mind" will not be reassured by the reference to an English "civilization"—a distinctive and, it may be surmised, superior civilization.

Edited by Lord Blake, the author of an important biography of Disraeli and of a history of the Conservative Party, and formerly a Conservative member of Parliament, the volume might be thought to reflect the political disposition of the editor—were it not for the fact that its contributors include historians of quite different political convictions. Nor is this the celebratory volume its physical appearance might lead one to suppose. The editor, as well as the contributors, are too learned and sophisticated for that.

While making much of the individualism that he regards as the most enduring and valuable feature of the English character, Blake also exposes some of the less endearing, and no less enduring, aspects of that individualism. There was, for example, the peculiar English custom (commented upon by the Venetian ambassador to the court of Henry VII) of boarding out children at the age of seven or eight as servants or apprentices for as long as eight years, after which they would make their own way with the help of their patrons more often than of their parents. The ambassador was assured that this was done so that children would learn better manners than they might at home; but he himself was convinced that it was because the parents would be better served by strange children, and at less cost since strangers need not be fed as well as family. The system, Blake remarks, prefigures the boarding schools of modern times—the practice, still common among middle-class and upper-class English families, of sending boys of "teddy-bear age" away from home for three-quarters of the year (and, until recently, of relegating little girls to the care of nannies and governesses). It was a system conducive to much anxiety and insecurity. But it was also conducive, Blake observes, to the social mobility that was so much more prevalent in England than on the Continent—a mobility both upward and downward for younger sons sent out into the world to seek their fortunes.[64]

Other contributors cite other manifestations of individualism and social mobility: the absence of a caste system or "nobility of blood" (the grandson of a duke might be a plain Mister, and knights are excluded from the House of Lords), the bestowal of titles for public service, the intermarriage of money and birth and of mercantile and landed wealth. Still others find England more distinctive in its response to change, habitually disposed to preserve the old in the midst of the new. "England's green and pleasant land," Richard Muir points out, was never quite destroyed even after the radical transformation brought about by the Industrial Revolution. The villages in some parts of northern England are still set out in a fashion that might date from the Conquest; private houses continue to exist, and to be cherished, in the heart of the metropolis; and the passion for flowers and gardens defies both urbanization and industrialization. "Throughout this story," Muir remarks, "the landscape historian is confronted by the two key themes of his calling: continuity and change."[65]

As in *The Oxford Illustrated History*, the dual theme of continuity and change is echoed throughout the book. But it takes on a special meaning here because of the thematic organization of *The English World*. In addition to the continuity and change that coexist in any one period, the book testifies to the continuity and change that characterize each aspect of history—landscape history, for example, as much as political, economic, social, cultural, or religious history. Moreover, the continuity and change spill over from one realm to another, so that a continuity of one kind may be seen to facilitate or mitigate a change of another.

One of the staple questions in modern history is why it was England rather than any other country that had the distinction of being the "first industrial nation." The answer is to be found not only in the usual facts adduced by the economic historian—the availability of capital, technological innovations, natural resources, the growth of population—but also in England's unique polity, society, culture, and religion. Perhaps the most significant fact about the first industrial nation is that it was also the oldest parliamentary nation, thus providing the political stability and harmony essential to economic progress. During the hundred years from 1621 to 1721, Lawrence Stone has pointed out, the English had the reputation of being "the most fickle and volatile people in the western world." He cites the contemporary saying: "An Englishman by his continued stirring of the fire shows that he never knows when a thing is well."[66] But this was the period when England's parliamentary institutions and traditions were being forged. By 1721 or thereabouts it had entered the period of "political stability" so well described by J. H. Plumb.[67] Its Parliament, like its economy, was peculiarly accommodating and adaptable, capable of embracing the new without abandoning the old—of democratizing the House of Commons, for example, while retaining the House of Lords, and eventually "meritocracizing" the House of Lords, at least in part (always in part), by creating life peerages in place of hereditary titles.

The conjunction of continuity and change explains the ability of the English to tolerate, indeed thrive on, contradictions and anomalies. Blake's characterization of the English tradition as "libertarian individualism" strikes a wrong note precisely because it is too rigorous, too consistent;[68] one wants a formula that will combine individualism and tradition, liberty and community. Asa Briggs quotes Tocqueville's puzzlement over one of the many contradictions in the English character: "I cannot completely understand how the spirit of association and the spirit of exclusion came to be so highly developed in the same people, and often to be so intimately combined." Tocqueville's examples were clubs that were cohesive for their members and exclusive in relation to nonmembers, and families that "divide up when the birds are able to leave the nest." Indeed, he took that amalgam of association and dissociation to be the essential feature of England's polity as well as society.[69] Briggs finds a similar penchant for contrariness in the enthusiasm for and resistance to technological change, in the ambivalence toward moneymaking even at the height of the Industrial Revolution and among the most enterprising industrialists, in the continued prominence of the aristocracy and gentry well into the nineteenth century, in an "open society" that is acutely class-conscious, in an established church that is tolerant and latitudinarian. And so too those other disparate, even contradictory, qualities associated with England: individuality and deference, eccentricity and conformity, secularism and evangelicalism, idealism and materialism.

To be sure, one can make too much of the national genius for compromise and complication that makes it possible to assimilate so much diversity, and to do so in a spirit of moderation and civility. In 1955 Geoffrey Gorer paid tribute to the English people as "among the most peaceful, gentle, courteous and orderly populations that the civilized world has ever seen"; he was especially impressed by the football crowds that were "as orderly as church meetings."[70] In view of recent events this would appear to be a singularly unfortunate example. Today "football hooliganism" is a subject of acute dismay for sports fans and of scholarly interest for sociologists and social psychologists.[71] Yet by and large, and compared with other peoples, the generalization has some merit. Briggs reminds us of the riots of 1736, 1768, and 1780, which gave London the reputation at the time of being more turbulent than Paris.[72] That reputation, however, hardly survived the French Revolution of 1789—or 1830, or 1848, or 1870. Even by nonrevolutionary standards, riots in England were not all that riotous, as another historian has observed: "A nation which commemorates 10th May, 1768, when about half a dozen rioters were killed, as the 'massacre' of St. George's Fields, 15th August, 1819, when eleven people were killed, as the 'massacre' of Peterloo, and 13th November, 1887, when no one was killed, as 'Bloody Sunday,' measures its public violence by high standards."[73]

The English World has provoked the sharpest, most sustained attack on the "tyranny" of national history.[74] As it happens, that critique (in the *Times Literary Supplement*) was followed by a much shorter review of Arthur Bryant's *Spirit of England*. This book was curtly dismissed: "This is patriotic history, not objective history." Patriotic history, the reviewer went on to say, is far less common in England than, for example, in Russia or Argentina; indeed, Bryant is "almost its only exponent in England."[75] One is tempted to add that if such history is less common in England, it is in part because the distrust of patriotism is more common. And it is this distrust that contributes to the animus against national history. National history has been identified with patriotic, or nationalist, history, just as the idea of nationality has been identified with the ideology of nationalism.

Lord Acton implicitly distinguished between nationality and nationalism when he differentiated the two ideas of nationality: the old idea which regarded nationality as "an essential, but not a supreme element in determining the forms of the state," and the modern idea which makes it supreme, almost identical with the state—the first being a warrant for liberty, the second an invitation to tyranny.[76] It is nationality in the second sense that he hoped would be rendered obsolete by the progress of civilization. "The process of civilization depends on transcending Nationality . . . Influences which are accidental yield to those which are rational."[77] Whatever the fate of nationality, Acton had no doubt of the reality of "national character": "Nobody doubts it who knows schools or armies."[78]

Since Acton's time we have witnessed the most debased and brutal exhibitions of nationalism, so that now it requires a special exercise of precision and prudence to distinguish between a natural, proper, legitimate sense of nationality and a pathological, tyrannical, even murderous nationalism. During the Second World War, George Orwell was moved to reassert the simple truth that intellectuals, above all progressive-minded intellectuals, had managed to forget or deny: "Yes, there *is* something distinctive and recognizable in English civilization." Only in England, he added, were intellectuals "ashamed of their own nationality."[79]

There is another truth that the war has taught us: the precariousness of the kind of civilization represented by England and its impotence when confronted with the most virulent form of nationalism. Far from "transcending" nationality, as Acton thought, civilization more often reflects it. Whatever other circumstances affect the level of civilization of a people—its geography, technology, economics, religion, politics—something remains that is not accounted for, some quality that is not reducible to anything else, some feature that, on the average and over the long run, distinguishes one people from another. For want of a better word, that quality may be identified as "nationality."

Nationality in this sense is a historical fact; nationalism, a political ideology. It may be, as Elie Kedourie has said, that "nationalism is a doctrine invented in Europe at the beginning of the nineteenth century."[80] But the nation-state and the sense of nationality antedated that doctrine by several centuries. One does not have to subscribe to the doctrine of nationalism in its usual forms—national self-determination, or national assertiveness, or national aggrandizement—to accept the fact of the nation as a historical entity (in those times and places where it was such an entity), and the fact of nationality as the sense of identity or communality among the people constituting the nation. It is the function of the historian to show that nationality, like nationalism (and like the nation itself), has a history, changing over the course of time and varying from place to place, even taking different forms at the same time and place—providing the impulse, for example, behind Little Englandism as well as imperialism, behind liberalism as well as conservatism.

It was John Stuart Mill, England's foremost philosopher of liberalism and individualism, who insisted on the importance of nationality and thus of national history:

> A portion of mankind may be said to constitute a Nationality if they are united among themselves by common sympathies which do not exist between them and any others—which make them co-operate with each other more willingly than with other people, desire to be under the same government, and desire that it should be government by themselves or a portion of themselves exclusively. This feeling of nationality may have been generated by various causes. Sometimes it is the effect of identity of race and descent. Community of language, and community of religion, greatly contribute to it. Geographical limits are one of its causes. But the strongest of all is identity of political antecedents; the possession of a national history, and consequent community of recollections; collective pride and humiliation, pleasure and regret, connected with the same incidents in the past.[81]

Who Now Reads Macaulay?   ·8·

"Who now reads Bolingbroke?" Burke asked, thus casually, irrevocably, consigning him to the ash heap of history.[1] So the modern historian may be tempted to ask, "Who now reads Macaulay?" Who, that is, except those who have a professional interest in him—and professional in a special sense: not historians who might be expected to take pride in one of their most illustrious ancestors, but only those who happen to be writing treatises about him. In fact, most professional historians have long since given up reading Macaulay, as they have given up writing the kind of history he wrote and thinking about history as he did.

Yet there was a time when anyone with any pretension to cultivation read Macaulay. It is often said that he was so widely read because he was so brilliant a stylist, so readable. This should not be taken to mean that he was easy to read, "a good read," as the English say. Even his essays were formidable—fifty-page disquisitions on the *Diary and Letters of Madame D'Arblay* or Lord Mahon's *History of the War of the Succession in Spain,* or the controversial hundred-and-twenty-page essay on Bacon. More popular, and more formidable still, were the five volumes of the *History of England from the Succession of James II* (1848–62). Had Macaulay never written the *History,* he would have been remembered as a brilliant essayist. But the *History* is so impressive that it quite properly overshadows the essays, and it did so in his time as in ours. Its success is all the more remarkable because its scope is so narrow. Originally Macaulay had intended to carry the story "down to a time which is within the memory of men still living"[2]—that is, through the reign of George IV, a period of a century and a half. In fact, the fifth volume (uncompleted and posthumously published) ends with the death of William III, a mere seventeen years after the accession of James II.*

It is this work, five substantial volumes of five to six hundred pages each, covering seventeen years of English history (with two long introductory chapters surveying the history of England before 1685), that became a best-seller in mid-Victorian England and continued to be reprinted throughout the century. The first two volumes sold 22,000 copies within a year, and by 1875 the first volume alone had sold over 133,000 copies. Macaulay was as impressed by the quantitative evidence of its popularity as we may be. When the third and fourth volumes were published, he noted in his diary: "The stock lying at the bookbinders' is insured for ten thousand pounds. The whole weight is fifty-six tons. It seems that no such edition was ever published of any work of the same bulk."[3]

Even more impressive were the kinds of readers it attracted. It was bought not only by the leisured classes—and not only, as one might suspect, to be bound and displayed. The lending libraries did a thriving trade in it. Mudie's, the largest, bought over two thousand copies of the volumes as they appeared, and business was so brisk that a special room was set aside to handle them. A gentleman living on the outskirts of Manchester invited his poorer neighbors to his house every evening after work and read the entire *History* aloud to them. At the end of the last reading, one of them rose and moved a vote of thanks to the author "for having written a history which working men can understand," a motion the gentleman dutifully reported to Macaulay—and Macaulay proudly entered in his journal.[4] It is no wonder that he prized this testimonial in view of the pains he took to make his work perfectly "pellucid," to have his pages read "as if they had been spoken off" and to "flow as easily as table-talk."[5]

---

*It has been estimated that on the scale of the existing volumes, the complete work would have required something like fifty volumes; and at the speed at which Macaulay wrote—three years a volume, which, considering the density and originality of the work, is no mean feat— would have taken 150 years, almost exactly the same time for the writing as for the unfolding of those historic events. (He had planned a faster pace: five volumes bringing him to the beginning of Walpole's administration, a period of thirty-five years. But even at that rate, Macaulay would have had to live to a ripe old age.)

Today it is all one can do to get a graduate student in history to read, let alone appreciate, Macaulay. If the *History* is, as is commonly thought, a paean to progress, the history of the *History* is a sad testimonial to the cultural regression of our own times. Macaulay was pleased to think of his work as in a direct line of descent from Thucydides' *History of the Peloponnesian War;* he admitted that his was far inferior to that greatest of all histories, but it aspired to the same standard of greatness. He also privately confessed that he had been sustained, through all his years of research and writing, by the hope that his work would be remembered in the year 2000 or even 3000[6]—not as arrogant a thought as it might seem, considering the fact that Thucydides has survived considerably longer than that. That remark was quoted in 1959, the centenary of his death, by a commentator who thought it safe to predict that Macaulay would indeed be read half a century hence, "if there are any readers left."[7] It is not clear whether that ominous proviso referred to a nuclear catastrophe or simply to the death of the written word as the result of television or a debased mass culture. What was not anticipated was that professional historians would turn against Macaulay, making him seem as unreadable and unmemorable as Bolingbroke.

A notable exception is John Burrow, who has made a valiant attempt to revive our interest in Macaulay, along with three historians of a later generation: William Stubbs, Edward Freeman, and James Anthony Froude. *A Liberal Descent: Victorian Historians and the English Past* is a subtle, sympathetic, thoughtful account; if it has a fault, it is that it makes too modest a claim on our attention. For we are invited to consider these historians not so much as historians recording momentous events in England's past—Macaulay on the Revolution, Stubbs on the "ancient constitution," Freeman on the Norman Conquest, Froude on the Reformation—but as Victorians reflecting in their histories ideas and attitudes peculiar to their own times. Thus Macaulay and his successors are assimilated into Victorian culture "on the premise that one of the ways in which a society reveals itself, and its assumptions and beliefs about its own character and destiny, is by its attitudes to and uses of the past."[8] This is surely not what Macaulay had in mind when he hoped to be read in centuries to come—as a specimen of Victorian society rather than as a historian of the Glorious Revolution. Yet he and the others could hardly complain, for they themselves insisted on the continuity of past and present, the relevance of their subjects and their works to their own times.

The break in continuity comes in our time. Ruefully, almost elegiacally, Burrow describes the kind of history, and the kind of culture producing that history, which is over and done with, which we can understand and enjoy only in its "remoteness." Macaulay, possibly even Stubbs, may continue to be read. But for the most part the great Victorian histories are the "triumphal arches of a past empire, their vaunting inscriptions unintelligible to the modern inhabitants"—monuments occasionally visited, Burrow comments in an uncharacteristically brutal expression, "as a *pissoir*, a species of visit naturally brief."[9]

"A liberal descent" is meant to encapsulate the essential principles of Whig history, the idea of liberty and the idea of continuity. The expression is Burke's: "This idea of a liberal descent inspires us with a sense of habitual native dignity, which prevents that upstart insolence almost inevitably adhering to and disgracing those who are the first acquirers of any distinction."[10] Burke's idea of liberty derived from and depended on the idea of descent. This was his quarrel with Paine, who believed that liberty inhered in man as a natural right, thus was an attribute of each individual and of each generation de novo. For Paine the idea of descent was not only unnecessary, it was pernicious; for it implied the "usurpation" of a right that was innate and natural and that could only be diminished and distorted through descent. For Burke the only real, reliable, worthy liberty—or better yet, liberties—came by way of descent. The historic liberties of Englishmen were in the form of a "patrimony," a "hereditary title," an "entailed inheritance," a "pedigree" from their "canonized forefathers."[11] Such liberties were not only legitimized by the past; they were secured and extended by the same process of inheritance that brought them into the present.

> The idea of inheritance furnishes a sure principle of conservation, and a sure principle of transmission; without at all excluding a principle of improvement. It leaves acquisition free; but it secures what it acquires . . . By a constitutional policy, working after the pattern of nature, we receive, we hold, we transmit our government and privileges, in the same manner in which we enjoy and transmit our property and our lives.[12]

The Burkean idea of the inheritance of liberty is very different from the familiar idea of the progress of liberty. "Progress" says nothing about the mechanism by which liberty advances, nothing about the means by which the past evolves into the present. It only asserts that there is such an evolution, as if it were foreordained, inherent in the nature of man and history. In this sense progress resembles the kind of metaphysical principle Burke so abhorred. The inheritance of liberty, on the analogy of the inheritance of property, is more concrete and substantive. It suggests the several stages through which liberty, like property, passes: the original act of acquisition, the protection of that acquisition, the acquisition of additional liberty (or liberties—the plural is more appropriate to this metaphor), and the transmission of those liberties that have been so laboriously acquired and preserved. It also suggests, as the idea of progress does not, that what has been acquired can be lost or taken away, in whole or in part (again the plural form is more fitting). Far from being assured by some providential order, liberty in this image is seen as vulnerable and precarious, in need of all the laws, institutions, conventions, and principles that encourage its acquisition, preservation, and transmission.

It might have been Burke writing the magnificent passage in Macaulay's *History:*

> As our Revolution was a vindication of ancient rights, so it was conducted with strict attention to ancient formalities. In almost every word and act may be discerned a profound reverence for the past. The Estates of the Realm deliberated in the old halls and according to the old rules . . . Both the English parties agreed in treating with solemn respect the ancient constitutional traditions of the state. The only question was, in what sense those traditions were to be understood. The assertors of liberty said not a word about the natural equality of men and the inalienable sovereignty of the people . . . When at length the dispute had been accommodated, the new sovereigns were proclaimed with the old pageantry . . . To us, who have lived in the year 1848, it may seem almost an abuse of terms to call a proceeding, conducted with so much deliberation, with so much sobriety, and with such minute attention to prescriptive etiquette, by the terrible name of Revolution.[13]

Yet Macaulay, as Joseph Hamburger has shown, was an imperfect Burkean, more of a "trimmer," a compromiser and conciliator, than was proper for a true Whig.[14] Burke's reverence for tradition, history, established institutions, and conventions was rooted in a theory of natural law: "the great primeval contract of eternal society, linking the lower with the higher natures, connecting the visible and invisible world, according to a fixed compact sanctioned by the inviolable oath which holds all physical and moral natures, each in their appointed place."[15] For Burke expediency, compromise, prudence, and the pragmatic accommodation to "circumstances" were the means, not the ends, of policy. For Macaulay, lacking any such commitment to natural law, they were the ends, the only principles of government.*

Macaulay was not even comfortable, Burrow points out, with the idea of the "ancient constitution," although he sometimes invoked it for rhetorical and polemical purposes.[16] It had for him the double liability of being reactionary and revolutionary: reactionary in not acknowledging the debt liberty owed to modernity; revolutionary in threatening to subvert the distinctive institutions of modernity—the monarchy, most notably—by appealing to the ancient ideal of a republic. In the battle of the ancients and moderns Macaulay was unequivocally on the side of the moderns. (His *Lays of Ancient Rome*, in this view, was a *jeu d'esprit*.) Liberty, he insisted, was not ancient; it was peculiarly modern. "In almost all the little commonwealths of antiquity, liberty was used as a pretext for measures directed against everything which makes liberty valuable."[17] It was England, not Greece or Rome, that gave birth to the traditions he cherished.

> Senate has not to our ears a sound so venerable as Parliament. We respect the Great Charter more than the laws of Solon. The Capitol and the Forum impress us with less awe than our own Westminster Hall and Westminster Abbey . . . Our liberty is neither Greek nor Roman; but essentially English. It has a character of its own—a character which has taken a tinge from the sentiments of the chivalrous ages, and which accords with the peculiarities of our manners and of our insular situation. It has a language, too, of its own, and a language so singularly idiomatic, full of meaning to ourselves, scarcely intelligible to strangers.[18]

For all their differences, Macaulay and Burke belonged to a common tradition, that "liberal descent" which both took to be the glory of

---

*It is revealing that Macaulay twice contemplated writing about Burke and twice abandoned the project, once after being well into it. That missing essay is a conspicuous and tantalizing gap in his corpus.

England. And so too, Burrow maintains, for all their more considerable differences, did those later Victorian historians, Stubbs, Freeman,
and Froude. On the surface, "liberal" hardly seems an apt label for any
of them, least of all for the Tory high-churchman William Stubbs, who
resigned the Regius Professorship of Modern History at Oxford in
1884 to become Bishop of Chester (and later Bishop of Oxford).
While Stubbs's own political views were decidedly conservative, his
Constitutional History of England (1873–78) was generally acknowl-
edged to be fair and judicious. Yet it did have political implications,
even Whiggish implications.

The ancient constitution described by Stubbs, with its local assem-
blies, legal institutions such as the jury, and a property system favoring
the independent freeholder, was designed to secure those principles of
personal freedom and political rights that were an essential part of the
Whig tradition. Later developments, to be sure—the Norman Conquest, feudalism, and the rise of the nation-state—altered that ancient
heritage, but enough survived to preserve some continuity with the
past and to give promise of some continuity with the future. Stubbs,
no less than Macaulay, looked forward to that "truer and brighter day,
the season of more general conscious life, higher longings, more for-
bearing, more sympathetic, purer, riper liberty," indeed "unto the perfect day."[19] If his was not quite the Whig view of history, it was a Tory
view that made conservatism itself, the appeal to the past, the guaran-
tor of progress and freedom.

When Edward Freeman, in his *History of the Norman Conquest*
(1867–79), extolled the ancient constitution, it was from the point of
view not of a Whig or Tory but of a radical and democrat. Having
coined the epigram, "History is past politics, and politics is present
history,"[20] Freeman was suspected by some of his contemporaries of
making of history not so much past politics as present politics. Burrow
reverses this judgment, arguing that it was not his politics that determined his history but his history that determined his politics. (This was
also the view of William Lecky, yet another Victorian historian: "We
are Cavaliers or Roundheads before we are Conservatives or Liberals."[21] Freeman's enthusiasm for the national liberation movements of
his own day derived from his reading of the early history of those
nations. "Every stage that has been taken towards the unity of Germany and Italy is not a step towards something new but a step back

towards something old."[22] Unlike Macaulay and like Stubbs, Freeman believed liberty to be ancient rather than modern. "As far at least as our race is concerned, freedom is everywhere older than bondage . . . Our ancient history is the possession of the liberal."[23] This was a distinctly un-Macaulayite kind of progress, a progress toward the restoration of the past. And it was an un-Macaulayite kind of liberalism—not pluralistic, pragmatic, latitudinarian, but homogeneous, doctrinaire, restrictive. This proponent of democracy and freedom, of republicanism and national self-determination, was also an avowed racist, xenophobe, and anti-Semite; only the Aryan race, he insisted, and only special breeds of Aryans at that, could aspire to the ancient liberties and privileges of the ancient constitution.

In this odd company of historians, James Anthony Froude is the odd man out. He and Freeman were bitter enemies, his contempt for Freeman's politics being matched by Freeman's contempt for Froude's scholarship. "Mr. Froude," Freeman wrote in the *Saturday Review*, "is not an historian. His work consists of four volumes of ingenious paradox and eight of ecclesiastical pamphlet. The blemishes which cut it off from any title to the name of history are utter carelessness as to facts and utter incapacity to distinguish right from wrong."[24] In fact, Froude's *History of England from the Fall of Wolsey to the Defeat of the Spanish Armada* (1856–70) was not as inaccurate as Freeman made it out to be, and it was based, as Freeman's work was not, on extensive archival research. Froude's reputation, however, was such that it seemed plausible to attribute to him the sentence that was said to have concluded his contribution to John Henry Newman's series, *Lives of the Saints:* "This is all, and perhaps more than all, that is known of the life of the blessed St. Neot." That sentence did not actually appear in Froude's book, but a variant of it did appear in one of the other *Lives* coauthored by Newman himself: "And this is all that is known, and more than all—yet nothing to what the angels know—of the life of a servant of God."[25] It is ironic that a favorable review of Froude should have generated one of the most memorable controversies of the century. Almost in passing, Charles Kingsley made the comment that was to provoke Newman to write his *Apologia Pro Vita Sua:* "Truth for its own sake had never been a virtue with the Roman clergy. Father Newman informs us that it need not, and on the whole ought not to be."[26]

More controversial than Froude's scholarship was the interpretation that colored his *History*. Where Stubbs and Freeman exalted the ancient constitution and Macaulay the modern, Froude, like his mentor Carlyle, despised constitutionalism itself—"constitution-mongering," Carlyle called it. And where the others exalted some idea of liberty, Froude proudly traced England's descent from the Tudors, whom he saw as benevolent despots, strong, natural, paternal rulers presiding over a strong, confident, imperial nation. It was a romantic history he wrote and a heroic past he celebrated, a past that threw into sharp relief everything he disliked in Victorian England: industrialism, liberalism, materialism, laissez-faireism. But while he did not share the Whigs' enthusiasm for liberty and representative government, he did share their admiration for Protestantism, and in this respect he contributed a vital ingredient to the Whig interpretation of history. As Macaulay legitimized the Revolution, so Froude legitimized the Reformation, a Reformation that was Whiggishly undoctrinaire and unsectarian, more moral than theological and more national than ecclesiastical.

Today it is not only the Whig interpretation of history that is in disrepute, not only the idea of a "liberal descent," but the idea of any "descent." If the Victorian historian could take for granted the continuity of the past, it was because he took for granted the political nature of that continuity, which is to say, the essentially political nature of history. Whatever period he chose to trace his descent from— medieval England, or the Reformation, or the Revolution—he identified that period with political principles, and he saw those principles transmitted (and in the process altered) by way of political institutions and traditions. Only now, with the displacement of political history by social history, can we appreciate how crucial that political dimension was both to Victorian history and to Victorian culture— and to the continuity between history and culture, the past and the present.

Historians have always written social history, in some form and to some degree. Macaulay himself did so. The famous third chapter of his *History,* on England in 1685, deals with social classes, standards of living, the condition of the poor, the state of agriculture and industry, the growth of population and of towns, child labor, pauperism, science, art, travel, newspapers, and books. But it is only one chapter of one volume, in what is otherwise an essentially political narrative. This is very different from the current mode of social history, which, if it does not lay claim to all of history, "total history," at the very least professes to be the dominant, determinant part of history. Even when "the people" appear as the dominant subject of Victorian history, it is not to the exclusion or depreciation of political history.

J. R. Green wrote an entire history of the people—indeed, two such histories, a one-volume *Short History of the English People* (1874) and a four-volume *History of the English People* (1877–80). Although he himself was something of a radical, he was well within the Whig tradition of history. A good friend of Freeman, he criticized him for having too narrow a view of history. "He passes silently by religion, intellect, society. He admires the people gathered in its Witan, but he never takes us to the thegn's hall or the peasant's hut. Of the actual life of our forefathers the book tells us nothing."[27] Yet Green himself, on the very first page of his book, admitted that "of the temper and life of these English folk in this Old England we know little."[28] And the reader of his book was never shown the inside of the thane's hall or peasant's hut, for the good reason that Green had no more evidence than Freeman to warrant such domestic intrusions.

In fact, Green's enormously popular *Short History* (the best-selling work of history since Macaulay) was not nearly so populist as he made out. "It is a history," his preface announced, "not of English Kings or English Conquests, but of the English People," which was why he proposed to devote more space "to Chaucer than to Cressy, to Caxton than to the petty strife of Yorkist and Lancastrian, to the Poor Law of Elizabeth than to her victory at Cadiz, to the Methodist revival than to the escape of the Young Pretender."[29] The statement is somewhat misleading; while he did make room for other subjects, royalty and war continue to dominate the book as a whole.* This becomes most con-

---

*Chaucer does occupy more space than Cressy, but not than the Hundred Years' War, in which the Battle of Cressy was only one incident. The three pages on the printer Caxton are notable, but they are half the number devoted to the "petty strife" of the Wars of the Roses. The half-page on the Elizabethan Poor Law compares favorably with the few sentences on Cadiz, but not with the three pages on the Spanish Armada. And while the actual escape of the Young Pretender is given short shrift, the Jacobite revolts take up about as much space as the Methodist revival, and both are enmeshed in a lengthier account of the wars of the period.

spicuous in his treatment of recent times, where the agricultural and industrial "revolutions" (as they were already being called by his contemporaries) occupy little more than two pages, while the wars with France take almost twenty. Moreover, the subjects he prided himself on including—and criticized Freeman for neglecting—were not social issues as we now use that term, but religious and intellectual ones. Of the four examples he gave, only one (the Poor Law) belongs to social history proper; the others are intellectual (Chaucer and Caxton) and religious (Methodism). "I dare say you would stare," he wrote to Freeman, "to see seven pages devoted to the Wars of the Roses and fifteen to Colet, Erasmus and More."[30] Today such a "history of the people" would be deplored as "elitist."

Nor did Green belittle political history. He explained that he gave so much space to Colet, Erasmus, and More because these were formative influences on English political life. And he sacrificed the colorful details of court intrigues in order to dwell at greater length on the "constitutional, intellectual, and social advance in which we read the history of the nation itself."[31] Even social conditions were often less important in themselves than in relation to the polity. The economic and social changes of the "New Monarchy," for example (which Green dated from the reign of Edward IV), were important because they sapped "the social organization from which our political constitution had hitherto sprung and on which it still rested."[32] As much as Freeman (indeed, Freeman was a major source for much of the early part of his book), Green admired the primitive democracy of old England, "the people gathered in its Witan." And as much as any Whig, he sought to discover the sources of modern parliamentary government.

> Here, too, the "witan," the Wise Men of the village, met to settle questions of peace and war, to judge just judgment, and frame wise laws, as their descendants, the Wise men of a later England, meet in Parliament at Westminster, to frame laws and do justice for the great empire which has sprung from this little body of farmer-commonwealths in Sleswick.[33]

Compared with their modern counterparts, Victorian historians, even when they were writing social history, were insistently political. In this sense too they maintained their continuity with the past, and not only with the history of their country but with the history of their discipline. Like Herodotus and Thucydides, they assumed that the polity—some kind of polity, ancient or modern, folk or state, Whig, Tory, or Radical—was the bearer of that "entailed inheritance" which ensured the continuity of the past and the present, and of the present and the future. They had different conceptions of the past, different views of the present, different hopes for the future. But they shared this essential ingredient of Whig history: an overriding respect for the "Noble Science of Politics."[34]

History and the Idea of Progress .9.

T he idea of Progress—Progress with a capital *P*—has been in disrepute for a long time now. And with good reason, one would think. The experiences of this century hardly dispose us to any complacency about the present, still less about the future. A pessimistic, even apocalyptic, view comes more naturally to a generation which has learned at great pain that the most impressive scientific discoveries may be put to the most grotesque use; that material prosperity sometimes has an inverse relationship to the "quality of life"; that a generous social policy may create as many problems as it solves; that even the most benign governments succumb to the dead weight of bureaucracy while the least benign ones are ingenious in devising new and horrendous means of tyranny; that religious passions are exacerbated in a world that is increasingly secular, and national passions in a world that is fatally interdependent; that the most advanced and powerful countries may be held hostage by a handful of primitive terrorists; that our most cherished principles—liberty, equality, fraternity, justice, even peace—have been perverted and degraded in ways our forefathers never dreamed of. At every point we are confronted with shattered promises, blighted hopes, irreconcilable dilemmas, good intentions gone astray, a choice between evils, a world perched on the brink of disaster—all the familiar clichés, which are all too true and which seem to give the lie to the idea of progress.

Yet it is just this idea that we are invited to contemplate and to embrace. And we are being urged to do so by one of our major social philosophers, a man who has not only shared these dismal experiences but taught us how to think about them. William James made much of the distinction between the "once-born" and the "twice-born": the once-born, simple, innocent, healthy-minded, having faith in a beneficent God and a harmonious universe; the twice-born, self-conscious and self-critical, experiencing life as a tragic mystery, acutely aware of the potentiality for evil and of the heroic effort required to overcome it.[1] Robert Nisbet is preeminently the twice-born man. He knows all that can be known about the treacherous simplicities of grand ideas. His work has taken him into three distinct disciplines, and from each he has learned the critical lesson: the sociologist's respect for the complexities of society, the historian's for the uniqueness of historical events, the philosopher's for the irreducibility of ideas to easy formulas. Each has made him wary of generalizations. Yet it is the largest, most ambitious of all generalizations, a single idea encompassing all of society through all of history, that he now asks us to entertain: "The idea of progress holds that mankind has advanced in the past—from some aboriginal condition of primitiveness, barbarism, or even nullity—is now advancing, and will continue to advance, through the foreseeable future."[2]

This may seem to be the worst of all times to propose this idea. The last time it was seriously proposed was not much more auspicious— from which, perhaps, there is a lesson to be learned about the relation of ideas and events. J. B. Bury's *Idea of Progress* appeared just two years after the end of World War I, while England was mourning the loss of the best and the brightest of the generation. Perhaps Bury was intimating some sense of unease when, at the very end of the book, he raised the possibility that just as the idea of providence had been discredited by the progress of civilization, so the idea of progress might be rendered obsolete by progress itself. But this supposition, he hastened to add, might be a "trick of dialectic," the implication being that the idea would survive in some other form.[3]

A dozen years later, again by some mischief of fate, Bury's book was published in America, this time at the depth of the Depression and in the shadow of the rise of Nazism. The irony was compounded by Charles Beard's introduction, the first sentence of which announced, "The world is largely ruled by ideas, true and false."[4] This dictum was followed by the equally unlikely one (considering the source) that it was only because ideas have this power that constitutional and democratic government is possible, because only ideas can resolve social conflict without violence. (This from the author of *An Economic Interpretation of the Constitution,* which was not especially respectful of the ideas of the Founding Fathers, nor, for that matter, of ideas in general as the moving force of history.)

The American edition of Bury coincided with the publication of another book that was more in keeping with the spirit of the times, Carl Becker's *Heavenly City of the Eighteenth-Century Philosophers.* Becker had earlier written a largely favorable review of Bury, but his own book was far more pessimistic. "Posterity," he quoted Diderot, "is for the philosopher what the other world is for the religious man."[5] This later emerged as the theme of his own book. In a deceptively casual tone, with a great show of urbanity and good humor (and without ever mentioning Bury), Becker delivered the coup de grace to the idea of progress. The *philosophes* who prided themselves on their modernity and enlightenment, who thought they had discovered the secret of the universe in the happy congruence of nature and reason, who hoped to liberate men from the forces of darkness—religion, superstition, convention, authority—succeeded only in creating a new "age of faith" under the guise of an "age of reason."[6] Theirs was only another version of Augustine's Heavenly City.

Becker's thesis was (and still is, in spite of the criticisms that have been leveled against it) enormously seductive. And not only because it sounds so sophisticated that any attempt to quarrel with it seems boorish and naive, but also because it is so thoroughly modern in its skepticism and relativism. "Whirl is king," Becker echoed Aristophanes.[7] All is relative. There is no progress, reason, natural law, or indeed any pattern, meaning, or sense in the universe. The only legitimate questions are "What?" and "How?" "If sometimes, in a moment of absent-mindedness or idle diversion, we ask the question 'Why?' the answer escapes us. Our supreme object is to measure and master the world rather than to understand it."[8] The only truth we can be confident of is that today's truths will be belied tomorrow. There is no higher wisdom than that of Marcus Aurelius: "The man of forty years, if he have a grain of sense, in view of this sameness, has seen all that has been and shall be."[9]

As Becker does not mention Bury, so Robert Nisbet, in his *History of the Idea of Progress,* does not mention Becker. Yet every page of Nisbet's book constitutes a powerful indictment not only of Becker's ideas but of his manner—cool, skeptical, uncommitted, bemused. This is not to say that Nisbet is returning the argument to where Bury left it. In paying tribute to Bury, Nisbet alludes to his differences with him, but so graciously that the gravity of their differences, and therefore the novelty of Nisbet's own work, may be muted. While Nisbet, like Bury, must be counted among the champions of the idea of progress, his progress is so different that it might almost be another idea.

A clue to the difference lies in the title: Nisbet's *History of the Idea of Progress* compared with Bury's *The Idea of Progress: An Inquiry into Its Origin and Growth*. For Bury, the early manifestations of the idea were significant only for what it was later to become; indeed, he did not find even the germ of the idea until the sixteenth century. For Nisbet, the idea existed in a complete and mature form in antiquity as well as in the Middle Ages; and far from seeing the earlier idea as a weak approximation of the later, he interprets the later, Enlightenment idea in terms of the earlier one. Thus where Bury was able to dispose of twenty centuries or so in a brief introductory chapter, Nisbet devotes a considerable portion of his book to that period.

The longest and most provocative section is on Augustine. Aware of just how provocative it is, Nisbet discusses those ideas in *The City of God* that would seem to belie the theory of progress: the stages of history corresponding to the ages of man and concluding with decay and death, and the universal conflagration that would precede universal redemption. In spite of this eschatology, Nisbet finds in Augustine the "vital, essential elements of the Western idea of progress":

> Mankind or the human race; the unfolding, cumulative advancement of mankind, materially and spiritually through time; a single time frame into which all the civilizations, cultures, and peoples which have ever existed on earth, or now exist, can be compressed; the idea of time as a unilinear flow; the conception of stages and epochs, each reflected by some historic civilization or group of civilizations or a level of cultural development; the conception of social reform rooted in historical awareness; the belief in the necessary character of history and in the inevitability of some future end or objective; the idea of conflict of cities, nations, and classes as the motor spring of the historical process; and finally, the raptured picture of the future, set by Augustine in the psychological, cultural, and economic terms which would remain the essential terms of nearly all utopias in later

centuries: affluence, security, equity, freedom, and tranquility. And justice![10]

This is no pallid progressivism. It is the full-blooded variety we have come to associate with the Enlightenment. It may also appear to be a highly secularized interpretation of Augustine. And perhaps it is. But if so, it prepares the way for a more religious view of the Enlightenment itself—and of all philosophies that claim to be truly progressive. Nisbet has turned Becker on his head. If the eighteenth-century *philosophes* were merely reconstructing Augustine's City of God, and if Augustine himself derived his "raptured picture of the future" from the dialectical relationship between the City of God and the City of Man, then the idea of progress—the modern idea as much as the ancient—must be infused with an authentic spirit of religiosity, a sense of man's worth that is predicated on a transcendent reality. Becker thought that in attributing a religious quality to the Enlightenment, in establishing its similarity to the Heavenly City, he was "exposing" it, revealing its fatal flaw, its unscientific, unhistorical, unmodern character. What Nisbet has done is to make a virtue out of Becker's vice.

The scholar fixated upon one or another figure in this history may lose sight of the whole, and that would be a great misfortune. On its own, for example, the account of Augustine may seem overly secularized. But if the story is permitted to unfold—"progressively," one might say—the larger configuration corrects whatever distortions may appear in the separate parts. The shadow of Augustine hovers behind the entire book, throwing into relief a variety of later figures, and in the process fleshing out Augustine himself. It is his ghostly presence that helps explain some of the other revisionist highlights of the book— most notably the reversal of the conventional interpretations of the Renaissance and the Reformation.

Recalling Samuel Johnson's paraphrase of a chapter of *The Natural History of Iceland*—"There are no snakes to be met with throughout the whole of Iceland"—Nisbet pronounces a similar unequivocal judgment on the Renaissance: "Nor are there any ideas of progress to be met with throughout the whole Renaissance."[11] After a brief discussion of some "crosscurrents" of the Renaissance, represented by Machiavelli, Erasmus, More, Bacon, and Descartes, Nisbet turns with obvious relief to the Reformation—"The Great Renewal," as he is pleased to call it, a renewal of the idea of progress and with it, not by accident, of religion.[12]

It is at this point that one can begin to appreciate the larger revisionist enterprise in which Nisbet is engaged—the revision not only of the received wisdom about individual thinkers and movements of thought but of the idea of progress itself. His initial definition of progress sounds innocent enough: "Mankind has advanced in the past, . . . is now advancing, and will continue to advance through the foreseeable future."[13] Nor is there anything startling in his description of the two lines of advance: the gradual, cumulative improvement in knowledge; and the realization on earth of man's spiritual, moral, and material aspirations. But as soon as he enters the classical and Christian worlds, the conventional picture fades and the lineaments of Nisbet's distinctive idea of progress begin to emerge. Knowledge, we are told, had an important practical, even technological, dimension from the beginning. This-worldly concerns were prominent even when the ultimate goal was other-worldly; the spirit of social reform inspired even the attempts to reform the church; and Christian millenarianism, combined with the ancient idea of development, made for a unilinear idea of progress in which past, present, and future were inextricably connected. The Renaissance, in denying its own immediate past and demeaning it as the Dark Ages, broke the chain of progress. Without the commitment to the past there was no warrant for progress in the future; all that remained were cycles of rise and decline. The rejection of tradition, authority, and doctrine led to a subjectivism that could find reality and redemption only in the inner consciousness of man, and to varieties of irrationality manifested in a fascination with the occult, witchcraft, magic, and the devil. "Fate or fortune" thus replaced "reason and probity" as the forces determining man's lot on earth.[14]

If the early history of the idea of progress is much altered by this reading, the later history is no less so. There is a deceptive familiarity in Nisbet's pronouncement that the Enlightenment witnessed the triumph of the idea of progress in its secularized form, a progress liberated from any reliance upon providence. But he includes among the leaders of the Enlightenment and the proponents of the idea of progress those who did in fact believe in providence, even those who believed in it in its most orthodox forms. And, more significantly, he insists that even the more secular, scientific creeds were imbued with a religious spirit, an idea of the sacred, that belies the conventional image of rationalism and secularism.

It is a perilous path Nisbet treads in this modern period. He has no difficulty in establishing the idea of progress as the common denominator among a wide variety of thinkers: materialists and idealists, romantics and positivists, evolutionists and revolutionists, reformers and millenarians, individualists and socialists, economists and anthropologists, poets and scientists. The difficulty lies in respecting their differences, differences that vitally affected their ideas of progress, while preserving the identity of the idea itself. He copes with this problem by distinguishing between two major groups: those who saw progress as the means for the achievement of freedom, and those who saw it as the means for the attainment of power. The "progress-as-freedom" school includes Turgot, Condorcet, Smith, Malthus, the Founding Fathers, Godwin, Kant, Mill, Spencer; the "progress-as-power" group includes Rousseau, Fichte, Hegel, Saint-Simon, Comte, Marx, Gobineau. Nisbet makes no secret of his preference for the first group and his wariness, in some cases abhorrence, of the second. Yet in both he finds much to praise as well as to criticize, so that the two categories do not correspond to an honor roll and a blacklist. The typology is useful, allowing for great latitude and subtlety. But in some instances, it is so latitudinarian that it obscures other important differences—between, for example, utopianism and progressivism.

As it stands, there are utopians on both sides of the great divide: Condorcet and Godwin on one side, Saint-Simon, Comte, and Marx on the other. Condorcet and Godwin are assigned to the first group because they looked to progress for the emancipation of individuals qua individuals; they remained libertarian to the end—indeed, to the end of history. Saint-Simon, Comte, and Marx, on the other hand, had as their end the emergence of a community in which individuals would find fulfillment only at the sacrifice of their liberty and individuality. One can argue, however, that even in the case of Godwin and Condorcet, the utopian impulse, radically individualistic and anarchic as it may seem, ultimately succumbs to the same failings that bedevil the power-oriented utopians. And for reasons that Nisbet can well appreciate: the break in the continuum of history, not only between the past and the present but between the all-too-real, all-too-imperfect present and the utopian future, the final state of perfection.

At one point Nisbet cites Leszek Kolakowski on the utopian mentality: "Utopia is a desperate desire to attain absolute perfection; this desire is a degraded remnant of the religious legacy in nonreligious minds." In the service of that ideal end and in defiance of the real desires of real people, the utopian is ready to use the most violent and despotic means. He is all the more ready to do so, Kolakowski says, because he sees nothing in the past or present that is worth salvaging: "There is a radical discontinuity between the world as it is and as it will be; a violent leap is needed to do away with the past; a new time will start."[15] Nisbet agrees with the first part of this critique but not the second. The utopian, he insists, has always been able to combine a philosophy of cumulative progress with a belief in catastrophic violence as a necessary prelude to the Golden Age. That argument, however, can be taken as a damning indictment of the idea of progress. If the idea of progress can coexist so readily with the disposition to violence, the idea of progress is gravely flawed. It is Kolakowski who, by denying to the utopians the idea of progress, by emphasizing the radical discontinuity in their view of history, redeems progress from the violence and despotism that have all too often accompanied utopianism.

From this perspective the libertarian utopians are as culpable as the socialist utopians. While Nisbet is well disposed toward Condorcet and Godwin, he does not shy away from the fact that they were genuine utopians. They were not merely liberals who carried their liberalism somewhat further than conventional liberals did. They did not simply look forward to a time when things would be better, even very much better. Their progress was nothing less than progress toward "perfectibility." Anything short of that they regarded as radically imperfect, hence evil. The future they anticipated was one in which all disease would be conquered, decay overcome, and life prolonged to an "indefinite," "infinite" extent tantamount to immortality. The only thing that would keep the world of the future from being intolerably overcrowded by all those immortal beings was the simultaneous and equally infinite progress in rationality, a rationality that would liberate men from selfish interests and irrational passions, including sexuality. Eventually these totally rational people would "probably cease to propagate," Godwin predicted. "The whole will be a people of men, and not of children. Generation will not succeed generation, nor truth have in a certain degree to recommence her career every thirty years."[16] The triumph of absolute rationality would also bring with it as a necessary corollary the triumph of absolute liberty. Thus the individual would be freed from all social, legal, political, domestic, even cultural bonds. (Concerts and plays, Godwin maintained, were forms of cooperation, hence as pernicious as law, government, family, and all other repressive institutions.)

A doctrine of perfectibility that regards interest and passion as irrational and immoral, law and government (not this or that law or government, but law and government per se) as illegitimate and tyrannical, the family as repressive, and even voluntary institutions as intolerable infringements upon the freedom of the individual, has political consequences that are not very different from those attending the progress-as-power utopias. One does not have to be an admirer of Burke or Tocqueville—although it helps—to appreciate the fact that liberty depends on the vitality and multiplicity of institutions which mediate between the individual and the state. Nisbet himself once proposed as the crucial test of a social philosophy its attitude toward the family; if there were only one criterion by which to distinguish between liberal and authoritarian philosophies, it would be the degree to which they supported or subverted the family. By that test, the progress-as-freedom utopias are as noxious as the progress-as-power ones. For it is utopianism itself that, finally, militates against the pluralism required for freedom. The ideal of a utopia not only belittles any kind of progress that can be achieved short of utopia, making anything less than perfection seem radically evil, but the pursuit of that idea— whether in the form of absolute reason, absolute liberty, absolute virtue, or any combination of these—makes it all too easy to justify the use of absolute power.

The only kind of utopia that escapes this fatal perversion is a religious one that is avowedly otherworldly. This suggests that it is not utopianism itself that is dangerous; what is dangerous is a utopianism that locates its ultimate ideal, its dream of perfection, in this world. The religious imagination at its best is able to retain the spark of divinity, the transcendent vision of perfection, without seeking to realize it on earth. Those utopians who deplore the lack of absolute ideals in the modern world, who find it spiritually debilitating not to have such ideals, are testifying to an important truth about human nature. But in belittling those ideals that are located in the realm of spirit, in insisting that the ideals are not real unless they infuse and transform the temporal world, utopians belie the reality of the spiritual aspect of human nature that they professedly value. And by trying to make them a reality in the here and now, they lend themselves to a grotesque perversion of the ideals themselves. It takes a subtle religious imagination to encompass both the idea of progress in this world and the idea of the millennium in the other.

It is not only the prominence given to religion that distinguishes Nisbet's idea of progress from the conventional idea. It is also the "remembered past," which is neither superseded by the present nor negated by the future but which continues to inform both the past and the future.[17] Thus progress is gradual and cumulative, material and moral, reflected in improved conditions and prospects for an ever-increasing number of people.

The idea of material progress brings Adam Smith to the center of this history. Some years ago Joseph Cropsey developed the interesting thesis that Smith advocated capitalism "because it makes freedom possible—not because it *is* freedom."[18] In another sense, however, Smith may be said to have identified capitalism with freedom. A "system of natural liberty" was the prerequisite for a "progressive" economy, and only such an economy could ensure the "natural progress of opulence"—an opulence that would inevitably affect, not equally, to be sure, but in some measure, all classes of the population.[19]

We are so accustomed to thinking of classic political economy as a "dismal science" governed by "iron laws" beyond human control—an amoral, asocial, apolitical ideology—that the real Adam Smith may come as a surprise. Nisbet properly restores Smith to the status he had in his own time, as a moral philosopher for whom wealth was a precondition of the well-being of society as well as of the individual. And by society Smith meant all people. "Servants, laborers, and workmen of different kinds make up the far greater part of every great political society," he wrote in the *Wealth of Nations*. "No society can surely be flourishing and happy, of which the far greater part of the members are poor and miserable."[20] Moreover, that greater part of society had essentially the same nature, needs, and aspirations as the smaller part, the rich and well-born. Nisbet quotes Smith on the basic equality of all men: "The difference of natural talents in different men is, in reality, much less than we are aware of," such difference as does exist deriving "not so much from nature, as from habit, custom, and education." The rest of the passage is even more striking: "By nature a philosopher is not in genius and disposition half so different from a street porter as a mastiff is from a greyhound."[21]

Yet there was a "dismal science," even if Smith had no part in it. It was Malthus who transformed political economy from the expansive, optimistic, melioristic, progressive creed of Adam Smith into a profoundly pessimistic doctrine.[22] Nisbet is right to say that the second edition of Malthus' *Essay on Population* was not as fatalistic as the first. The original version of the law of population had posited a discrepancy between population and food supply—population tending to increase geometrically while food supply increased only arithmetically—which was corrected or kept in balance by a series of "checks" (famine, disease, and various immoral means of preventing procreation), all of which, in one way or another, contributed to "misery and vice." The second edition introduced an additional check on population which did not result in misery and vice: "moral restraint," a voluntary delay of marriage and hence of procreation. This new check opened a possibility which had been earlier foreclosed, that at some future time there might be real improvement in the condition of the lower classes.

That second edition, however, was not so radically different from the first as may be supposed. Like the first, it attacked Smith for supposing that industrialism would benefit the working classes; it equivocated on the degree of improvement that might realistically be expected from moral restraint; and the thrust of its argument, its dramatic and memorable message, continued to be the inexorability of the law of population and the misery and vice resulting from that law. The benign vision of Smith, in which an "invisible hand" made the self-interest of individuals conducive to the best interests of all and in which a "progressive" economy led to a progressive expansion of "opulence" for all, was replaced by the image of a society engaged in a desperate struggle for existence, with each individual pitted against every other, and where even the fortunate survivors in this "lottery of life" were doomed to misery and vice. It was this Hobbesian scene— "solitary, poor, nasty, brutish, and short"—that haunted England for at least half a century, and made industrialism a terror to the very people who were to be, as Smith had predicted, its main beneficiaries.

In his introduction Nisbet explains why the idea of progress is so important: "The history of all that is greatest in the West—religion, science, reason, freedom, equality, justice, philosophy, the arts, and so on—is grounded deeply in the belief that what one does in one's own time is at once tribute to the greatness and indispensability of the past, and confidence in an ever more golden future." It might be argued, he continues, that all that is required for progress lies in the individual alone, in his will, aspirations, and actions. But this view he rejects: "The springs of human action, will, and ambition lie for the most part in beliefs about universe, world, society, and man which defy rational expectations"—in "dogmas," in short.[23] The idea of progress is such a dogma. It is this dogma that has permitted the West to attain the heights it has, and the waning of this dogma that is one of the most ominous facts of the present and a tragic portent of the future.

At this point one has to confront what may seem an anomaly in this work, one that Nisbet, perhaps out of modesty, does not allude to. This is its place in his own intellectual history. It is surely worthy of note that this tribute to the idea of progress should have been written by the author of those other memorable books: *The Quest for Community, Community and Power, The Social Bond, Tradition and Revolt, The Degradation of the Academic Dogma,* and *Twilight of Authority.* The last two titles hardly signify an overweening faith in progress, and the others suggest a mode of thought that is not usually associated with that idea. Nor are the heroes of those earlier books the heroes of this one. Tocqueville and Weber appear here as critics of the idea of progress—antiheroes, so to speak. Durkheim, the subject of another of Nisbet's books, makes only one fleeting appearance, and Simmel and Tönnies are not present at all; if they were, it could only have been as witnesses for the prosecution. So too with Nisbet's lesser heroes— Burke, Lamennais, Burckhardt, LePlay—who are either conspicuously absent here or in the opposition.

Nor is there much room for the concepts that figured so prominently in Nisbet's other influential work, *The Sociological Tradition* (1966): community, authority, status, the sacred, alienation. By an effort of imagination they might be made consonant with the idea of progress; they are, after all, part of the past that Nisbet insists upon as an essential aspect of progress. Yet there is clearly a tension between them and the idea of progress. In that book progress, liberty, individuality, reason, and nature, the typical products of the Enlightenment, were seen as contributing to the release of the individual from social ties and moral and intellectual traditions, ties and traditions that Nisbet himself valued for the sake of the individual as well as of society.

Social Change and History (1969) presents still more difficulties, for its subject is even more closely related to the idea of progress. In the foreword to *The Idea of Progress* Nisbet speaks of going over some of the same "intellectual ground" he had covered in the earlier book, although with a "different objective."[24] That qualification hardly prepares us for the extent of the difference, a difference all the more striking in view of the similarities in the accounts of some individual thinkers (Augustine, for example). A token of the difference is the use of the word "metaphor" in the earlier book to describe the idea of development or progress. The metaphor, Nisbet explained, was useful in characterizing an abstraction, an intellectual construct rather than an empirical fact. But the metaphor, like the idea it signified, was easily abused.

Dedicated to his teacher, Frederick Teggart, *Social Change and History* reflected Teggart's own suspicion of any overriding idea—the idea of progress being the most egregious example—that tried to impose an artificial unity upon either history or society, thus violating the particularity of historical events and the plurality and complexity of social institutions. Expanding on this view, Nisbet suggested that the true premises of social behavior were the "very opposite" of those posited by developmental theories. "Fixity," not change, was the natural, normal condition; and the "event," rather than any law or theory, was the crucial concept in the understanding of change. The event itself was resistant to generalization because it was, as often as not, external, adventitious, intrusive, intermittent. Whatever "linear directionality" might be found in history was in the "beholder's eye," not in the events themselves. The quest for such a "unified theory of change" had been going on for twenty-five hundred years and was "as vain as the quest for perpetual youth or for the means of transmuting base metals into gold."[25]

History of the Idea of Progress (perhaps so titled to distinguish it as much from Teggart's *The Idea of Progress* as from Bury's book) would seem to be doing exactly what *Social Change and History* had decried: seeking a "unified theory of change"—and finding it, moreover, in the twenty-five-hundred-year history of the idea of progress. Yet in an important sense the two books are complementary rather than contradictory. In *Social Change and History*, Nisbet was addressing himself to theories of history and society, attempts to understand historical events and social facts, and in that context the idea of progress was obfuscatory and misleading. It substituted metaphor for explanation, assumed some kind of determinism or necessity where there was more often chance and contingency, and made light of concrete events and circumstances. But even in that book, Nisbet conceded that the metaphor of progress was useful in illuminating patterns on the largest scale, so long as it was confined to metaphor—or "metahistory," one might say. "It is as inevitable in modern Western consciousness (perhaps in all human consciousness) to ask the question, whither Civilization? . . . as it is to ask the question, what is the meaning of life? Not the most resolutely empirical or pragmatic mind, surely, can resist the occasional allure of such questions."[26]

If Nisbet has now succumbed to the allure of those large questions, he has done so without falling into the fallacies he had earlier cautioned against. *History of the Idea of Progress* is a pure, classic exercise in metahistory. At no point is the idea of progress used to explain any particular historical event or even any complex or sequence of events. Nor does it pretend to be empirically demonstrable or verifiable. It is as he had earlier described it: an idea, a dogma. It is not, however, a metaphor. And here lies the difference between the books. They are entirely consistent, although quite dissimilar in intent and "affect." In the earlier book, the idea of progress was something to be wary of, to use, if at all, with circumspection, to keep at a safe distance, as history itself had to be distanced from it—hence, "metaphor," a literary term to emphasize its divorce from reality (and also, perhaps, to belittle and trivialize it). In the later book, the idea has been restored to its status as an idea and invested with the power of a dogma—a dogma essential to the well-being of society.

However metaphorical or metahistorical the idea may be, it now comes to us with all the urgency of a specific, highly charged, indeed explosive historical situation. Nisbet has not succumbed to the allure of metahistory. History itself has done so, has called metahistory onto the stage of history. A decade or so earlier, when *Social Change and History* was published, the clear and present danger was the contempt for the specific and the concrete—for particular events which could properly be explained only in particularistic terms, for social problems which could be alleviated only by small, pragmatic, incremental re-forms. Today the danger is a lack of faith so monumental that it can be met only by invoking an idea on the same grand scale. It is precisely the "totality" of history, society, culture, civilization, that is at stake. And it is at stake, Nisbet now believes, because the idea that once gave meaning to it—and with meaning, a sense of dignity, confidence, pride, power—has been fatally undermined.

Toward the end of the book, Nisbet quotes Friedrich Hayek: "Prog-ress is movement for movement's sake, for it is in the process of learn-ing, and in the effects of having learned something new, that man enjoys the gifts of his intelligence."[27] One hears the echo of Mill's theory of liberty for its own sake and individuality for its own sake. Nisbet does not explicitly take issue with Hayek, but his own idea of progress is more substantive and concrete. For him "movement" is a necessary but not a sufficient condition for the idea of progress. In-deed, he posits five "crucial premises" of the idea: "belief in the value of the past; conviction of the nobility, even superiority, of Western civili-zation; acceptance of the worth of economic and technological growth; faith in reason and in the kind of scientific and scholarly knowledge that can come from reason alone; and, finally, belief in the intrinsic importance, the ineffaceable *worth* of life on this earth."[28] It is because each of these premises is now being widely denied—not, as in the past, by a few historians, philosophers, and artists, but by a large and extremely influential body of opinion—that the situation has be-come so critical. "Progress at Bay" is the title of the penultimate chap-ter. But it could as well have been called "Western Civilization at Bay."

It is not so much Nisbet who has changed his views as history that has given them an ironic twist. In *The Sociological Tradition* he ex-plained how the ideals of the Enlightenment had become perverted— how democracy had resulted in a "tyranny imposed by the mass," liberty in a "morbid isolation" of the individual, reason in a "rational-ization of spirit," secularism in "sterile disenchantment."[29] It was this perversion that had so distressed Burke, Tocqueville, Burckhardt, Weber, Durkheim, and the others in the great "sociological tradition," and that had made them so skeptical of any theory of progress.

> What we see, beginning with the conservatives in their general distrust of modernism, is the tragic view of life set in time perspective. It is a view

that draws its melancholy forecast of the future, not from extraneous or fortuitous factors, but from the very substance of history, from the very forces that the rationalists had hailed as promising liberation and the new empire of reason. In this view history is conceived as being periodically seized by deep moral crises which do not—as the thinkers of inexorable progress argued—automatically resolve themselves but remain instead to haunt and mock man's hopes of secular salvation.[30]

We are now witnessing one of those "deep moral crises" that has periodically assailed us, a crisis so deep that it may signal the end of Western civilization. In this situation of "disbelief, doubt, disillusionment, and despair"[31] (one can go on with those negatives—a distrust of ourselves, a discontent with what we have achieved, a disrespect for our principles and institutions, a debasement of our culture), Nisbet calls for a return to the idea of progress, perhaps not so much to signify our faith in the future as to reaffirm our faith in ourselves—which is to say, in our own past and present. Only by reestablishing that continuity can we prevent ourselves from being engulfed by a new "wave of the future" that is not our future at all.

There is scarcely anyone else who could make so powerful a case for the idea of progress. If Nisbet now commends that idea to us, it is from the vantage point of one who knows everything that can be said against it. It is as a "twice-born," temperamentally and philosophically committed to a tragic view of life, that he is proposing to rehabilitate an idea that we had consigned, perhaps too glibly, to the dustbin of history. He does not pretend to be sanguine about our prospects. History itself, he reminds us, provides few examples of cultures as debilitated as ours which were not destroyed by the very forces they set in motion. The only optimistic sign he can point to is the "faint, possibly illusory," beginnings of a religious revival.[32] There is, however, another heartening sign. This book, and the favorable reception it has had, may itself be symptomatic of a new sensibility, one that is post-Enlightenment, postmodernist—but not post-Western.

Does History Talk Sense? *·10·*

"Supposing truth is a woman—what then?"[1] Nietzsche's question may well be the most tantalizing introduction to any philosophical text. It is also the prelude to one of the most arresting images in philosophy. The philosopher pursuing truth, Nietzsche explains in *Beyond Good and Evil,* is like an earnest, clumsy man trying to win over a woman. Just as woman has always resisted heavy-handed attempts at seduction, so truth has always resisted the importunities of philosophers, which is why philosophical dogmas always end up in a state of disarray. The philosopher's "will to truth" has proved as unavailing as the fumblings of an inept suitor. Only the "free spirit" has the strength of will to abandon this unseemly quest and liberate himself from the "tyranny" of truth as from any other tyranny. For he knows that whatever else woman wants, "she does not *want* truth."

> What is truth to woman? From the beginning, nothing has been more alien, repugnant, and hostile to woman than truth—her great art is the lie, her highest concern is mere appearance and beauty. Let us men confess it: we honor and love precisely *this* art and *this* instinct in woman: we who have a hard time and for our relief like to associate with beings under whose hands, eyes, and tender follies our seriousness, our gravity and profundity almost appear to us like folly.[2]

Nietzsche's image recalls another that is no less provocative. The English philosopher Michael Oakeshott would seem to have little in common with Nietzsche. His philosophical roots are in Hegel, his

171

political roots in England, a combination that makes him the very antithesis of Nietzsche.[3] Yet we are irresistibly reminded of Nietzsche in the metaphor that provides the climax to one of Oakeshott's most interesting essays, "The Activity of Being an Historian." The historian, Oakeshott tells us, "adores the past," but the world cannot understand that kind of love.

> It [the world] deals with the "past" as with a man, expecting it to talk sense and have something to say apposite to its plebeian "causes" and engagements. But for the "historian," for whom the past is dead and irreproachable, the past is feminine. He loves it as a mistress of whom he never tires and whom he never expects to talk sense.[4]

Oakeshott's essay was first published in 1955 when it was still possible—but only barely—to use such sexual imagery. Even then it was provocative, as much for the implication that history does not "talk sense" as for the image of the beloved mistress whom one does not expect to talk sense. With each reprinting of the essay in *Rationalism in Politics* (in 1962, 1974, and 1981), the implication and provocation became greater. In Oakeshott's latest work, *On History*, the image does not appear but the idea evoked by it is essentially the same. Today, with Oakeshott emerging as a major figure in English philosophy, and with history itself being transformed by all the varieties of the new history, his views are more pertinent than ever.*

The image of the mistress appears toward the end of "The Activity of Being an Historian," following an analysis of the three modes of experience corresponding to three modes of history. The practical mode of experience is that which occupies most of us most of the time; it is the realm of cause and effect, necessity and accident, good and bad, and whatever other concepts are needed to understand our world in relation to ourselves. The scientific mode understands these concepts, especially cause and effect, in another sense, not in relation to ourselves but independently of ourselves, "objectively," as is said. The contemplative mode is typical of the poet or artist who sees in the world not signs or portents, causes or effects, but only "'images' of delight," images which may be real or fictitious—the distinction is irrelevant to him—and which call neither for his approval nor for his disapproval.[5]

---

*Oakeshott is sometimes described as both historian and philosopher, having started his career as a lecturer in history at Cambridge University. Although he has written about history and has reviewed a great many books on history, he has never written any work of history.

The same modes are said to govern our attitudes toward the past. As there are different presents, so there are different pasts and different ways of viewing the past. Indeed, all pasts are constructions made out of the present, the present world providing evidence for past events. Yet there are distinctive attitudes toward those events. The practical attitude interprets the past in relation to the present, reading the past backward from the present (or from a more recent past), seeking in the past the origins of whatever appears in the present, judging the past in terms derived from the present. The scientific attitude tries to understand the past by subsuming individual events under general laws, so that the past it deals with is not the real past but a "timeless world, a world, not of actual events, but of hypothetical situations." The contemplative attitude is exemplified in its purest form in the historical novel, where the past is neither practical nor scientific but a "storehouse of mere images."[6]

While most historians display in their work a combination of these attitudes, Oakeshott finds a single attitude unique to history as such. The kind of statements historians (but not others) sometimes (but not always) make about the past is neither practical, scientific, nor contemplative. In the specifically historical attitude the past is not viewed from the perspective of the present or of a more recent past. No event is placed, judged, explained, or criticized in relation to later events. No evidence is excluded, nothing is irrelevant, whether or not it "contributed" to later history. A pope cannot be said to have "intervened" to change the course of events; his action was part of the course of events, hence not an intervention. Nor did a king "waste" his resources in "useless" wars; the wars were what they were, part of the actual course of events, not of some imaginary course of events that would deem them wasteful and useless. "In 'history' no man dies too soon or by 'accident'; there are no successes and no failures and no illegitimate children."[7]

Like the scientific attitude, the historical is neither practical nor present-minded. But unlike science, history has no room for any kind of general causes. If there are no accidents in history, neither is there anything in history that is "necessary" or "inevitable"—concepts implicit in the idea of general causes. The historian knows no general causes that are the necessary and sufficient causes of war; he knows only the particular course of events which made a particular war not accidental and not inevitable but simply "intelligible." Nor is the historian's attitude truly contemplative, although it may sometimes appear to be so. For the historian, unlike the historical novelist, sees past events as "facts" rather than mere "images."[8]

It is an austere and difficult regimen Oakeshott imposes upon the historian, requiring him to think about the past in ways that are utterly foreign to his usual ways of thinking about the present. Not only must he refrain from assimilating the past into the present, from making the past inform the present or the present the past, he must also refrain from understanding the past in terms that have generally been thought necessary to make the past itself intelligible—in terms of cause and effect, beginnings and ends, accidents and necessities. The historical past, as Oakeshott sees it, is so complicated, so entirely composed of contingencies, that it has no "unity or feeling or clear outline," no "over-all pattern or purpose." The only intelligibility it has is that given it by the "circumstantial relations" established by the historian. Each piece of historical writing is an independent exercise, a picture drawn to its own scale, eliciting a "coherence in a group of contingencies of similar magnitude." There is no single picture that may be said to be true to the exclusion of all others; there are only a multitude of "coherences" of different orders and on different scales.[9]

This conception of the historical enterprise is in one sense exceedingly modest, aspiring to no large visions or enduring truths, producing only a kaleidoscope of changing pictures. In another sense, however, it is enormously ambitious, for it requires the historian to resist the overwhelming tendency of all time, and of the present time most especially. In resisting the present, the historian demonstrates his true love of the past, a past that is all the more "adorable" because it is untainted by the present and the practical. It is in this context that Oakeshott introduces the image of history as mistress.

> The "historian" adores the past; but the world today has perhaps less place for those who love the past than ever before. Indeed, it is determined not to allow events to remove themselves securely into the past; it is determined to keep them alive by a process of artificial respiration or (if need be) to recall them from the dead so that they may deliver their messages. For it wishes only to learn from the past and it constructs a "living past" which repeats with spurious authority the utterances put into its mouth. But to the "historian" this is a piece of obscene necromancy: the past he adores is dead. The world has neither love nor respect

for what is dead, wishing only to recall it to life again. It deals with the "past" as with a man, expecting it to talk sense and have something to say apposite to its plebeian "causes" and engagements. But for the "historian," for whom the past is dead and irreproachable, the past is feminine. He loves it as a mistress of whom he never tires and whom he never expects to talk sense.[10]

Like an imminent hanging, this passage concentrates the mind wonderfully. It obliges the reader to confront the implications of Oakeshott's argument as no prosaic exposition of it would have done. If the historian is startled to be told that history is a "mistress . . . whom he never expects to talk sense," he is still more provoked by the idea that in doing what historians have always done, he is engaged in an act of "obscene necromancy." The metaphor is even more provocative than Oakeshott may have intended. If the conventional historian seeking to resuscitate the dead is guilty of necromancy, Oakeshott himself may be charged with the no less obscene perversion of necrophilia. For Oakeshott's mistress, the past, whom he adores and who never talks sense, is—he leaves us in no doubt about this—irrevocably, if also irreproachably, dead.

There are no such titillating images in Oakeshott's recent volume of essays, *On History,* perhaps out of regard for current sensibilities.* His essential thesis about history is the same as in the early essay, but it is developed more soberly and systematically, in prose that is all too often dense and abstract. (Thus a historical event requires "the situation itself to be transformed by being understood as the outcome of an uncovenanted circumstantial confluence of vicissitudes.")[11] It is with relief that one comes upon the occasional metaphor, such as the "dry wall" constructed by the historian, a wall created by placing the stones of events in such a fashion that they are held together by shape and contiguity rather than by mortar.[12] At another point the historical

---

*Or not-so-current sensibilities. More than two centuries ago David Hume confessed to Adam Smith that he regretted having published an essay in which he recommended that women study history in order to learn from it two important truths: that the male sex was far from perfect and that love was not the only passion governing the male world. Hume withdrew the essay from later editions of his works. ("Of the Study of History" [1741], in *David Hume: Philosophical Historian,* ed. David F. Norton and Richard H. Popkin [New York, 1965], p. 35.)

work is said to resemble not a jigsaw puzzle in which fixed pieces are fitted together so as to constitute a picture, but rather "ambiguous echoes which wind in and out, touch and modify one another . . . more like a tune (which may be carried away by the wind) than a neatly fitted together, solid structure."[13]

Both of these metaphors are meant to convey Oakeshott's sense of the "evanescence" of the historical enterprise.[14] But they contradict each other in interesting ways. The "dry wall" is, in fact, a solid structure that will not be carried away by the wind, not even, if it is at all skillfully constructed, by a severe storm. Indeed, it has a good deal in common with the jigsaw puzzle that Oakeshott eschews, the stones having fixed shapes and the wall created from them also having a fixed (although not necessarily predetermined) shape. The conventional historian might well seize upon this metaphor to describe his own enterprise, which depends not upon the artificial use of mortar to make the facts adhere in an arbitrary manner, but rather upon the selection and connection of facts that come together easily and naturally. Oakeshott's distinctive idea of history is more accurately conveyed in the second metaphor—the "ambiguous echoes" resembling a tune that at any moment may be dissipated by the wind.

To appreciate the full implications of this idea of history, to see it in its most radical and uncompromising form, one must return to Oakeshott's first major work, *Experience and Its Modes,* published half a century ago (and republished twice since, most recently in 1978). The chapter "Historical Experience" makes many of the same points as the later essays—about cause and effect, accident and necessity, origin and development, the practical mode and the scientific. But the thesis is even bolder. Whatever "truth or validity" adheres to history, we are told, does not derive, as the conventional historian might assume, from an "objective" world, a world of past events waiting to be discovered and reconstructed by the historian. For there is no such objective world, no historical events independent of the experience of the historian, no events or facts that are not also ideas. "History is the historian's experience. It is 'made' by nobody save the historian; to write history is the only way of making it."[15] The function of the historian is to make coherent a multitude of past acts and events, and this coherence alone defines historical truth. "To be true is to belong to a coherent world."[16] There is no essential difference between the facts or "texts" of history and the historian's interpretation or "experience" of them. In a memorable sentence Oakeshott anticipated the latest and most modish of literary theories: "The text is the interpretation and the interpretation is the text."[17]

If Oakeshott (and this account of him) so often seems to blur the distinction between the two meanings of history—history as the past and history as writing about or reflecting upon the past—it is because this is his intention. "No distinction whatever can be allowed between the raw material of history and history itself, save a distinction of relative coherence. There is no fact in history which is not a judgment, no event which is not an inference. There is nothing whatever outside the historian's experience."[18] Far from celebrating a past that is over and finished, Oakeshott here actually rejects the conception of a "dead past." Such a past, one that has no links to the present and is totally differentiated from the present, "suffers from a fatal defect: it implies that history is not experience."

> A fixed and finished past, a past divorced from and uninfluenced by the present, is a past divorced from evidence (for evidence is always present) and is consequently nothing and unknowable. If the historical past be knowable, it must belong to the present world of experience; if it be unknowable, history is worse than futile, it is impossible. The fact is, then, that the past in history varies with the present, rests upon the present, is the present.[19]

The historical past, then, instead of being irrevocably past, seems to be irrevocably present, and this even when it has no "practical" import. It is present simply because it is a form of experience and all experience is in the present. "Its facts are present facts, its world a present world of ideas."[20] And whatever coherence may be given it by the historian is necessarily part of that present world of ideas.

Earlier in this chapter of *Experience and Its Modes* we are confronted with a paradox that "must be taken absolutely": the paradox that "the historical past is not past at all," that it is very much part of the present. "It is not merely that the past must survive into the present in order to become the historical past; the past must *be* the present before it is historical."[21] By the end of the chapter that paradox has made of historical experience a "defective mode of experience." Caught up in a "radical contradiction" between a historical world whose specific and distinctive characteristic is that it is in the past, and a historical experience that is necessarily in the present, history is fatally flawed. From the perspective of the "totality of experience," historical experience is "an arrest in experience and a renunciation of the full, unmitigated character of experience." It is "a failure and consequently an absolute failure." It is "a backwater, and, from the standpoint of experience, a mistake." It "leads nowhere," and the path to satisfactory experience can be regained "only by superseding and destroying it."[22]

There is no suggestion in Oakeshott's later work that he meant to repudiate or significantly alter this chapter. (He twice reissued *Experience and Its Modes* unchanged.) But there is an interesting shift in the argument. For where the earlier discussion of history concludes in a radical critique of history, on the ground that there is no historical past and that the past as experienced by the historian is always and necessarily implicated in the present, the later essays attack those modes of history, especially the practical, which do not respect the inviolable pastness of the past. In "The Activity of Being an Historian," Oakeshott affirms both a "specifically 'historical' past" and a specifically historical "attitude towards the past."[23] This historical attitude is relatively modern, "the product of a severe and sophisticated manner of thinking about the world." At best it gives rise to a "tentative and intermediate kind of intelligibility," a dreamlike history "without unity of feeling or clear outline."[24] Such as it is, however, it is possible and it is available to us. The same message emerges from *On History,* where we are assured that "historical understanding is not a hopeless enterprise doomed to succumb to distraction," that "the circumstances of perception and the self-understanding of the subject may go some way towards promoting and protecting the integrity of the undertaking."[25] Again, it is a tenuous and ephemeral understanding that awaits us. But it is not a hopeless undertaking—and not, as in *Experience and Its Modes,* a futile and radically defective form of experience.

If the difference between *Experience and Its Modes* and the later essays is not to be explained in terms of an "early" and a "late" Oakeshott, it may perhaps be attributed to the different nature of the works. The book, a metaphysical treatise, looks at history from the point of view of the "totality of experience," and in that light judges it to be an "arrest in experience," hence an "absolute failure." The essays, concerned with history as a practical enterprise, an "activity," have a different standard of judgment. From this perspective history is seen to be commonly flawed but not irredeemably so, and the historian, alerted to the flaws, is encouraged to make the best he can of imperfect materials and an imperfect medium.

Oakeshott's strictures on history inevitably recall those of Herbert Butterfield. Yet it is curious that, except for one passing reference, Oakeshott does not mention Butterfield's *Whig Interpretation of History*[26]—perhaps because his own critique went so much further than Butterfield's that he did not want the two to be identified or confused with each other. Published in 1931, two years before *Experience and Its Modes,* and reprinted twice before "The Activity of Being an Historian" appeared, Butterfield's little book has long been the most influential critique of the practical, present-minded, progressive, judgmental mode of history; indeed, its title is the accepted, shorthand description of that mode. Although Butterfield himself took the Whig historians as the classic exemplars of the Whig interpretation or "Whig fallacy," the concept is now understood generically to apply to any present-minded or future-minded reading of the past. The fallacy, as he describes it, has two sources: the distortions that come from the processes of selection, abridgment, generalization, and interpretation that are inevitable in the writing of history; and the natural tendency to read the past in terms of the present—to select, abridge, generalize, and interpret in accord with the knowledge of hindsight and the predisposition of the historian. In both respects the fallacy pertains to the writing of history, not to the past itself. And while Butterfield adjures the historian to be wary of that fallacy and to avoid it as far as possible, he does not take it as vitiating the independence and integrity of the past. The evidence of the past, the historical record, is inadequate and inaccurate, and the historian's use of it inevitably aggravates these flaws. Yet the past itself is real and objective, and it is this past that the historian tries to discover and reconstruct. If the ideal always eludes him, it never ceases to inspire him.

On the surface this may also be taken to be Oakeshott's message. But only on the surface, for Oakeshott's past is not only past but dead and buried, and the historian who tries to disinter it will recover dry bones that disintegrate and ashes that blow away with the wind. Oakeshott is not so much cautioning the historian against the Whig fallacy as cautioning him against the past itself. The very idea of a past purged of its presentness appears to him a fallacy. And because the past is so tenuous, the writing of history becomes not only difficult, as it is for Butterfield, but almost impossible. This is evident in the list of subjects cited by Oakeshott as instances of the fallacy of present-mindedness. Some of the items on that blacklist are familiar to us from Butterfield's interdictions, and while the historian may find them hard to avoid, he can understand and respect the reasons for distrusting them:

> King John was a bad King.
> The death of William the Conqueror was accidental.
> The Factory Acts of the early nineteenth century culminated in the Welfare State of the twentieth century.[27]

Others, however, are so restrictive as to inhibit almost all historical discourse:

> The loss of markets for British goods on the Continent was the most serious consequence of the Napoleonic Wars.
> The effect of the Boer War was to make clear the necessity for radical reform in the British Army.
> The evolution of Parliament.
> The development of industrial society in Great Britain.[28]

By the time the reader gets to the one historical text cited in praise, an extract from F. W. Maitland, he has become so sensitive and suspicious that he may find even this passage tainted by the vice of present-mindedness, and thus an appropriate candidate for the blacklist:

> Towards such a theory English law had been tending for a long while past, very possibly the time was fast approaching when the logic of the facts would have generated this idea . . . Still this principle had not been evolved. It came to us from abroad.[29]

The skepticism induced by Oakeshott's view of history is so unmitigated, the inhibiting effect it has (or would have if taken literally) on the practice of history so devastating, that one can hardly face up to it. Perhaps this is why Oakeshott's admirers have shied away from its real import. The philosopher R. G. Collingwood praised *Experience and Its Modes* for vindicating the "autonomy of historical thought" and making the historian "master in his own house." Although he was not entirely happy with Oakeshott's insistence upon the absolute presentness of the past (because the past is to some extent present, he pointed out, this does not prevent it from also being past), he saw this as a minor "limitation" in a theory that was "full of hope for the future of English historiography."[30]

In fact, the most striking thing about Oakeshott's theory is how little hope it holds out, either for the future of English historiography or for the past. There is no future in it because it is more a prescription for the nonwriting of history than for the writing of it. And there is no past because it illegitimizes almost the entire corpus of historical writing. Oakeshott himself has criticized another theory of history as defective on two counts: it posits a kind of history that "has never been written" and one that "never could be written." The first he takes to be a suggestive although not conclusive defect; the second the critical defect.[31] If Oakeshott's own view of history suffers from the same defects, the first—the fact that it prescribes a kind of history that has never been written—is, in his case, the more critical. For his philosophy in general assigns a paramount importance to the given, to what is and has been, as opposed to what might or should be.

Whatever metaphysical or epistemological status Oakeshott gives to history, one might expect him to treat the practical discipline of history, the "activity of being an historian," in the same fashion as other practical activities (to cite his own examples), such as poetry, cookery, and horse racing. These activities he insists upon subjecting to the test of "practical knowledge," of experience and tradition in contrast to theory or "reason." In the essay that gives the title to the volume *Rationalism in Politics* (the same volume in which "The Activity of Being an Historian" appears), he exposes the fallacy of "rationalism" that is the peculiar and insidious heresy of modernity. Yet in ignoring or dismissing the practical knowledge of history, in belittling the experience, practice, and "art" of real historians, in imposing upon them restrictions that even the greatest of them have never imposed upon themselves, in setting up as an ideal a kind of history that "has never been written," Oakeshott may be guilty of the fallacy of rationalism that he himself has so brilliantly diagnosed. And rationalism, as he has also pointed out, is the prelude to anarchism.

It is interesting that although both *Rationalism in Politics* and *On History* contain essays entitled "The Tower of Babel," they are substantively different. In the first, the tower is a metaphor for moral perfection, the pursuit of rational, conscious moral ideals; in the second, it represents material perfection, the total gratification of material and sensory ideals. Yet the message of both essays is the same: the attempt to construct such a tower leads to chaos because it seeks to substitute a utopian rationality for the practical reality of habit, custom, and tradition. So too, it may be argued, an ideal of historical "activity," entirely divorced from any kind of history that has been written or could be written, is an invitation to historical nihilism. It signifies the death of the past and the futility of any meaningful writing about the past.

Nietzsche, curiously enough, proves to be less a nihilist, in this respect at least, than Oakeshott. In *Beyond Good and Evil* Nietzsche ridicules the philosopher who courts truth as a fumbling suitor might court a woman. In *The Use and Abuse of History* he criticizes the historian who courts history in the same clumsy, ineffectual manner. The philosopher is inept because he does not realize that the object of his affections "does not *want* truth" and because he himself is not enough of a "free spirit" to resist the tyranny of truth; the historian, because he misunderstands the "use and abuse" of history and because he is not strong enough to master history instead of being mastered by it.

"Only strong personalities," Nietzsche tells us, "can endure history; the weak are extinguished by it."[32] To understand and profit by the past, one must live fully in the present. It takes a man of experience and character to write history. "He who has not lived through something greater and nobler than others will not be able to explain anything great and noble in the past."[33] The historian who burrows in the past because he has no confidence in the present, who thinks he has to empty himself of his "subjectivity" in order to understand the past "objectively," who believes that the proper disposition with which to approach any event in the past is by not being affected at all by it—he makes of history a "harem" presided over by a "race of eunuchs." And to the eunuch "one woman is the same as another, merely a woman, 'woman in herself,' the Ever-unapproachable." Because he himself is unable to make history, history remains for him "beautifully 'objective'." Incapable of being drawn upward to the "Eternal Feminine," he draws it down, making history as "neuter" as he is. Uncomfortable with the "Eternal Masculine," he emasculates history by associating it with the "Eternal Objective."[34]

"We do need history," Nietzsche insists, although not the variety cultivated by the "jaded idlers in the garden of knowledge." "We need it for life and action, not as a convenient way to avoid life and action, or to excuse a selfish life and a cowardly or base action."[35] And it can promote life and action—to a point. Beyond that point it becomes enervating and destructive. "We must know the right time to forget as well as the right time to remember, and instinctively see when it is necessary to feel historically and when unhistorically."[36] Rightly understood, history serves living man in three ways: in his "action and struggle," his "conservatism and reverence," and his "suffering and his desire for deliverance." These three purposes correspond to three kinds of history: the "monumental," dwelling upon the greatness of the past; the "antiquarian," connecting the individual with a "we" (a town, people, or civilization) larger than himself; and the "critical," passing judgment upon the past, explaining what is worth preserving and what is not.[37] Each has its abuses as well as its uses, monumental history tending to glorify a mythical past, antiquarian history to preserve a trivial past, and critical history to destroy the past by an excessive zeal for criticism. But the worst abuse is the emasculation of history by eunuchs who are themselves emasculated and have no more use for history, the kind of history that would truly animate "life and action," than they have for women.

Nietzsche's is a severe indictment of history but not a fatal one. And it is history that is under indictment—a way of thinking and writing about the past, not the past itself. For Nietzsche the past has a real and independent existence, however difficult it may be for the historian to discover it; and the past is a vital part of the present, however rare the historian who can recognize its presence. Far from being dead, the past is very much alive, sometimes all too much alive. The test of the good historian is to know when to remember and when to forget, when to embrace the past and when to disengage from it. "This is the point that the reader is asked to consider: that the unhistorical and the historical are equally necessary to the health of an individual, a community, and a system of culture."[38]

The feminist may take as little satisfaction from Nietzsche's sexual imagery as from Oakeshott's; but the historian may take more.* Oake-

---

*The metaphor of woman occurs again and again in Nietzsche's writings. If he often reduces woman to the role of playmate, bedmate, or housemaid, he also sometimes elevates her to a position of superiority. "Wisdom," he has Zarathustra say, "likes men who are reckless, scornful and violent; being a woman, her heart goes out to a soldier." (*The Genealogy of Morals* [New York, 1956], p. 231.) Even the identification of woman with wisdom, in shott's historian, for all his talk of adoring and loving the past (and loving her as a man loves a mistress rather than a wife), seems to be capable of loving her only after she is dead. And he does so not even in the illusion that she is alive or in the hope of resurrecting her, but knowing that she is dead and loving her because of that. Even Nietzsche did not anticipate so macabre an obsession. The worst perversity he could imagine was the historian who was a eunuch, as impotent in dealing with real history as with a real woman, who was "neither man nor woman, nor even hermaphrodite, but mere neuter."[39]

"Supposing history is a woman—what then?" That supposition has often been made, starting in antiquity with Clio, the muse of history.* Schopenhauer, whom Nietzsche believed to be the real nihilist because he denied life as well as truth, was all too willing to think the worst of Clio. In addition to all the other imperfections he found in history, "there is also the fact that Clio, the muse of history, is as thoroughly infected with lies and falsehood as is a common prostitute with syphilis."[40] Oakeshott's muse is infinitely more agreeable. His mistress is no prostitute; she is, in fact, "irreproachable." But while she does not tell lies, neither does she talk sense. (The metaphor gets mixed here, for she is also dead and therefore presumably incapable of talking either sense or nonsense.) Only Nietzsche pays Clio the compliment of thinking her capable of telling, not the truth—there is no truth in history any more than in philosophy—but something important about the past and therefore about the present.

Nietzsche's muse turns out to be unexpectedly modest, sensible, even domesticated, one that most historians may find more congenial than Oakeshott's. If the historian can learn to dispense with absolute truth, to pursue not "woman in herself" but a real woman, not the chimera of the "Eternal Objective" but the reality of something only partially knowable, he can love the past and live happily with her. He can even expect her to talk sense, quite as if she were a sensible wife instead of a frivolous mistress.

---

contrast to the lowly soldier who is her suitor, may be objectionable to feminists who want nothing more than not to be identified or distinguished at all.

   * But then all the muses, of science as well as art, were feminine. Only in late antiquity did Clio become differentiated from the muses of poetry, comedy, tragedy, and the rest. One also recalls that Metis, Zeus's first wife, was the wisest of mortals and gods; indeed, it was because she was potentially mightier than Zeus that he swallowed her (while she was with child), thus producing Athena, the goddess of war.

Notes

Introduction

1. Charles Tilly, "The Old New Social History and the New Old Social History," *Review* [journal of the Fernand Braudel Center, Binghamton, N.Y.], Winter 1984.

2. James Harvey Robinson, *The New History: Essays Illustrating the Modern Historical Outlook* (New York, 1965 [1st ed., 1912]), pp. 132, 8, 24.

3. For a discussion of the actual content of this *History,* see Chapter 8.

4. H. G. Wells, *Outline of History* (New York, 1971 [1st ed., 1920]), pp. 779–780.

5. Ibid. (1st ed.), preface.

6. Carl L. Becker, "Mr. Wells and the New History" (1921), reprinted in Becker, *Everyman His Own Historian: Essays on History and Politics* (Chicago, 1966), pp. 169–190.

7. H. G. Wells, *Experiment in Autobiography: Discoveries and Conclusions of a Very Ordinary Brain* (New York, 1934), pp. 551–552.

8. The title of the journal has changed several times; it is currently *Annales. Economies. Sociétés. Civilisations.* For the French literature on this school, see the bibliographies in Hervé Coutau-Bégarie, *Le phénomène "Nouvelle Histoire": stratégie et idéologie des nouveaux historiens* (Paris, 1983); and Traian Stoianovich, *French Historical Method: The Annales Paradigm* (Ithaca, 1976). One of the earliest serious critiques in America was by Bernard Bailyn, "Braudel's Geohistory—A Reconsideration," *Journal of Economic History,* Summer 1951. Among the notable English critiques are Richard Cobb, "Nous des *Annales*" (1966), reprinted in Cobb, *A Second Identity: Essays on France and French History* (London, 1969); J. H. Hexter, "Fernand Braudel and the *Monde Braudellien*," *Journal of Modern History,* December 1972; Samuel Kinser, "*Annaliste* Paradigm? The Geohistorical Structuralism of Fernand Braudel," *American Historical Review,* February 1981; David Gress,

"The Pride and Prejudice of Fernand Braudel," *New Criterion,* April 1983. Some of these authors (Kinser, for example) offset their criticism with effusive praise, and others deal with Braudel rather than the Annalistes in general.

9. *The Journals of Francis Parkman,* ed. Mason Wade (New York, 1947), p. xi. A more recent "classic" in the same vein is Walter Prescott Webb, *The Great Plains* (Boston, 1931), where the chief protagonists are the soil and the climate.

10. G. R. Elton, "Two Kinds of History," in Robert William Fogel and G. R. Elton, *Which Road to the Past? Two Views of History* (New Haven, 1983), p. 83.

11. Emmanuel Le Roy Ladurie described this "total" history as exercising a "near total hegemony." Coutau-Bégarie, *Le phénomène,* p. 16.

12. *American Historical Review,* December 1985. See also the contents of the April 1986 issue: "Cotton Mill People: Work, Community, and Protest in the Textile South, 1880–1940"; "Atrocious Misery: The African Origins of Famine in Northern Somalia, 1839–1884"; "Anglo-Indian Medical Theory and the Origins of Segregation in West Africa"; and "Psychohistory as History."

13. Gertrude Himmelfarb, review of *The Past before Us, New York Times Book Review,* August 17, 1980, p. 3.

14. Carl Degler, "Women and the Family," in *The Past before Us: Contemporary Historical Writing in the United States,* ed. Michael Kammen (Ithaca, 1980), p. 326.

15. Colin Lucas, "Introduction," *Constructing the Past: Essays in Historical Methodology,* ed. Jacques Le Goff and Pierre Nora (Cambridge, 1985), p. 10. Lucas is quoting the introduction by Le Goff and Nora to the original four-volume collection of essays, *Faire de l'histoire* (Paris, 1974), from which *Constructing the Past* is a selection.

16. Pierre Nora, "Le retour de l'événement," in *Faire de l'histoire,* I, 227. The "return of the event"—in this special sense of "event"—was a subject much discussed among the Annalistes at this time. Stoianovich, *French Historical Method,* pp. 228–231. The "return of politics" has also been heralded by a prominent Annaliste—but again, in a very special sense (see Chapter 1, note 6).

17. *Perspectives* [newsletter of the American Historical Association], February 1986. Report of comments by E. J. Hobsbawm during a conference at the New School for Social Research, October 30, 1985.

18. The phrase is generally attributed to Henri Berr. See Fernand Braudel, "Personal Testimony," *Journal of Modern History,* December 1972, p. 467; idem, *On History,* trans. Sarah Matthews (Chicago, 1980), p. 64.

19. Warren I. Susman, *Culture as History: The Transformation of American Society in the Twentieth Century* (New York, 1985), pp. 103, 197.

20. Peter N. Stearns, "Coming of Age," *Journal of Social History,* Winter 1976, p. 250.

21. Marc Bloch, *Strange Defeat: A Statement of Evidence Written in 1940,* trans. Gerard Hopkins (New York, 1968), pp. 172–173.

22. Braudel assigns this term to Paul Lacombe and Francois Simiand. See his "Personal Testimony," p. 467, and *On History,* p. 27.

23. Braudel, *The Mediterranean and the Mediterranean World in the Age of Philip II*, trans. Sian Reynolds (New York, 1972), I, 21 (preface to 1st French ed., 1946).

24. Braudel, "Personal Testimony," p. 454.

25. Braudel, *Mediterranean*, II, 1244.

26. Robert Nisbet, *Prejudices: A Philosophical Dictionary* (Cambridge, Mass., 1982), pp. 22, 28.

1. "History with the Politics Left Out"

1. François Furet, "Introduction," *In the Workshop of History*, trans. Jonathan Mandelbaum (Chicago, 1984 [originally published 1981]); Lawrence Stone, "The Revival of Narrative: Reflections on a New Old History" (1979), reprinted in idem, *The Past and the Present* (London, 1981).

2. Carl L. Becker, *Everyman His Own Historian: Essays on History and Politics* (Chicago, 1966 [1st ed., New York, 1935]).

3. Emmanuel Le Roy Ladurie, *The Peasants of Languedoc*, trans. John Day (Urbana, 1974 [1st ed., 1966]), p. 8; Peter Stearns, "Coming of Age," *Journal of Social History*, Winter 1976, p. 246; idem, "The New Social History: An Overview," in *Ordinary People and Everyday Life: Perspectives on the New Social History*, ed. James B. Gardner and George Rollie Adams (Nashville, 1983), p. 7; Furet, "Introduction," pp. 5–6; Traian Stoianovich, *French Historical Method: The Annales Paradigm* (Ithaca, 1976), pp. 102ff.; Hervé Coutau-Bégarie, *Le phénomène "Nouvelle Histoire": stratégie et idéologie des nouveaux historiens* (Paris, 1983), pp. 92ff. One Annaliste, Pierre Vilar, concludes his discussion of Marxist history by observing that it too, like all "true history," must become "new history" and thus "total history." "Any 'new' history which has no ambition to be total in its scope is a history that is obsolete before it even begins." Vilar, "Constructing Marxist History," in *Constructing the Past: Essays in Historical Methodology*, ed. Jacques Le Goff and Pierre Nora (Cambridge, 1985), p. 80.

4. G. M. Trevelyan, *English Social History* (New York, 1941), p. vii.

5. Herbert Butterfield, *The Whig Interpretation of History* (London, 1931).

6. See, for example, Jacques Le Goff, "Is Politics Still the Backbone of History?" *Daedalus*, Winter 1971; Allan G. Bogue, "The New Political History in the 1970s," in *The Past before Us: Contemporary Historical Writing in the United States*, ed. Michael Kammen (Ithaca, 1980); Samuel P. Hays, "Politics and Social History: Toward a New Synthesis," in Gardner and Adams, *Ordinary People and Everyday Life*; J. Morgan Kousser, "Restoring Politics to Political History," *Journal of Interdisciplinary History*, Spring 1982, and comments on this article by Paul F. Bourke and Donald A. DeBats in the same journal, Winter 1985; Philip R. Vandermeer, "The New Political History: Progress and Prospects," in *International Handbook of Historical Studies: Contemporary Research and Theory*, ed. Georg S. Iggers and Harold T. Parker (Westport, 1979); Alan Brinkley, "Writing the History of Contemporary America: Dilemmas and Challenges," *Daedalus*, Summer

1984; "Political History in the 1980s," in *The New History: The 1980s and Beyond,* ed. Theodore K. Rabb and Robert I. Rotberg (Princeton, 1982).

One Annaliste has gone so far as to call for a "return to politics." But he then goes on to define the new political history as incorporating political economics, political geography, political science, political sociology, and political ethnography. See Jacques Julliard, "La politique," in Le Goff and Nora, *Faire de l'histoire* (Paris, 1974), II, 227–250. Even David Potter's tribute to Roy Nichols for the "rehabilitation of political history" has something of this character, the rehabilitation involving the denigration of traditional or conventional history, as narrow, superficial, desiccated—"a miscellany of chronology punctuated with anecdote." See "Roy F. Nichols and the Rehabilitation of American Political History" (1971), in *History and American Society: Essays of David M. Potter,* ed. Don E. Fehrenbacher (New York, 1973), pp. 194, 206–207.

7. G. R. Elton, *The Future of the Past* (Cambridge, 1968), p. 4.

8. Ibid., pp. 24–25.

9. Ibid., p. 27.

10. Ibid., p. 22.

11. College Board Examination, 1981; *Perspectives,* January 1982, p. 12.

12. In 1985 the documentary question on the European examination dealt with juvenile offenders in Britain in the nineteenth century.

13. T. R. Macaulay, *Works,* ed. Lady Trevelyan (London, 1875), I, 3. On the "dignity of history" see also Lord Bolingbroke, *Letters on the Study and Use of History* (New York, 1970 [1st ed., 1738]), I, 159 (letter 5).

14. Review by Roy Porter, in *New Society,* July 15, 1982, p. 110.

15. Elizabeth Fox-Genovese and Eugene D. Genovese, "The Political Crisis of Social History: A Marxian Perspective," *Journal of Social History,* Winter 1976, pp. 213–215. For a similar criticism of social history from a Socialist perspective see Tony Judt, "A Clown in Regal Purple: Social History and the Historians," *History Workshop: A Journal of Socialist Historians,* Spring 1979.

16. H. J. Perkin, "Social History," in *Approaches to History,* ed. H. P. R. Finberg (London, 1962), p. 81.

17. Aristotle, *Politics,* bk. I, chap. 2. The historian who mistranslated Aristotle is in good company. Hannah Arendt, who in her own work tried to restore a sense of the importance of political life, traced the perversion of Aristotle's dictum to Seneca and Thomas Aquinas, and thence to modernity. See her *Human Condition* (Chicago, 1958), p. 23.

18. Lawrence Stone, luncheon talk, American Historical Association convention, December 1982; idem, *Newsletter,* American Council of Learned Societies, Winter-Spring 1985, pp. 18–19.

19. Gordon A. Craig, "The Historian and the Study of International Relations," *American Historical Review,* February 1983, p. 2.

20. Robert Darnton, "Intellectual and Cultural History," in Kammen, *The Past before Us,* pp. 350–351.

21. Michael S. Henry, "The Intellectual Origins and Impact of the Document-Based Question," *Perspectives,* February 1986, pp. 15–16.

22. *The Economist*, September 24, 1983.

23. Marc Ferro, *The Use and Abuse of History; or, How the Past is Taught* (London, 1984), pp. 239–240.

24. Furet, "Introduction," p. 11.

25. Eric Hobsbawm, report of conference on "The Impact of the *Annales* School on the Social Sciences," *Review*, Winter-Spring 1978, p. 65.

26. Mildred Alpern, "AP European History for Able Sophomores," *Perspectives*, December 1985, p. 16.

27. Carl Degler, in *Philosophy and History*, ed. Sidney Hook (New York, 1963), pp. 205–211.

28. Herbert Butterfield, *George III and the Historians* (London, 1957), p. 206.

29. Furet, "Introduction," p. 9.

2. Clio and the New History

1. G. R. Elton, *The Practice of History* (New York, 1967), p. 25. This statement is even truer today than when Elton made it.

2. Clifford Geertz, "Waddling In," *Times Literary Supplement*, June 7, 1985, p. 624. See also Louis A. Sass, "Anthropology's Native Problems," *Harper's*, May 1986.

3. Jacques Barzun, *Clio and the Doctors: Psycho-History, Quanto-History, and History* (Chicago, 1974). See also idem, "Where Is History Now?" *Proceedings of the Massachusetts Historical Society*, 1983.

4. Emmanuel Le Roy Ladurie, "History That Stands Still," in Le Roy Ladurie, *The Mind and Method of the Historian*, trans. Sian and Ben Reynolds (Chicago, 1981), pp. 1–27; idem, "History without People: The Climate as a New Province of Research," in Le Roy Ladurie, *The Territory of the Historian*, trans. Sian and Ben Reynolds (Chicago, 1979), p. 286.

5. Rudolph Binion, "Hitler's Concept of Lebensraum: The Psychological Basis," *History of Childhood Quarterly*, Fall 1973, pp. 189–190. Of the several comments appended to this article, the only one seriously critical of the method was by George Mosse.

6. Ibid., p. 193.

7. Erik H. Erikson, *Young Man Luther: A Study in Psychoanalysis and History* (New York, 1958), p. 247.

8. Ibid., p. 37.

9. Ibid., p. 50.

10. Ibid., p. 48.

11. Bruce Mazlish, "Toward a Psychohistorical Inquiry: The 'Real' Richard Nixon," *Journal of Interdisciplinary History*, Autumn 1970, pp. 49–105; idem, *In Search of Nixon: A Psychological Inquiry* (New York, 1972).

12. Richard T. Vann, "Literacy in Seventeenth-Century England: Some Hearth-Tax Evidence," *Journal of Interdisciplinary History*, Autumn 1974, pp. 287–293.

13. Robert W. Fogel and Stanley L. Engerman, *Time on the Cross: The Economics of American Negro Slavery* (Boston, 1974).

14. Fogel, for example, has recently criticized the idea that any single kind of evidence, quantitative or literary, is "sufficient." Robert W. Fogel and G. R. Elton, *Which Road to the Past? Two Views of History* (New Haven, 1983), p. 48.

15. See, for example, the essays of William Aydelotte correlating the economic interests and voting patterns of members of parliament in mid-nineteenth-century England: "The House of Commons in the 1840s," *History,* 1954 (vol. 39, no. 137); "Voting Patterns in the British House of Commons in the 1840s," *Comparative Studies in Society and History,* 1963 (vol. 5); "Parties and Issues in Early-Victorian England," *Journal of British Studies,* May 1966.

16. David Landes, "On Avoiding Babel," *Journal of Economic History,* March 1978, p. 10.

17. Le Roy Ladurie, *The Territory of the Historian,* pp. 6, 15.

18. Emmanuel Le Roy Ladurie, *Montaillou: The Promised Land of Error,* trans. Barbara Bray (New York, 1979).

19. Fernand Braudel, *On History,* trans. Sarah Matthews (Chicago, 1980), pp. 10–11.

20. Ibid., p. 28.

21. Ibid., pp. 28, 67, 177.

3. Two Nations or Five Classes

1. "New Trends in History," *Daedalus,* Fall 1969, p. 894.

2. Lionel Trilling, *The Liberal Imagination* (New York, 1950), pp. 213ff., 222.

3. Matthew Arnold, *Culture and Anarchy* (1869).

4. S. G. Checkland, "The Historian as Model Builder," *Philosophical Journal,* January 1969, p. 37.

5. R. S. Neale, "Class-Consciousness in Early Nineteenth-Century England: Three Classes or Five?" *Victorian Studies,* September 1968; reprinted in *Class and Ideology in the Nineteenth Century* (London, 1972). Citations are to the original article. See also Neale's comments on my essay in *Class in English History: 1680–1850* (Oxford, 1981), pp. 137–144.

6. Neale, "Class-Consciousness," pp. 23–24.

7. Ibid., p. 23.

8. G. Kitson Clark, *The Making of Victorian England* (Cambridge, Mass., 1962), p. 5.

9. Neale, "Class-Consciousness," p. 9.

10. Ibid., p. 10.

11. George Eliot, *The Leader* (October 1855); quoted by John Mander, *Our German Cousins* (London, 1974), p. 84.

12. Thomas Carlyle, *Reminiscences,* ed. J. A. Froude (New York, 1881), p. 226.

13. Carlyle, "Chartism" (1839), reprinted in *English and Other Critical Essays* (Everyman's ed., London, n.d.), p. 170.

14. Ibid., pp. 165–167, 188. (Italics in original.)

15. Ibid., p. 208.

16. Ibid.

17. Carlyle, *Past and Present* (Everyman's ed., London, 1941 [1st ed., 1843]), pp. 1, 5.

18. Ibid., p. 199.

19. Ibid., p. 193.

20. Ibid., p. 147.

21. James Anthony Froude, *Thomas Carlyle: A History of His Life in London, 1834–1881* (London, 1884), I, 174; letter of February 11, 1840.

22. James Pope-Hennessy, *Monckton Milnes: The Years of Promise, 1809–1851* (London, 1949), p. 184. Milnes was passing off as his own a comment Harriet Martineau had made in a letter to him.

23. Carlyle, *Sartor Resartus* (Everyman's ed., London, 1940 [1st ed., 1834]), pp. 214–215.

24. Kathleen Tillotson, *Novels of the Eighteen-Forties* (Oxford, 1965), p. 80; Robert Blake, *Disraeli* (London, 1966), p. 201.

25. Asa Briggs, "The Language of 'Class' in Early Nineteenth-Century England," in *Essays in Labour History,* ed. A. Briggs and J. Saville (New York, 1960), p. 48.

26. Benjamin Disraeli, *Coningsby; or, The New Generation* (London, 1948), p. 78.

27. W. F. Monypenny and G. E. Buckle, *The Life of Benjamin Disraeli, Earl of Beaconsfield* (London, 1929), I, 629. The allusion, his biographers tell us, was to his novel *The Voyage of Captain Popanilla,* published in 1828. But neither the term nor the subject in the usual sense appears in that novel.

28. For an analysis of his indebtedness to the commission report, see Sheila M. Smith, "Willenhall and Wodgate: Disraeli's Use of Blue Book Evidence," *Review of English Studies,* 1962 (vol. 13, no. 2).

29. Disraeli, *Sybil; or, The Two Nations* (London, 1954 [1st ed., 1845]), pp. 72–73.

30. Ibid., p. 73.

31. Ibid., p. 15.

32. Ibid., p. 126.

33. Ibid., p. 71.

34. Ibid., p. 190.

35. Ibid., p. 88.

36. Ibid., p. 179.

37. Disraeli, *Coningsby,* p. 116.

38. Disraeli, *Sybil,* p. 264.

39. Ibid., p. 270.

40. Ibid., p. 272.

41. Ibid., p. 281.

42. G. M. Young, *Victorian Essays* (London, 1962), p. 163.

43. Gareth Stedman Jones, *Outcast London: A Study in the Relationship between Classes in Victorian Society* (Oxford, 1971), pp. 16, 196, 344.

4. The "Group"

1. Ross McKibbin, "Why Was There No Marxism in Great Britain?" *English Historical Review*, April 1984.

2. Elie Halévy, *A History of the English People in the Nineteenth Century*, trans. E. I. Watkin and D. A. Barker (London, 1960), I, 387.

3. Christopher Hill, R. H. Hilton, and E. J. Hobsbawm, "Past and Present: Origins and Early Years," *Past and Present*, August 1983, p. 3; interview with E. P. Thompson, in *Visions of History*, ed. Henry Abelove et al. (Manchester, 1983), p. 22.

4. "Past and Present," p. 3.

5. Eric Hobsbawm, "The Historians' Group of the Communist Party," in *Rebels and Their Causes: Essays in Honor of A. L. Morton*, ed. Maurice Cornforth (London, 1978), pp. 21, 27.

6. Bill Schwarz, "'The People' in History: The Communist Party Historians' Group, 1946–56," in *Making Histories*, ed. Richard Johnson et al. (Minneapolis, 1982), p. 46.

7. Hobsbawm, "The Historians' Group," p. 23.

8. Ibid., pp. 30–31.

9. Ibid., p. 26.

10. Ibid., pp. 31–34.

11. Harvey J. Kaye, *The British Marxist Historians* (Cambridge, 1984). This nostalgia is also reflected, though to a lesser extent, in the essay by the young English historian Bill Schwarz, who looks back to that earlier time when the Group had a "securely founded conception of the politics of intellectual work." Schwarz, "'The People' in History," p. 44.

12. Kaye, *The British Marxist Historians*, p. x.

13. Hobsbawm, "The Historians' Group," p. 17. It is curious that in the Festschrift for Dobb published in 1969, Hobsbawm discusses Dobb's ideas and career, his relations with other Marxists and with Hobsbawm himself, without ever mentioning the Communist Party Historians' Group. See *Socialism, Capitalism and Economic Growth: Essays Presented to Maurice Dobb*, ed. C. H. Feinstein (Cambridge, 1969).

14. Schwarz, "'The People' in History," p. 331, n. 7.

15. Kaye, *The British Marxist Historians*, p. 33.

16. Maurice Dobb, *Studies in the Development of Capitalism* (New York, 1963), pp. 18–19, 176.

17. Parts of the debate have been reprinted in *The Transition from Feudalism to Capitalism*, ed. Rodney Hilton (London, 1976).

18. Kaye, *The British Marxist Historians*, p. 68.

19. Ibid., pp. 71–72.

20. Hilton, *Transition,* p. 30.

21. Ibid., pp. 26–27; Kaye, *The British Marxist Historians,* p. 84.

22. Karl Marx, *The Eighteenth Brumaire of Louis Bonaparte,* in Karl Marx and Friedrich Engels, *Collected Works* (New York, 1975–), XI, 187.

23. Friedrich Engels, *The Condition of the Working Class in England,* in *Collected Works,* IV, 309.

24. Engels, *The Peasant War in Germany,* in *Collected Works,* X, 471.

25. K. E. Holme, *Two Commonwealths* (London, 1945). This is a glowing account of the Soviet Union written in the spirit of the Webbs.

26. Christopher Hill, ed., *The English Revolution, 1640: Three Essays* (London, 1941), p. 9. (This is a reprint of the 1940 edition, which includes essays by two other historians.)

27. Ibid.

28. The most recent statement of this thesis is an essay by Hill, "A Bourgeois Revolution?" in *Three British Revolutions: 1641, 1688, 1776,* ed. J. G. A. Pocock (Princeton, 1980), pp. 109–139.

29. Hill, *English Revolution,* 1st ed., p. 15; 3rd ed. (London, 1976), p. 10.

30. Hill, *The World Turned Upside Down: Radical Ideas during the English Revolution* (New York, 1972), p. 274.

31. Hill, *Intellectual Origins of the English Revolution* (Oxford, 1965), p. 289.

32. Quoted by Raphael Samuel, "British Marxist Historians, 1880–1980: Part One," *New Left Review,* March-April 1980, p. 75, n. 250.

33. Kaye, *The British Marxist Historians,* p. 102.

34. Thompson, in Abelove et al., *Visions of History,* p. 19.

35. Hobsbawm, "The Historians' Group," p. 44.

36. Eugene Genovese and Warren I. Susman, editorial statement in the first issue of *Marxist Perspectives,* Spring 1978, p. 9; James Cronin, "Creating a Marxist Historiography: The Contribution of Hobsbawm," *Radical History Review,* Winter 1978–79, p. 88.

37. The main sources are the interview with Hobsbawm in Abelove et al., *Visions of History,* pp. 30–43; some comments in Hobsbawm, *Revolutionaries: Contemporary Essays* (New York, 1973), pp. 250–251; a profile by Pieter Keuneman written while Hobsbawm was an undergraduate at Cambridge and reprinted in *Culture, Ideology and Politics: Essays for Eric Hobsbawm,* ed. Raphael Samuel and Gareth Stedman Jones (London, 1982), pp. 366–368; and a few remarks in an interview with Miriam Gross in *Time and Tide,* Autumn 1985.

38. Hobsbawm, in Abelove et al., *Visions of History,* p. 30.

39. The key essays appear in Hobsbawm, *Labouring Men: Studies in the History of Labour* (London, 1964), and idem, *Workers: Worlds of Labor* (New York, 1984).

40. Hobsbawm, *Primitive Rebels: Studies in Archaic Forms of Social Movement in the Nineteenth and Twentieth Centuries* (Manchester, 1959), passim.

41. Ibid., pp. 2–3, 9.

42. Eugene D. Genovese, "The Politics of Class Struggle in the History of Society: An Appraisal of the Work of Eric Hobsbawm," in *The Power of the Past: Essays for Eric Hobsbawm*, ed. Pat Thane et al. (Cambridge, 1984), p. 13.

43. Kaye, *The British Marxist Historians*, p. 146 (quoting letter by Hobsbawm); Hobsbawm, in Abelove et al., *Visions of History*, pp. 32–33.

44. Hobsbawm, in Abelove et al., *Visions of History*, p. 33.

45. Hobsbawm's major synthetic works are *The Age of Revolution: Europe, 1789–1848* (London, 1962); *Industry and Empire: An Economic History of Britain since 1750* (London, 1968); and *The Age of Capital, 1848–1875* (London, 1975).

46. E. P. Thompson, *William Morris: Romantic to Revolutionary*, 2nd ed. (New York, 1977), p. 810.

47. Thompson, in Abelove et al., *Visions of History*, p. 21.

48. Thompson, *William Morris*, p. 769.

49. Ibid., 1st ed. (London, 1955), p. 270.

50. Ibid., p. 795.

51. Ibid., p. 760.

52. Ibid.

53. Ibid., p. 485.

54. Ibid., 1st ed., p. 840; 2nd ed., p. 726.

55. Ibid., 1st ed., pp. 731, 881.

56. Kaye, *The British Marxist Historians*, p. 173.

57. Thompson, *The Making of the English Working Class* (New York, 1964), p. 194. (The English edition was published in 1963.)

58. Ibid., p. 12.

59. Thompson, in Abelove et al., *Visions of History*, p. 21.

60. Thompson, *Making of the English Working Class*, pp. 375, 381, 385.

61. Ibid., pp. 367–368.

62. Thompson, "The Moral Economy of the English Crowd in the Eighteenth Century," *Past and Present*, February 1971; idem, "Patrician Society, Plebeian Culture," *Journal of Social History*, Summer 1974.

63. Thompson, *The Poverty of Theory and Other Essays* (New York, 1978), pp. 4, 111.

64. Perry Anderson, *Arguments within English Marxism* (London, 1980), p. 1; Thompson, in Abelove et al., *Visions of History*, p. 17.

65. See, for example, the review by David Landes of Hobsbawm's *Age of Capital* in the *Times Literary Supplement*, June 4, 1976, pp. 662–664.

66. J. H. Hexter, "Reply to Mr. Palmer: A Vision of Files," *Journal of British Studies*, Fall 1979, pp. 132–136. This is a reply to a critique of his critique. The original review appeared in the *Times Literary Supplement*, October 24, 1975, and was reprinted in Hexter, *On Historians* (Cambridge, Mass., 1979).

67. Christopher Hill, *Change and Continuity in Seventeenth-Century England* (Cambridge, Mass., 1975), p. 279.

68. Anderson, *Arguments*, p. 2.

69. Abelove et al., *Visions of History*, pp. x–xi.

70. Hobsbawm, "The Historians' Group," p. 31.

71. Abelove et al., *Visions of History,* p. x.

72. Hobsbawm, in Abelove et al., *Visions of History,* pp. 33–34; idem, "The Historians' Group," pp. 44, 29. Hobsbawm was obviously speaking of the Group's scholarly work. In journalistic articles and popular books some of its members did deal with more recent history. See, for example, Christopher Hill, *Lenin and the Russian Revolution* (London, 1947; rev. ed., 1971). Hobsbawm himself has recently published a scholarly essay, "The 'Moscow Line' and International Communist Policy, 1933–47," in *Warfare, Diplomacy and Politics: Essays in Honour of A. J. P. Taylor,* ed. Chris Wrigley (London, 1986). It is an oddly ambiguous essay, for while he claims to have exposed the "myth" that Communist parties were the "agents of Moscow," much of the evidence he cites seems to substantiate that myth.

73. J. P. Kenyon, "*Past and Present* No. 100," *Times Literary Supplement,* August 5, 1983.

74. Hobsbawm, "The Historians' Group," p. 26.

75. *Time and Tide,* Autumn 1985, p. 53.

76. Hobsbawm, "The Historians' Group," p. 42.

77. Ibid., p. 41.

78. Thompson, *Poverty of Theory,* p. i.

79. Ibid., p. 305.

80. Kaye, *The British Marxist Historians,* p. 248; Marx, *Eighteenth Brumaire,* in *Collected Works,* XI, 106.

81. Kaye, *The British Marxist Historians,* pp. 248–249.

82. Abelove et al., *Visions of History,* p. xi.

83. See, for example, Emmanuel Le Roy Ladurie, *Paris-Montpellier: P.C.-P.S.U. 1945–1963* (Paris, 1982); Natacha Dioujeva and François George, *Staline à Paris* (Paris, 1982); François Furet, "French Intellectuals: From Marxism to Structuralism" (1967), in Furet, *In the Workshop of History* (Chicago, 1984).

5. Social History in Retrospect

1. T. H. Huxley, "The Coming of Age of 'The Origin of Species'," in Huxley, *Darwiniana: Essays* (New York, 1893), p. 229.

2. Lawrence Stone, *The Past and the Present* (London, 1981), pp. xi–xii.

3. Ibid., pp. 81, 30.

4. Ibid., p. 86.

5. Ibid., pp. 31–32.

6. See, for example, Jacques Le Goff, "Mentalities: A History of Ambiguities," in *Constructing the Past: Essays in Historical Methodology,* ed. Jacques Le Goff and Pierre Nora (Cambridge, 1985), pp. 166–180.

7. Stone, *The Family, Sex and Marriage in England, 1500–1800* (New York, 1977), p. vii, quoting Clifford Geertz, *The Interpretation of Cultures* (New York, 1973), p. 363.

8. The exemplar of this method is Geertz's account of a Balinese cockfight in his *Interpretation of Cultures.*

9. Stone, *Past and Present,* p. 80.

10. Ibid.

11. Ibid., p. 81.

12. Ibid., pp. 74ff.

13. Ibid., p. 89. The phrase "history in microcosm" was used by Peter Burke in a review of another such work, Natalie Davis' *Return of Martin Guerre* (Cambridge, Mass., 1983) in the *London Review of Books,* May 2, 1984, p. 12. Hobsbawm himself doubts that the "revival of narrative" is as extensive as Stone suggests; see Hobsbawm, "The Revival of Narrative: Some Comments," *Past and Present,* February 1980, pp. 3–8.

14. Stone, *Past and Present,* p. 96. Perhaps this is what is meant by the neologism "narrativist" used by Hayden White, "Between Science and Symbol," *Times Literary Supplement,* January 31, 1986, p. 109.

15. Stone, *Past and Present,* p. 91.

16. See, for example, Stone's reviews of two books by Alan Macfarlane, the first concluding that the author's thesis is "an unlikely consequence of an implausible hypothesis based on a far-fetched connection with one still unproved fact of limited general significance"; the second claiming that all the flaws of the earlier book had been repeated "in if anything a still more reductionist and implausible form" (*New York Review of Books,* April 19, 1979, p. 41; *Times Literary Supplement,* May 16, 1986, p. 526). The second review concludes by attributing to the author a "hidden ideology," which has the doubly unfortunate effect of misrepresenting the ideology itself and suggesting an ideological animus on Stone's part.

17. Stone, *Past and Present,* pp. 131, 256.

18. Review by E. P. Thompson in *New Society,* September 8, 1977, pp. 499–501.

19. Stone, *Past and Present,* p. 86.

20. Ibid.

21. Ibid., p. 30.

22. "The Book of Numbers," *Times Literary Supplement,* December 9, 1965, pp. 1117–18.

23. Peter Laslett, *The World We Have Lost: Further Explored* (New York, 1984).

24. Ibid., p. 151.

25. Ibid., pp. 151–152.

26. Ibid., pp. 81ff.

27. Ibid., pp. 22ff., 182ff.

28. Ibid., p. 42.

29. Ibid., p. 247.

30. Ibid., p. 8.

31. Ibid., pp. 55–56.

32. Ibid.

33. Ibid., p. 21.

34. Ibid., pp. 5–6.

6. Case Studies in Psychohistory

1. Peter Gay, *Freud for Historians* (New York, 1985), p. 7.

2. Ibid., p. 4.

3. Edmund Burke, *Reflections on the Revolution in France,* ed. Conor Cruise O'Brien (London, 1968), pp. 34–35.

4. Ruth A. Bevan, *Marx and Burke: A Revisionist View* (La Salle, Illinois, 1973), p. 171 and passim.

5. Isaac Kramnick, *The Rage of Edmund Burke: Portrait of an Ambivalent Conservative* (New York, 1977).

6. Ibid., pp. 4, 11.

7. Ibid., pp. 4, 10.

8. Ibid., p. 70.

9. Ibid., p. 112.

10. Ibid., p. 114.

11. Ibid., pp. 119–120.

12. Ibid., pp. 120–121.

13. Ibid., pp. 134, 151, 157.

14. Ibid., pp. 157, 160.

15. Ibid., p. 122.

16. Ibid., p. 140.

17. Ibid., p. 85.

18. Ibid.

19. Ibid., p. 53.

20. Ibid., p. 56.

21. Ibid.

22. Ibid., p. 87.

23. Burke, *Reflections,* pp. 139–140.

24. Bruce Mazlish, *In Search of Nixon: A Psychological Inquiry* (New York, 1972), p. 154.

25. Mazlish, *The Meaning of Karl Marx* (New York, 1984), p. 3. See also Gertrude Himmelfarb, "The 'Real' Marx," *Commentary,* April 1985.

26. Mazlish, "Toward a Psychohistorical Inquiry: The 'Real' Richard Nixon," *Journal of Interdisciplinary History,* Autumn 1970, p. 53.

27. Mazlish, *Nixon,* p. 152.

28. Mazlish, *James and John Stuart Mill: Father and Son in the Nineteenth Century* (New York, 1975), p. 48.

29. Ibid., p. 49.

30. Ibid.

31. Ibid.

32. Ibid.

33. Alexander Bain, *James Mill: A Biography* (New York, 1967 [1st ed., 1882]), p. 5.

34. Mazlish, *Mill,* p. 51.

35. Ibid.
36. Ibid., p. 16.
37. Ibid., p. 18.
38. Ibid., pp.18–19.
39. Ibid., p. 53.
40. Ibid., p. 42.
41. Ibid., p. 75.
42. Mazlish, *Marx,* p. 26.
43. Mazlish, *Mill,* p. 82.
44. Ibid., p. 114.
45. Ibid., p. 115.
46. Ibid., p. 372.
47. Ibid., p. 379.

7. Is National History Obsolete?

1. The saying is often attributed to Cesare Beccaria, *Essay on Crimes and Punishments* (Eng. trans., London, 1767 [1st ed., 1764]). Carlyle quotes Montesquieu's version of it, then improves upon that with yet another version of his own. Thomas Carlyle, *The French Revolution* (Everyman ed., London, 1955 [1st ed., 1837]), I, 22; idem, *History of Friedrich II of Prussia, called Frederick the Great* (London, n.d. [7-vol. ed.]), IV, 272.

2. According to the Leicester school, local history is not merely a subdivision of national history but a substantively different mode of history. H. P. R. Finberg, "Local History," in *Approaches to History: A Symposium,* ed. Finberg (London, 1965), p. 120.

3. The original idea of universal history was inimical not to national history but only to the exclusive concern with Western history. Voltaire's *Essai sur les moeurs et l'esprit des nations,* often regarded as the progenitor of universal history, earned that reputation because it dealt with the Orient, the Near East, and Africa, in addition to the Western nations. Geoffrey Barraclough cautiously states the case for a world history that is more than the sum of national histories, but at the same time is not "history with national history left out." Barraclough, "Universal History," in Finberg, *Approaches to History,* p. 89.

4. See, for example, Carl N. Degler, "Remaking American History," *Journal of American History,* June 1980.

5. Geoff Eley, "Nationalism and Social History," *Social History,* January 1981, pp. 83–84.

6. Karl Marx, *Communist Manifesto* (New York, 1955 [1st ed., 1848]), pp. 21, 29.

7. Michael Oakeshott, *On History and Other Essays* (Oxford, 1983), p. 100. See Chapter 10 for a discussion of Oakeshott's philosophy of history.

8. Theodore Zeldin, *France 1848–1945,* 2 vols. (Oxford, 1973–77); idem, *The French* (New York, 1982).

9. Zeldin, "Social History and Total History," *Journal of Social History*, Winter 1976, pp. 242–243.

10. Ibid., pp. 243–244.

11. Robert Blake, ed., *The English World: History, Character, and People* (New York, 1982). See the second part of this chapter for a discussion of this book.

12. Zeldin, "Ourselves, as We See Us," *Times Literary Supplement*, December 31, 1982, p. 1436.

13. Ibid., p. 1435.

14. Ibid.

15. Zeldin, *France*, I, 285.

16. Ibid., p. 385.

17. Ibid., p. 3.

18. Ibid., p. 1.

19. Ibid., p. 8.

20. Ibid., II, 1.

21. Ibid., pp. 1–2.

22. Zeldin's tables on foreign residents and naturalization (ibid., p. 16) are typical of his cavalier way with statistics. The first table covers the period 1851 to 1931; the following one stops short, with no explanation, in 1911. Because there are no accompanying statistics for the population as a whole, and no percentage figures, there is no way of knowing whether and to what extent the proportion of foreign residents and naturalized citizens increased.

23. Zeldin, *France*, II, 1154.

24. Ibid., p. 1155.

25. Quoted from *Time*.

26. Zeldin, *The French*, pp. 507–508.

27. Ibid., pp. 509–510.

28. Ibid., p. 143.

29. Ibid., p. 36.

30. Ibid., p. 3.

31. Ibid., p. 506. The disdain for statistics seems to have communicated itself to the editor who, on the back flap of the jacket, praises the book for being "much more than a portrait of twenty-five million people."

32. Ibid., p. 36.

33. Ibid., p. 45.

34. Ibid., p. 214.

35. Ibid., p. 303.

36. Ibid., p. 348.

37. Ibid., p. 456.

38. Ibid., p. 508.

39. Marc Bloch, *Strange Defeat* (New York, 1968), p. 3.

40. Q. D. Leavis, "The Englishness of the English Novel" (1981), in *Collected Essays*, ed. G. Singh (Cambridge, 1983), I, 303, 306–307, 318.

41. Theodore Zeldin, "Social History and Total History," *Journal of Social*

History, Winter 1976; idem, "Ourselves, as We See Us," *Times Literary Supplement,* December 31, 1982; Eric Hobsbawm and Terence Ranger, eds., *The Invention of Tradition* (Cambridge, 1983), p. 13 and passim; Geoff Eley, "Nationalism and Social History," *Social History,* January 1981; Olivier Zunz, ed., *Reliving the Past: The Worlds of Social History* (Chapel Hill, 1985), p. 57. For a recent affirmation of the idea of "Englishness" see *Englishness: Politics and Culture 1880–1920,* ed. Robert Coles and Philip Dodd (London, 1986).

42. Kenneth O. Morgan, ed., *The Oxford Illustrated History of Britain* (Oxford, 1984); Robert Blake, ed., *The English World: History, Character, and People* (New York, 1982).

43. Eley speaks of the "nationalist problematic" ("Nationalism," p. 83).

44. See the first part of this chapter.

45. Morgan, *Oxford Illustrated History,* p. v.

46. Ibid.

47. Ibid., p. viii.

48. Ibid.

49. Ibid., p. 111.

50. Ibid., p. 149.

51. Ibid., p. 230.

52. Ibid., pp. 265, 307.

53. Ibid., p. 325.

54. Ibid., p. 351.

55. Ibid., pp. 371, 416–417.

56. Ibid., pp. 388, 419.

57. Ibid., pp. 419, 430.

58. Ibid., pp. 496, 523.

59. Ibid., p. 567.

60. Ibid., p. 588.

61. Ibid., p. 222.

62. Ibid.

63. Blake, *English World,* pp. 25, 30.

64. Ibid., pp. 25–26.

65. Ibid., p. 229.

66. Lawrence Stone, in *Three British Revolutions: 1641, 1688, 1776,* ed. J. G. A. Pocock (Princeton, 1980), p. 24.

67. J. H. Plumb, *The Growth of Political Stability in England, 1675–1725* (London, 1967).

68. Blake, *English World,* p. 30.

69. Ibid., p. 248.

70. Ibid., p. 250.

71. See, for example, Jeffrey Richards, "The Hooligan Culture," *Encounter,* November 1985.

72. Blake, *English World,* p. 250.

73. T. A. Critchley, *The Conquest of Violence: Order and Liberty in Britain* (New York, 1970), pp. 1–2.

74. See the critique by Theodore Zeldin discussed in the first part of this chapter.

75. Review by Jasper Ridley, *Times Literary Supplement,* December 31, 1982, p. 1436.

76. Lord Acton, "Nationality" (1862), in *Essays on Freedom and Power,* ed. Gertrude Himmelfarb (Boston, 1948), p. 184.

77. Lord Acton, Cambridge University MS. 4908; quoted in Gertrude Himmelfarb, *Lord Acton: A Study in Conscience and Politics* (Chicago, 1952), p. 183.

78. Ibid. (MS. 4939).

79. George Orwell, *The Lion and the Unicorn: Socialism and the English Genius* (1941), in *The Collected Essays, Journalism and Letters of George Orwell,* ed. Sonia Orwell and Ian Angus (New York, 1968), II, 57, 75.

80. Elie Kedourie, *Nationalism* (London, 1971 [1st ed., 1960]), p. 9. This has been much quoted and endorsed. See, for example, K. R. Minogue, *Nationalism* (New York, 1967), p. 17. The idea that nationalism was "invented" is the main theme of Hobsbawm and Ranger, *Invention of Tradition.*

81. John Stuart Mill, *Representative Government* (Everyman ed., London, 1940 [1st ed., 1861]), pp. 359–360. For a similar sentiment see his essay on Coleridge (1840), in *Essays on Politics and Culture,* ed. Gertrude Himmelfarb (New York, 1962), pp. 151–153. Mill repeated this passage toward the end of *A System of Logic* (London, 1949 [1st ed., 1843]), pp. 602–603.

8. Who Now Reads Macaulay?

1. Edmund Burke, *Reflections on the Revolution in France* (New York, 1961), p. 103. Burke was perhaps echoing Alexander Pope, who said of another unfortunate predecessor, "Who now reads Cowley?"

2. Thomas Babington Macaulay, *History of England from the Succession of James II,* in *Works,* ed. Lady Trevelyan (London, 1875), I, 1.

3. G. Otto Trevelyan, *The Life and Letters of Lord Macaulay* (New York, 1875), II, 323.

4. Ibid., pp. 207–208.

5. Ibid., pp. 234, 238.

6. Ibid., pp. 215–216.

7. Mark A. Thomson, Macaulay (London, 1959), p. 25.

8. J. W. Burrow, *A Liberal Descent: Victorian Historians and the English Past* (Cambridge, 1981), pp. 1–2.

9. Ibid., p. 300.

10. Burke, *Reflections,* p. 46.

11. Ibid., pp. 44–46.

12. Ibid., p. 46.

13. Macaulay, *History of England,* II, 395–396.

14. Joseph Hamburger, *Macaulay and the Whig Tradition* (Chicago, 1976).

15. Burke, *Reflections,* p. 110.

16. Burrow, *A Liberal Descent,* pp. 55ff.

17. Macaulay, "History" (1828), in *Works,* V, 136.

18. Ibid., p. 138.

19. Robert Brentano, "The Sound of Stubbs," *Journal of British Studies,* May 1967, p. 4.

20. Burrow, *A Liberal Descent,* p. 164.

21. Ibid., p. 14.

22. Ibid., p. 224.

23. Ibid., p. 102.

24. Quoted in G. P. Gooch, *History and Historians in the Nineteenth Century* (London, 1952), pp. 313–314.

25. Quoted in Gertrude Himmelfarb, *Victorian Minds* (New York, 1968), p. 241.

26. Wilfrid Ward, *The Life of John Henry Cardinal Newman* (London, 1912), II, 1 (quoting *Macmillan's,* December 1863).

27. Quoted in Gooch, *History and Historians,* p. 325.

28. John Richard Green, *A Short History of the English People* (London, 1964), I, 1.

29. Ibid., p. xi.

30. Gooch, *History and Historians,* p. 330.

31. Green, *Short History,* I, xi.

32. Ibid., p. 274.

33. Ibid., pp. 3–4.

34. Macaulay, "Mill's Essay on Government" (1829), in *Works,* V, 270.

9. History and the Idea of Progress

1. William James, *The Varieties of Religious Experience* (London, 1902), pp. 80ff. (The terms "once-born" and "twice-born" were Francis Newman's.)

2. Robert Nisbet, *History of the Idea of Progress* (New York, 1980), pp. 4–5.

3. J. B. Bury, *The Idea of Progress: An Inquiry into Its Origin and Growth* (New York, 1960 [1st ed., 1920]), p. 352.

4. Ibid., pp. ix–x.

5. Carl L. Becker, *The Heavenly City of the Eighteenth-Century Philosophers* (New Haven, 1970 [1st ed., 1932]), p. 119.

6. Ibid., pp. 8, 29.

7. Ibid., p. 15.

8. Ibid., pp. 16–17.

9. Quoted in ibid., p. 168.

10. Nisbet, *Idea of Progress,* p. 76.

11. Ibid., p. 101.

12. Ibid., pp. 118ff.

13. Ibid., pp. 4–5.

14. Ibid., p. 105.

15. Ibid., p. 239.

16. William Godwin, *An Enquiry Concerning Political Justice, and Its Influence on General Virtue and Happiness* (1st ed., London, 1793), II, 871.

17. Nisbet, *Idea of Progress,* p. 323.

18. Joseph Cropsey, *Polity and Economy: An Interpretation of the Principles of Adam Smith* (The Hague, 1957), p. x.

19. Nisbet, *Idea of Progress,* p. 191.

20. Adam Smith, *An Inquiry into the Nature and Causes of the Wealth of Nations,* ed. Edwin Cannan (New York, 1937 [1st ed., 1776]), pp. 78–79.

21. Nisbet, *Idea of Progress,* p. 192; Smith, *Wealth of Nations,* pp. 15–16.

22. Gertrude Himmelfarb, *Victorian Minds* (New York, 1968), pp. 82ff.; idem, *The Idea of Poverty: England in the Early Industrial Age* (New York, 1983), pp. 100ff.

23. Nisbet, *Idea of Progress,* p. 8.

24. Ibid., p. ix.

25. Nisbet, *Social Change and History: Aspects of the Western Theory of Development* (New York, 1969), pp. 270, 284, 303.

26. Ibid., p. 242.

27. Nisbet, *Idea of Progress,* p. 300.

28. Ibid., p. 317.

29. Nisbet, *The Sociological Tradition* (New York, 1966), p. 268.

30. Ibid.

31. Ibid., p. 318.

32. Ibid., p. 356.

10. Does History Talk Sense?

1. Friedrich Nietzsche, *Beyond Good and Evil,* trans. Walter Kaufmann (New York, 1966 [1st ed., 1886]), p. 2.

2. Ibid., p. 163.

3. According to David Boucher, Oakeshott's philosophical roots were more immediately in the British idealists, especially F. H. Bradley. See Boucher, "The Creation of the Past: British Idealism and Michael Oakeshott's Philosophy of History," *History and Theory,* 1984 (no. 2).

4. Michael Oakeshott, *Rationalism in Politics* (London, 1962), p. 166.

5. Ibid., p. 143.

6. Ibid., p. 149.

7. Ibid., p. 154.

8. Ibid., pp. 157–158.

9. Ibid., pp. 166–167.

10. Ibid., p. 166.

11. Oakeshott, *On History and Other Essays* (Oxford, 1983), p. 64.

12. Ibid., p. 94.

13. Ibid., p. 117.

14. Ibid., p. 61.

15. Oakeshott, *Experience and Its Modes* (Cambridge, 1978 [1st ed., 1933]), p. 99.

16. Ibid., p. 100.

17. Ibid., p. 113.

18. Ibid., p. 100.

19. Ibid., p. 107.

20. Ibid., p. 111.

21. Ibid., p. 109.

22. Ibid., pp. 146–149.

23. Oakeshott, *Rationalism in Politics*, pp. 150, 158–159.

24. Ibid., pp. 159, 166.

25. Oakeshott, *On History*, p. 29.

26. Ibid., p. 106.

27. Oakeshott, *Rationalism in Politics*, p. 148.

28. Ibid.

29. Ibid., pp. 157–158. William H. Dray points out that Oakeshott sometimes praised history books that in fact violated his own prescriptions. See Dray, "Michael Oakeshott's Theory of History," in *Politics and Experience: Essays Presented to Professor Michael Oakeshott on the Occasion of His Retirement*, ed. Preston King and B. C. Parekh (Cambridge, 1968), p. 34.

30. R. G. Collingwood, *The Idea of History* (New York, 1956), pp. 155, 158–159.

31. Oakeshott, *Experience and Its Modes*, p. 119.

32. Nietzsche, *The Use and Abuse of History*, trans. Adrian Collins and Julius Kraft (New York, 1957), p. 32.

33. Ibid., p. 41.

34. Ibid., pp. 32–33.

35. Ibid., p. 3.

36. Ibid., p. 8.

37. Ibid., p. 12.

38. Ibid., p. 8.

39. Ibid., p. 33.

40. Arthur Schopenhauer, *Parerga and Paralipomena: Short Philosophical Essays*, trans. E. F. J. Payne (Oxford, 1974), II, 447.

Acknowledgments

I am grateful for permission to use revised versions of essays that originally appeared in the following publications:

Chapter 1—*Harper's,* April 1984

Chapters 2 and 9—*Commentary,* January 1975 and June 1980

Chapter 3—*Art, Politics and Will: Essays in Honor of Lionel Trilling,* ed. Quentin Anderson, Stephen Donadio, and Steven Marcus (copyright © 1977 by Basic Books, Inc., Publishers; reprinted by permission)

Chapters 4 and 6—*New Republic,* February 10, 1986, and November 19, 1977

Chapter 5—*New York Times Book Review,* January 10, 1982, and June 24, 1984 (copyright © 1982/1984 by The New York Times Company; reprinted by permission)

Chapter 6—*Times Literary Supplement,* May 23, 1975

Chapters 7 and 8—*New Criterion,* May 1983 and December 1982

Chapter 10—*American Scholar,* Summer 1976

Index of Names

DATE DUE
